Praise for

Where Joy is Found

I am so grateful that after 30 years, my passing acquaintance with Gary Best "the apostolic leader/ teacher'' has bloomed into an authentic and valued friendship. And I know exactly how that happened. Gary opened that door by (1) being vulnerable with his deepest questions about God, humanity and the structure of reality, and (2) by locating his BIG questions in the real story of his life and in the grand narrative of redemption. This beautiful work—so much more than a memoir—reflects and testifies to that Jacob-like journey. In *Where Joy is Found,* even readers who've known him well for decades will be introduced afresh to deep-faith Gary, the one who has wrestled with God, walks with a limp and has found his blessing.

-Brad Jersak, Author of *A More Christlike God*

Over the years, my wife Michelle and I have been amongst the chorus of voices urging Gary to consider writing another book. Our conviction was not so much in thinking Gary has something to say, as much as, Gary has something we need to hear. With equal parts wisdom, truth, humility, and humor, *Where Joy is Found*, is exactly the book we were hoping for. A thoughtful invitation to open our hearts and see the provision of God that is everywhere...even in the pain.

-Joe Vieira. Pastor Atlantic Beach Vineyard Church
Atlantic Beach, Florida

It has been my privilege to count Gary as a mentor through-out my twenties and now into my thirties. Few leader's lives have shaped me more than Gary and Joy's. I am so deeply grateful that Gary has captured so much of what I learn from him personally, into these pages, so that you might receive it as well.

Gary and Joy have taught me to ask better questions in life and faith, to rush to the place of anonymity and service, to seek the authority of God not power, to pursue the shalom of God in every area of my life, and to open my eyes to the provision that is everywhere. I miss Joy deeply, but this book really does honour who she was, how she and Gary discovered the way of the Kingdom together, and how she left Gary a better man than she found him, even if it felt like she was gone too soon.

Embrace this book as a story, to be followed, enjoyed, wrestled with and challenged by. May you discover where joy is found in your own life, within the mysterious and faithful presence of the God who longs to see us each take hold of all that he has for us. What a gift.

-Miriam Swanson, Global Student Mission Leader
Fusion Movement

I am incredibly thankful for all of the memories I have made with my Grandma and Grandpa. Reading this book has helped me better understand my Grandpa and his life, and I am very grateful to have this collection of stories to carry with me forever.

-Eden Wiebe
Granddaughter of Gary and Joy

Gary is a sensational storyteller. He is an advocate for the search and the journey. His ability to ask better questions is so needed in the social constructs we find ourselves in - where we're obsessed with quick fix solutions and one-size-fits-all answers. His straight talking embrace of curiosity and often doubt, leaves readers sighing "thank God it's not just me thinking that!". He's asking the questions we all want to ask but often lack the courage to.

I loved this book. It's a lot like life—you don't necessarily get or agree with it all and that's okay. It's hilarious at times; warm and witty then tragic and turbulent. But faith isn't thrown in just for good measure. There's power in these pages; there's hope to be received; there's an eternal longing in these words. Fine tune your eyes and get ready for a ride. We are welcomed into a story that's much much bigger than us. And I sure want to be a part of this journey of finding Jesus. I'm so thankful I've found this book at the age of 30, I know I'll keep going back to it as I grow up.

-Pippa Baker, One Hope Project
www.onehopeproject.co.uk

Seven years into church planting and knee deep in experiences of disillusionment, tension, and questions, we know hunger to learn and grow still lives within us, but also that it is clouded by residues of significant pain. It is in this exact place that we found ourselves picking up, "Where Joy is Found."

It's engaging, based in story, and invites the reader into a grander narrative then they may have been aware of. But instead of "3 Easy Steps to Find Joy," (which at this stage in life we would chuck into the trash can), Gary invited us into his story—full of tension, beauty, pain, and grace.

Because of Gary's willingness to tackle the paradoxes and questions of life, "Where Joy is Found" gave language to things we've been feeling for years, but haven't quite been able to put into words. It's like the words jumped off the page and spoke directly to us and we are sure they will for you!

-DJ and Vanessa Jergensen. Founding pastors
Durango Vineyard Church, Colorado

When my wife Stefanie and I began to get to know Gary, we were quickly drawn in by his ability to tell a story while also meeting us in ours. Yet, we've learned that Gary is not just a good storyteller, he also has a story to tell. Rich in wisdom and wit, Where Joy is Found takes us on a journey that meets us deeply in the our current cultural moment with an imagination that cuts through the fog and gives us eyes to see hope both around and in us, yet will no doubt serve as a guide to future generations, as this work is both timely and timeless.

-David Brickey, Lead Pastor, Church of the Open Door
Maple Grove, MN

Long time friends and colleagues, Gary and Joy Best have deeply influenced us since we first met. Gary's writing is easy and energising to read—but don't be fooled by that! This book packs a punch in the midst of beautiful stories, raw anecdotes, biblical narratives and leadership insights.

People are desperate for real, honest stories that encourage, restore hope, and inspire. Gary's book plumbs the depths of what it looks like to be a follower of Jesus, a servant leader, a spouse, a parent and more. This book is about learning to love well and invites you to pause and ponder and then stretch for the better way—we long for all current and future leaders to read it!

May you also find joy as you read this beautifully crafted and utterly disarming book.

-Lloyd & Victoria Rankin, Founders of Vineyard Churches
Aotearoa New Zealand

Gary Best has written a tribute to his late wife, Joy. She deserves it. Along the way, he tells the story of her affect on his life, and he includes his evolving thoughts about history, faith, interpretation of sacred texts, and the posture that he now finds himself taking as he approaches the latter seasons of life. Altogether, it is a masterpiece. There are elements of story and passages of significant thought. With astonishing vulnerability he shows himself as a young and gifted man, hoping to find belonging and success. The themes of the book tie together to show the result of a pilgrimage through ups and downs that leads to a confident simplicity. After all is said and done, he has found the strength to be himself.

-Dr. Peter Fitch, Professor of Religious Studies
St. Stephen's University

Where Joy is Found

BY GARY BEST

Where Joy Is Found
Copyright © 2020 by Gary Best
Published by Gary Best
garydebest@gmail.com

ISBN: 9798559579023

DEDICATION

To my irreplaceable Joy—
You lived with your eyes wide open,
seeing the provision of God everywhere.
Now you know fully what your heart
has always longed for.

(Experience the song, "Where Joy is Found" at
https://youtu.be/9HXnQWuQlll)

CONTENTS

Part 2: A Tale Of Two Stories

Part 3: Slip Slidin' Away

Part 4: The Road Less Travelled

Important Tips for Readers

Frequently during the week, I jump on my bike and head out for a brisk 20km cycle. The beginning is always a breeze—I'm heading along a nice level country road that winds past Tuscan Farms, with its exquisite gardens and fragrant fields of lavender. Next is a gradual uphill past the free-range chicken farm. It's always interesting because of the odd chicken that invariably makes it's escape to freedom...and then spends most of its remaining energies trying to figure out how to get back in with the others.

I turn right at the elementary school for a long somewhat gentle rise which eventually curves past the old country cemetery, where I pay my respects while continuing to ride. There's a bit of a reprieve when the road levels off a bit. Then comes the long uphill grind that mercifully crests the hill just as my legs are threatening to look for another body. Finally, there's a straight run to a magnificent view—here you can see all the way to the distant gem which is Vancouver and to the mountains that frame it.

It's here that I work my way through the Lord's Prayer in order to prepare myself for the rest of the day. I add some personal reflections and requests, listen a bit and then...it's mostly all downhill to home. Returning past the cemetery once again, I usually pop in for a longer conversation. Then, with my legs fully rested, I power the rest of the way through my ride.

It's a great routine—not quite the European cycling trip my wife Joy and I did in 2018, involving 60-70km a day for a week—but it keeps the blood circulating and the brain clear.

Reading this book is like my cycling route—there's some relatively easy reading, like downhill glides, but also some tougher, uphill stretches. If you are used to the rigour and rhythm of it all, it's quite easy. If it's a little out of the norm for you, then it can feel like getting through the book might be more work than it's worth.

In the last years, there has been an invention which has been a game changer for beginning cyclists—it's called the e-bike. You are really cycling with one notable difference. When the hill gets too long and fatigue sets in, you just flip a switch. Then the bike literally takes over, bringing you along for the ride. It's a great way to savour the experience without being overwhelmed by some of the harder sections.

That's probably the best way to approach the book. Enjoy the ease of the "downhill" story sections, where you almost feel like you can stop peddling and just coast. In the few segments with hills—you'll especially find these in Part 1 of the book—let me suggest this hint. If a section seems too long or difficult and you are finding it hard to stay focused and engaged, just flip an imaginary e-bike switch. Skim ahead, or even skip an entire chapter or two (or even three).

Maybe at some further point these chapters might be

important for you to engage with...and build some muscle doing so. But for now, the most important thing is to take in the full experience, the entire route. Make sure that the book serves you, and not vice versa!

So, in anticipation of the pages to come, I authorize all of you to utilize the literary equivalent of an e-bike and enjoy the ride! Hopefully, you will find that joy awaits you at the journey's end.

Author's Note

Twenty years or so ago—in what is possibly the most fruitful and productive season of my life—a good friend, Dan Wilt, encourages me as he so often does, to *finally* write a book. "What's in you has to be said," Dan pleads.

My response is one that I have rehearsed countless times in my own head: "I think I'll be content with leading the kind of life that others want to write about." I like the ring of that response. It sounds so...well, noble. And if others indeed *do* write about me? Isn't that how I will know that I've finally arrived, that I'm really significant?

Yet, here I am writing a book. And it's not even my first one. So much for that idealistic dream.

Why am I writing? Quite simply, it's a way for me to process my life so far, to face head-on the question, "What is true significance after all?" How else will I determine what kinds of things I need to adjust in order to live fully and well in what is now the final act of my life story? I am writing this book first of all for me.

I remember, many years ago, running across a book entitled, "Don't waste your sorrows." I think the actual writing is less memorable than the title—I remember little of its message. This unforgettable line, though, keeps near the front of my memory, always nudging when crucial decisions are to be made.

My writing is helping me process the tangled mix of success and sorrow that has defined the plot lines of my story. I'm not trying to *cement my legacy*—it's probably a bit late for that. What I'm trying to do is understand: myself, first of all, and then, hopefully, a little more of God's lifelong invitation.

Of course, to understand requires re-visiting. The warm memories—times of loving and being loved, the thrill of new adventures or accomplishments, rich encounters with God—they're the easy part. But to truly understand, I need to find the courage to go deeper. To even dare to remember parts of my story that I've been quite content to leave buried and undisturbed.

As Brené Brown writes in *Gifts of Imperfection,*

> Owning our story can be hard but not nearly as difficult as spending our lives running from it. Embracing our vulnerabilities is risky but not nearly as dangerous as giving up on love and belonging and joy—the experiences that make us the most vulnerable. Only when we are brave enough to explore the darkness will we discover the infinite power of our light.[1]

The light of which Brown speaks, is not the bank of stadium lights that I think I need to have certainty in my field of play. It's more like the Psalmist's lamp to my feet—always enough light to take the next step, but never

---

[1] Brené Brown, The Gifts of Imperfection. (Hazelden, 2010), 6.

enough to feel like I'm in control. It's impossible to follow without trust.

I'm approaching the twilight of my present journey, and I'm hopefully expectant that the strengthening light from over the horizon will overcome any remaining darkness. Is that radiance actually getting brighter, or is my trust simply growing deeper?

One thing is for sure. I'm more committed than ever to turn toward that light. Yet, in some mysterious way, I still fear joy and love. Is it simply the expectation of disappointment? Still, I know if I am to fully live, I must embrace them. I feel like I'm a little late to the game, but at least I'm playing.

The invitation to follow this path—the one that leads to joy—has pursued me my entire life. Yet, like Augustine, I find myself confessing, "Late have I loved you, O beauty so ancient and so new. Late have I loved you."[2] I write in the hope that, through journeying with me a bit, your own longings for joy, love, and belonging will be stirred and renewed. Thanks for your company![3]

---

[2] St. Augustine, The Confessions, Book X, Chapter 27. Of course, my late may be God's right on time.

[3] You have no doubt noticed that this Preface is written in the present tense. I'm doing this intentionally to help you get used to the book as a whole. Wherever a scene is set—whether Paul in a prison cell or me as a nine-year-old in a neighbour's basement—I'm inviting you to be present in that place and time. Don't worry, it gets easier to adapt to over time. What may be more difficult, particularly for my neighbours to the south, will be adjusting to my persistent Canadian spelling. Trust me—words, by any other spelling, still can smell as sweet.

Acknowledgements

If it takes a village to raise a child, how many more are necessary to sustain us through our entire life journey? I fear that tending my life has necessitated a larger than expected share of the world's human resources.

Most of all, of course, I'm grateful for my own precious Joy, my wife of 48 years—one Joy bequeathing another, as I write in the book. It's Joy who, more than any other, keeps calling me to embrace my deepest longings and to have the courage to live fully pursuing them.

Second, my family: Jon (with his beautiful young women, Maddie and Ellie) and Jaana (with Jeremy and their two special children, Eden—ballerina extraordinaire—and Asher, my special birthday buddy). I often say that I want to become like them if I ever grow up...and that is barely said in jest.

Jon has taken the lead in editing the book, helping to bring who I am to the surface. He worked with me for

---

You will also quickly recognize that I'm using a very informal writing style: using contractions whenever possible and not hesitating to use sentence fragments. This is again intentional as I want my writing style to invite you very personally into my thoughts and experiences. My hope is that, rather than being comfortable observing me, you will be truly with me in my journey.

many years and now has become one of my closest friends. Jaana is an incredibly thoughtful and wise woman—and excellent writer by the way—who again and again saves me from myself. It's so comforting to have her alongside while walking out this journey.

I've so appreciated my other two editors, Phil Kinnie (theatre background)—thanks Phil for the chapter divisions and titles!—and Josh Randhawa (literary background) who constantly pushes me to "show, not tell." Their interaction with me throughout the unfolding project has made the book immeasurably better. All the shortcomings still evident are the result of me ignoring their wise counsel.

Ben and Miriam Swanson are like a second set of kids. They have walked closely with me throughout the aftermath of Joy's passing to this present day. They have continued to believe in me—even to the point of making the final call on this book being published! May we have many more years journeying together!

I'm greatly privileged to have younger friends around the world who profoundly impact my life and help me to become the best version of myself. They graciously have committed time and energy to read through various stages of the manuscript and offer suggestions which have greatly strengthened the finished product. If you know any of these people, you are as privileged as I am: my daughter Jaana, her husband Jeremy, and her daughter Eden; my former co-worker Monique Tute; Lloyd and Vicki Rankin in New Zealand; Joe and Michelle Vieira in Jax Beach; DJ and Vanessa Jurgensen in Durango; Brad Jersak, Peter Fitch, and Allen Doerksen (my "academic" friends), and—last but not least—Anna Westin and Pippa Baker in the UK.

I'm deeply appreciative of DJ and Vanessa for creating the cover and overseeing the layout of the book (check out gingermoosephotography.com)—and kudos to author advocate Cindy Conger for walking us through the whole publishing journey! Speaking of photography, thanks Ron Peters for my personal cover photo—talk about being the best version of oneself!

I'm also so, so grateful for my fourteen-year-old grand-daughters Maddie and Eden who collaborated to produce the drawing at the end of the book—Maddie creating the art piece and Eden adding the scripting.

There are three writers that have had a significant impact on my personal journey, each in their own unique way. First, N.T. Wright made it possible for my wife Joy and I to actually read the Bible together through his *For Everyone* series. He may be a theological rock star but if you reach out to him, he answers. Who does that? (There's a great back story on that but I'd have to tell you over a glass of whiskey.)

Second, though I've never had the privilege of meeting him personally, Lesslie Newbigin. His writings came to me at a critical time in my wrestling with faith and doubt. Finally, Brad Jersak. As a young youth pastor, Brad used to hang around and listen to me speak. Now, I'd go anywhere to hear him. His book, *A More Christlike God* has been perhaps the critical piece in my coming to complete rest in believing that God is good and is for me. I can't recommend Brad or his books enough!

Finally, I am deeply humbled by the privilege of having so many friends that have helped form me in all the best ways throughout my life's journey. If to any small degree this book is able to touch and encourage the lives of still more fellow travellers, you share significantly in that reward.

Foreword

My name is "Jaana". It means "The Lord hears" and was chosen very carefully because it captured the very heart of how I came to live! I remember hearing the story of my birth repeatedly through my childhood, how my life has been a constant reminder of God's faithfulness, an answer to my dad's prayers. Perhaps this storytelling served as a root, which has helped to anchor me from being completely unearthed during the many storms I've encountered?

Dad has always been a safe place where I can find connection, safety and understanding. He is always cheering me on and tirelessly calling me forward. Often, he has wanted to take away my pain as 'Mr.Fix-It,' yet keeps pointing me towards my journey, knowing that healing, fulfillment, and freedom are earned through MY ability to choose hope in the darkness. Ever pointing me to trust the process—that God CAN produce good through hard circumstances, even those we'll never understand.

My parents modeled transparency and the willingness to keep growing and changing through all seasons of life and death. Of course, there were imperfections and struggles along the way, including some very turbulent teen years. This openness towards vulnerability and growth was the cord that held us together, leading towards restoration, healing and strength. I am learning to find my voice and that it matters.

Mom was such an example of truly living IN each day, not looking too far ahead or behind. The world was like a vast moving canvas—always reflecting our creator's beauty and teaching us how to walk each day. Her eyes were open to see His provision because she was looking. It was a choice she spent many years on, refocusing her thoughts, gratitude journaling, and mining for the beauty and truth around her. She dared to expect good things!

It's been a gift to walk alongside my dad and witness this beautiful, brave process of writing his story and the healing which has resulted. I am so very thankful for this legacy for our family to stand on and am grateful to share it with you. I know you will be captivated, challenged and inspired to wrestle through what stirrings arise. So get ready to be uncomfortable and enjoy the ride!

-Jaana Wiebe

Life is an unfathomable gift. This became permanently tattooed on my soul on March 20, 2019, but I have always been sensitive to this… the beauty of a dusting of snow on the mountains, a crocus pushing through dead leaves with glorious purple, the fractals of a jewel toned fern leaf unfurling towards the sun. It is all around us, and in us. My life is a miraculous gift. Given the odds, I should not have survived or, at the very least, should have serious cognitive and physical challenges from being born 10 weeks early (in the 1970's). My name Jonathan means "gift of God" or "God has given." As I have progressed through my life, I have many times asked, "What makes me a gift?" Or, "Who am I a gift to?

In the movie The Princess Bride, Miracle Max says loudly to the (mostly dead) Westley, "Hey! Hello in there. Hey! What's so important? What you got here that's worth living for?" As Max expresses the air he has forced in into Westley's lungs with a bellows, Westley replies in a faint wheeze, "Truuuueeee loooooooovvvveee...." Learning to love is something I believe is worth spending my life learning how to do. I can't say I'm good at it. I have failed many times, but I want to learn and keep on asking how I can get better.

Like Max, my dad (Gary) has asked great questions, and has done so all over the world for decades. He has journeyed with many people to ask the who, what, when, where, and why of life and faith. He has done his best to invite people to join him, not just in asking deep questions, but to live out the answers to those questions together. I deeply appreciate that he keeps on asking. In fact, the best questions are Inception like: the question beneath the question beneath the question...In the end, what is worth living for?

This book is a raw, candid, brave invitation for us all to join Gary in journeying towards the answer to that question. As you read these pages, jump into these stories like Lewis' pools in the world between the worlds. Enter in and make these questions your own. Leap, trust, hope... and find where you are found.

-Jon Best

The Patio

The Patio

It is unseasonably warm for the first day of Spring, even for Vancouver. Though almost certainly it won't last and the cool rains will return before giving way to an explosion of warmth and new life, my wife Joy and I feel compelled to welcome and enjoy it.

For this very reason, though I suspect I'll regret it later, I decide to pull out the patio furniture earlier than usual to take full advantage of the spring flowers—all of which seem to be competing with each other for recognition as the first and brightest.

Joy is euphoric, as for the first time of this calendar year she's able to dry our washing outside in the sunshine, letting it absorb the freshness of the spring breeze. This is always her favourite time of year. And when it's like this? A taste of heaven, certainly.

We joyfully step into the scheduled events of our day, after inviting our son Jon to join us later for dinner on the patio. Certainly this unanticipated blessing of spring must be shared. Joy spends her day just the way that she would if she knew that it would be her last. We go for a run in the forest; she delivers lunch to our church staff (of course presented with fresh flowers); she spends five hours with a refugee family that we're helping to sponsor.

She even finds time to wander the local thrift store for treasures to add to her trove of ready-made gifts.

On the way home after picking me up, she's effusive in noticing and remarking on God's presence everywhere around us. She sees God in the landscape, the swirling clouds, the new-born animals skipping in the fields. It's almost embarrassing. I think to myself, "What universe are you living in?"

The joy she feels continues through our dinner. Energized by the colours and scents around us, she takes it all in, especially feeding on the laughter and conversation. Some dear friends bring dessert and join our group. A night to remember.

And then her brain ruptures.

Within five minutes she's unconscious. In my frantic attempts to take charge—to save her—I never even have the presence of mind to say goodbye. Perhaps I can't let myself believe it. It will always be one of the greatest regrets of my life.

It's not unexpected. For over twenty years, Joy and I have been aware that she has an idiopathic condition that results in unbelievably high blood pressure. In spite of a very active lifestyle, careful eating habits, and attempts at various treatments, nothing is ever successful at bringing it to the place where her life will not be at risk. We know that each day can be her last.

In the beginning this brings me great anxiety. I want to find a way to fix it, to gain control over the narrative. Joy, in contrast, is always at great peace. She says over and over, "Can't you trust God for this?" My carefully considered response will inevitably be, "No!"

So we begin to learn to literally live one day at a time. Saying, "Goodbye" takes on new meaning. There are numbers of times when Joy is so overdue from a run along the river that I reluctantly take the car to go and pick up her body—only to find that she has been delayed, either from meditating on a flower or from picking up garbage from beside the road.

Certainly, our reality does wonders for our initially argumentative marriage. Again and again we will pause in the midst of disagreement and reflect, "If this is the last day, is this issue really worth it?" There aren't a lot of arguments truly worthy of continuing on a last day.

Yet, even though I've been expecting this for over two decades, when it happens I'm not ready. However, ready or not, it changes everything. Of course, for some time— actually quite a long time—I'm not in any way able to process this tragedy well enough to understand what has really happened. I am simply surviving.

I do know that my story has irrevocably changed. Well, to be honest, I first feel that my story is over. In a somewhat surreal way, I feel removed from my own life, even though I am still technically breathing. It's as though I'm watching myself continue the story of my life—one that I've spent a lifetime carefully crafting and molding— but now I'm somewhat just going through the motions.

It's now one year after that fateful evening. Like the previous spring, the flowers are casting their hopeful beauty, and the sun, low in the sky, is coaxing them with warmth and splashing them with radiant contrast. Beauty certainly hasn't died; life has proved once again stronger than death.

Yet I am looking at this scene from inside my kitchen window. It's close enough to touch, but I'm separated from it. It's as though something has quarantined me from the full experience of life, from my own story, and its hopeful possibilities.

Ironically, having just returned from the United States, I'm presently in quarantine because of the COVID-19 pandemic, an experience which is acting in some way as a springboard for my deeper thoughts and feelings. Looking out through the glass at the beauty outside, I feel lost and alone…the pain of a year ago still biting and bitter. At the same time, another realization forces itself into my conscious mind.

I know this feeling. I've felt it all my life.

The sense of being on the outside of the window looking in. This sense of loss runs far deeper than grief itself. It's always been with me, from my earliest childhood. My loss of Joy has unsealed a box that I don't know if I dare to open. Perhaps it would be better to simply close it up again.

Turn away from the window.

Yet, at the same time, I feel something rising up in me. Is it some form of "hope springs eternal," like we see each year in spring, inviting me to choose life? Something within me—could it be God's Spirit?—is challenging me to revisit my story, even though my illusion of being able to control my narrative has been shattered.

I know what's said about social organizations: when all

of their best days are in the past, the spirit of their movement is over. What's true of groups must be true of an individual. Do I dare to believe that my best days, the most fulfilling and meaningful part of my story, lies yet in my future? Something in me must believe that to be true.

But that will mean finding the courage to step back into the journey. I'm fully aware that it won't work to simply re-enter what was, picking up where I left off. Something has changed and I am left with more questions than answers. Perhaps that is the wonderful gift of tragedy — it ruins us for the status quo. It calls us to something more. It reminds us that our calling is not just to exist but to fully live.

This will mean having the courage to ask better questions.

Not just, "How can I get more done? How will I keep my anxieties at bay? How will I make sure that my story has at least a fair share of prominence and privilege?"

But, "What is it that makes a great story anyway? What is the whole point of all of this from God's perspective? And of all that I have experienced, what can I carry forward that will serve me well in this next stage of the adventure? What will need to be left behind?"

Near the end of his life, Dallas Willard wrote a simple paper reflecting on the challenge of staying connected to the vision that initially inspired our stories and kept them vitally joined to God's great story.[4] While coming to the sad conclusion that almost no movements manage to keep this connection vital over time, he did offer some hope. Some individuals do finish well, stay fully alive to

---

[4] Dallas Willard, Living In The Vision Of God

their last breath. Can I be one of those people? Can I avoid the cynicism of the disappointed but also the doubling down of the zealots?

I suspect it will mean being willing to dismantle some of the scaffolding I've built and tried to pass off as the real building I originally set out to construct. It will likely require more than simply relying on my old systems of control—instead learning, adapting, changing while somehow retaining my initial audacious hope and innocence. And that will mean revisiting my story—my journey so far—seeing it through new lenses and stepping forward into the light of what I see…with no guarantees.

I'm not even sure if I can find the courage to look at my life and try to understand what perhaps God has been trying to teach me all along. But something is hooking into my heart—like a faint and distant memory, inviting me to recall.

There is a deeper joy that I've yearned for my entire life—long before I met my wife. And at this moment, somehow I know that this joy is reaching for me.

Part 1

Searching For a Story

1 We are Made for Story

I've always been drawn to stories. And I've always dreamed of living in a great one. Of course, my perspective of a *great* story as a kid is not that informed but, given my limited understanding at the time, I certainly want to grow up to be Superman rather than Mr. Rogers. (I might choose differently now—so late, so smart.)

This shouldn't be surprising. I realize I'm made for stories. It almost seems like I'm hardwired to not only compulsively tell them, but to live within them. I don't think I'm alone in this. According to author Gene Fant, story pretty much defines all of us. It's right up there with walking on two legs and having opposable thumbs.[5]

Hardly a day goes by without me telling a story. If I'm not sharing about the details of my own life in story form, I'm relating someone else's story. It's largely how I make sense of the past and the present and determine how to navigate the future. So, I talk around the dinner table...a little more challenging these days, I converse over a coffee, or I spin tales to my grandchildren every time I get a chance. And, even at my age, I'm still enthralled by

[5] Gene C. Fant Jr., *God as Author: A Biblical Approach to Narrative* (B&H Publishing Group, 2010), 6.

stories that take me to other lives, times, and places.

There's a lot of buzz today about facts and data. I'm surrounded by experts and bombarded by information—all pronouncing judgment upon me and the way I am or am not living. So much so, that at times I feel like I am "drowning in a sea of data."[6]

Yet this isn't how I actually live my life day to day. As Eugene Peterson says, "...we don't live our lives by information. We live them in relationships in the context of a community of men and women...and of a personal God, who cannot be reduced to formula or definition."[7]

By the time I've gathered all the info and consulted all the experts, I realize that I've left just one thing out—me. And when I lose *me*, my own soul and longings and desires, it isn't analyzing data that helps me find my way home. As Peterson says, "story is the best way of getting us back in touch again."[8]

The best stories reach to something deep within me, something that I rarely consciously acknowledge but know instinctively is central to who I am. From the Ancient Greek philosopher Aristotle on, theorists have tried to explain what it is about the structure of certain stories that really *works*, resonates so deeply within the human soul. Though explained in slightly different

---

[6] A phrase used by Edwin H. Friedman, in a speech to the American Association of Marriage and Family Therapists to commemorate the 500th anniversary of Columbus discovering America—or was it the other way round? He develops those ideas further in his book, *A Failure of Nerve: Leadership in the Age of the Quick Fix,* (Seabury Books, 2007).

[7] Peterson, *Living into God's Story*, a pdf article located at: https://static1.squarespace.com/static/55a6400fe4b0062f1359e218/t/581ef178d2b85747b9dd2e7c/1478422904361/Living+into+God%27s+Story.pdf

[8] Peterson, Living into God's Story.

ways—much like variations on a common theme— stories that penetrate and stick have the following elements: setting, conflict, climax, and resolution.

Everyone knows that the best stories follow some variation of this progression. But why does it work? In *Blue Like Jazz,* Donald Miller explores this question and how it becomes a eureka moment for him. He muses that conflict in a story so resonates with us because we are part of some kind of universe-wide conflict that involves us in some way. We may not understand it, but we sense it, deep inside of ourselves. He concludes:

> If we were not experiencing some sort of conflict in our lives, our hearts would have no response to conflict in books or film. The idea of conflict, of having tension, suspense, or an enemy, would make no sense to us. But these things do make sense.[9]

Is it possible that the best stories are perceived by me in that way because they hook into what I am actually experiencing on a deeper, cosmic level? That I'm truly living within a time and place of separation—the reason for which goes far beyond my own willful choices? An alienation that has had and is having tragic con- sequences in my own life and in the lives of everyone? And could it be true that my hope of resolution—that I and the world in which I live could somehow be put right someday—is actually rooted in reality? That there is an actual plan…a strategy centered in and around love that is working to accomplish that very dream?

For many years, Joy and I watch the full extended version

---

[9] Miller, *Blue like Jazz: Nonreligious Thoughts on Christian Spirituality* (Nelson, 2003), 31-32. Jill Carattini has a great take on how C.S. Lewis saw this connection between the great myths and the Christian story - https://www.rzim.org/read/a-slice-of-infinity/myth-and-fact

of LOTR[10] over the Christmas holidays. Each year I wonder what it is that keeps me motivated to repeatedly invest that many hours. Not entertainment alone. Not a gratuitous violence fix for an otherwise pacifist soul.

I believe what draws me each year is a longing. A desire to see my own hope renewed. Hope for myself and for this world. That I'm not, and it isn't beyond saving. Somehow, I know that before heading into a new year I have to believe again. Something deep in me is reaching, longing.

Or is the story reaching for the deep parts in me that want to be found?

---

[10] *Lord Of The Rings*

2 An Inconsolable Longing

C.S. Lewis, the well-known twentieth century literature professor and popular author, understood this longing. He saw it as the central key to his journey toward faith.

Lewis once described himself as "the most reluctant convert in all of England."[11] While he would point back to a conversation with close friends and fellow professors J.R.R. Tolkien and Hugo Dyson as the precise turning point in his actual conversion, in fact it was simply one step in a gradual process of many. It was a journey in which Lewis would profess that he was far more pursued than pursuing.

Later reflecting on how this came about, Lewis realized that this pursuit had begun at an early age, and in ways that did not at first seem to be clearly connected with God. Even as a young boy, he could identify certain things that stirred his heart and put him in touch with a longing that existed deep within him. The catalysts varied: it might be Norse mythology, or a Beatrix Potter story, a moss garden, or an Autumn walk.

Initially, Lewis simply acknowledged these yearnings as

---

[11] C.S. Lewis, *Surprised by Joy: The Shape of My Early Life* (Harvest Books, 1955), 229.

emotions that just *were*. He described them as part of some kind of romanticism. Only later did he begin to understand them as signs along a path, placed there intentionally to lead him toward God.[12]

What hooked his heart was what he later described as joy—something he never confused with happiness or pleasure.[13] Joy, in his mind correlated with the German philosophic term *"sehnsucht"*: a deep desire for something that we've never experienced, like a longing for a home we've never known. But Lewis was quite aware that this longing was probably never going to be fully satisfied, at least in this world.

That nostalgic dissatisfaction, as much as anything, stirred spiritual hunger in him. "If I find in myself a desire which no experience in this world can satisfy, the most probable explanation is that I was made for another world," he reasoned. His longings were like markers pointing to another place.[14]

What's going on, I wonder, within Lewis? It's as though something mysterious from over the horizon has caught his eye, or even more important, has caught his heart. From a simple glance, something has hooked into him at the deepest core of his longings and desires. Almost compulsively he continues to look toward that horizon, longing for another glimpse. He knows instinctively that

---

[12] C.S. Lewis, *The Weight of Glory and Other Addresses* (McMillan, 1949). Various authors explore this same idea - Tim Keller writes about 'clues', Philip Yancey 'rumours', and N.T. Wright 'echoes of a voice.'

[13] Joy to Lewis was "an unsatisfied desire which itself is more desirable than any other satisfaction". *Surprised by Joy*, 18.

[14] https://blog.logos.com/2015/08/c-s-lewis-ingenious-apologetic-of-longing/ For further depth see: *Joy and Sehnsucht:The Laughter and Longings of C.S. Lewis* by Terry Lindvall
http://www.leaderu.com/marshill/mhr08/hall1.html

what he's "tasted" in these sightings is a vision of what could be...and perhaps will be one day.

Even more, he begins to believe that Someone from over that horizon is initiating these visions.[15]

Intending to draw him in. To lead him on a journey and invite him into a future...where joy will be found.

Could this be what happens to Abram and Sarah? Of course, initially they think—at least I imagine so—that the promised land will actually be a real plot of land in the here and now. Yet, when they arrive, the hook they felt in their hearts when they first heard God's call is still there.

Their eyes still keep looking toward the horizon.

Is their hoped-for city more heavenly than middle eastern?

It's hard, bone crushing hard, to keep longing for a lifetime. There's a reason that Lewis calls joy "an inconsolable longing." It's tempting to try on different stories along the way—those that distract, medicate, sedate, and tranquilize our deep desires in exchange for lesser pleasures.

Yet, at all times, if I will only look, there appear *pointers* that both encourage my desperate heart and show me a

---

[15] The theologian Karl Rahner asks why it is that we humans aren't satisfied with simply being human, but instead keep stretching outward to Being, to God. His best explanation is that God is reaching for us. See Karen Kilby's excellent summary of Rahner's thinking in *Karl Rahner: A Brief Introduction*.

path to follow. Like watering holes for someone dying of thirst. Refreshing my hope; giving life to my tired heart. Like the great myths that stirred a young Lewis' heart.

Others have travelled this path before and have left messages. Though cryptic, many are trustworthy. Connecting them all together, they seem to point back, as at the same time, they direct me onward.

Are they pointing ultimately to a meta-story...to a great myth which is, as Lewis put it, also a fact?[16] Or, as Donald Miller noted, guiding me to the narrative arc that I am searching to find?

Could there be a grand story in which I can become fully alive?

---

[16] C.S. Lewis, *God in the Dock* (Eerdmans, 1970).

3 Junior High

I remember it like it was yesterday—the first day of junior high school. It's a new experiment for our school district. Someone with "qualifications" has determined that it will be a wonderful idea to combine grades 7 through 10.

What could possibly go wrong?

In my particular case, actually a fair number of things. For one, as a boy who is slowly—and I mean *very* slowly— becoming a man, it's somewhat intimidating being mixed in with others who have been shaving for several years, and who because of their academic record—or lack of— are driving themselves to school.

What makes things worse are my mom's plans—no doubt because of a lack of finances—to ensure that my new school clothes will last for at least the duration of my junior high school career. So here I am in the gymnasium with everyone else waiting to be called into our classes with my catalog-ordered, extra large jeans, rolled up to expose—you have to visualize this—*red flannel lining*...at a time when everyone else has discovered skinny jeans.

It gets worse.

I'm sitting as inconspicuously as possible, trying to tuck my legs away from sight. I'm slightly distracted, my mind running through options of where I'll go after I've run away from home...something I seriously try to negotiate in the next few years.

Then the moment comes that I've been anxiously awaiting. I'm very aware that I only have one chance to get it right. I hear my name being called from the microphone. At least I think it is. Not knowing what else to do, I get up and follow this new group. I'm a bit concerned, since all of the people I'm following— including the girls—are at least a foot taller than me, and none of them have I ever seen before.

After a long, long walk through seemingly endless corridors, we arrive at a classroom. Literally numb, I stumble into a seat. Compulsively I feel like bolting and not stop running until I reach the safety of my bedroom. Sitting in my new class, while the teacher calls out names, I contemplate various methods of ending my life. Finally, he finishes confirming all the names on his class list. He then turns to me and demands, "You don't belong here. Go back to the gym. This is a grade 10 class."

In spite of the laughter following me, being turned out to the hallway is like being pardoned from prison. My deep sense of relief, however, quickly gives way to a new terror.

The only way back into the gym is from the front, forcing me to face the mocking gaze of everyone I know. I can't slip in unnoticed. The stinging mockery that follows touches something deep inside me. Strangely, after the first sense of utter humiliation and pain, it is as though I'm physically removed from what is going on around me. Even the sound seems muted and distant—like a dull echo or what a sound is like when heard from under water. I've had this experience before; it's like an old friend. It makes me feel safe. Though to be more accurate, perhaps I've found a way to be safe from my feelings.

Much of the following events is a blur to me. Eventually my name really is called, I finally get to the right class and am assigned a seat. I recognize a few faces, though sadly, there are no friends among them.

I'm put in the second to last seat closest to the door. Behind me is Barry. Barry has failed a few times and even though he is sitting, he still seems taller than me as I walk toward him. With his ducktail haircut, he's the epitome of cool. I look down at my jeans. This isn't going well.

I try to look straight ahead. Perhaps he'll simply forget about me. Even better, perhaps he'll forget about school and get a job somewhere.

Any temporary peace is fragile. I hear a snapping noise followed by a sting behind my right ear. I try to ignore it.

Snap! Snap!

Reluctantly, I turn around. There's a smiling Barry with what looks like a piece of rubber that he's stretching and then releasing in the direction of my ear.

Though it's only later that I discover that the piece of rubber is actually a condom, I know one thing for a fact: the story I've tried to live in—a decent Christian story passed on to me from my parents—isn't made for this jungle that I'm in. It's not going to help me to survive this school year, let alone this week. I don't know what I'll do but I'm going to have to find a whole new story. I'm going to have to take on a whole new identity. One that will enable me to hide within a secure facade. A story that will make it possible for me to belong.

And in this I'm completely alone. My parents will never, ever understand and can't help. As for God? God seems more part of the problem than a hopeful solution.[17]

---

[17] As Brené Brown writes, "Sometimes the most dangerous thing for kids is the silence that allows them to construct their own stories— stories that almost always cast them as alone and unworthy of love and belonging." *Braving The Wilderness: The Quest for True Belonging and the Courage to Stand Alone.* (Random House, 2017), 15.

4 The Genesis Of A Dispassionate Life

My memory of my childhood is limited to some fragmented pictures—some quite vivid, others more in the shadows. Perhaps, as is true for most of us, it's stories told to us later in life that help to thread these pictures together into some kind of understandable narrative.[18]

And it's this narrative that helps us understand our responses to things such as I've described, like my traumatic junior high school experience. We don't make decisions in isolation from what's gone before. Is it not more likely that these dramatic life choices are simply the tipping point, one last small step in a long process of action and reaction?

It always seems amazing to Joy that I can unemotionally recount early experiences in my life that, to her, would have been overwhelming. I describe them, she says, almost as though they've really taken place in someone else's life—with me simply witnessing them from a

---

[18] For an interesting discussion of how story-telling impacts memory, see https://theconversation.com/are-memories-reliable-expert-explains-how-they-change-more-than-we-realise-106461.

detached distance. My explanation, to Joy and to others, is that I'm consummately logical—left brain oriented. I lack emotional genes.

Joy is less convinced of my theory than I am, and fifteen years or so into our marriage I have an unexpected meltdown that appears to prove her right. It all starts with a deeply hurtful experience in which I feel I've been unfairly treated. Instead of supporting me, Joy seems to simply pile on with accusations of her own. And then, to my utter surprise, I completely unravel emotionally—I suppose that being curled up into a fetal position, racked with deep pain and howling like a dog for forty-five minutes, qualifies as "unraveled."

In this unanticipated encounter with myself, I have a seemingly unending stream of memories that come with incredible force—combined pictures and feelings that trace elements of my journey from before I was even born right through to adulthood. They're so vivid it's almost as though I'm re-living them.[19]

At one point in this primal experience, I'm "taken" to a time shortly after I move into a new neighbourhood in the third grade. I've already moved nine times by this point. I don't remember ever having a friend from my different homes—we didn't stay anywhere long enough I guess.

Shortly after arriving in my new neighbourhood, two boys invite me to join their club. They are older than me, and have lived there longer, and I can't believe my good fortune. They're including me! I'm not an outsider. I belong.

I have a vivid memory of being led through a small door

---

[19] Being reminded of Dickens' *A Christmas Carol* is not too big of a stretch here.

under their basement steps. There is a single light bulb that lights the small space, which is bare except for a pole in the center.

A pole to which I'm tied.

To this day everything up to that point remains a clear picture, and while I know that they then begin to do some things to me, my memory after that point is completely blank. All I know is that I never visit these boys again though we live across the street for many years.[20]

The other pictures are similar in nature. During the time I am curled up on the floor, there's one common theme running through all the unwanted memories crowding into my brain: a deep feeling of being unwanted and therefore rejected.

Of not belonging. Never belonging.

As dramatic as my "howling dog" experience is, somehow in the months that follow, I'm able to regain my sense of control and equilibrium. I diligently try to learn some life lessons about this, particularly trying to understand why rejection is such an important issue for me. But my emotions are neatly excluded from the learning process. I mostly get back to "normal."

I continue to live my life as I described in my opening introduction: on the other side of a window, observing

---

[20] I'm not trying to imply anything beyond what I am explicitly saying here. I simply don't have any memory of what happened after I was tied to the pole.

life, going through the motions of actually living, but somehow removed emotionally from it. My emotions are, like Snow White, lying dormant, against the odds waiting to be kissed.

When does this pattern start? For much of my life, I would say that I'm really not sure—that it seems like this has always been how I've lived. About a decade or so ago, though, I discover something that gives me a whole new level of understanding.

In the last couple of days that my Dad can talk, just before he dies, he relates to my son and his fiancée what a well-behaved baby I was. When asked how that came to be, he launches into a full explanation—one that, to his mind, would confirm what a brilliant parent he is.[21] One day, he explains, I was crying uncontrollably. Needing to be in charge, he sternly commanded me to stop crying. When I didn't respond according to his wishes, he put his strategy into action: he covered my mouth and nose and held that position until I succumbed and went limp.

When he took his hand away, I proceeded to scream again. He responded. I went limp.

This continued several more times, he says, until when he finally took his hand from my mouth, I didn't react. He had won. And I was well on my way to being an obedient child.

---

[21] I have to this day the greatest respect for my Dad. If you only take one snapshot of his life, it perhaps won't show him in a very good light. If you take a movie of his entire life, you can see more clearly just how much he learns and grows. In his last weeks of life, he confesses to me that the only time his father touched him was to hit him. My Dad never beat me. In fact he even told me that he loved me—the first time three days before he died and the last day in which he could still speak. Not much you say? He gave me what he never heard from his father for himself.

With a smile on his face, convinced he is sharing a helpful story to a young, soon to be married couple, he remarks, "Well after that, Gary wouldn't come to me for several months. But, from that point on, when he would cry, all I ever had to say to him was, 'Stop.'"

"And he would stop."

This explains a lot.

As I listen to this story being related, I understand more than ever before why I'm terrified of emotion. It's obviously a life and death issue for me.

Express and you die. You want to live, bottle it in.

I also understand why I have so much rage inside of me. I've spent my whole life trying to lock it down—deep, deep within—and throw away the key.

Of course, I can also see that once these feelings have been buried deep enough, and long enough, I eventually convince myself that I have no rage. No feelings.[22] I just choose and act. Like my father.

Almost.

---

[22] As Brené Brown notes, "We cannot selectively numb emotions, when we numb the painful emotions, we also numb the positive emotions." *The Gifts of Imperfection: Let Go of Who You Think You're Supposed to Be and Embrace Who You Are.* (Hazelden, 2010)

5 Strange Portents

Though in my post-Barry years I do everything I can to craft a cruel, uncaring persona, I'm always terrified that I'll be discovered. That others will realize that I'm vulnerable to being rejected and hurt, that I care deeply about belonging.

I try in every way to wall up this inner insecurity, to euthanize it by consciously choosing a lifestyle destructive to others and myself. Eventually, unable to contain my rage, I embrace it and make a virtue of it.

If I can never have my father's approval and acceptance, then I'll excel in the things of which he disapproves. I'll do the same with God.

I choose a Satanist girlfriend. I consume Jim Morrison and any music from the darker side that I can find. I learn to use my ability to craft words to carve weapons of destruction, designed to penetrate people in their places of greatest vulnerability.

All the while I see myself becoming less human, less alive. I compensate by pouring myself into competition. I'll prove to others that I'm better than any of them. Then they'll be forced to acknowledge that I belong.

And yet, while I'm doing all I can to cut myself off from heaven and from whatever gods may dwell there, heaven will not stop reaching for me. Though I've suffocated my deepest desires, believing that if I don't hope then I won't be disappointed, still my hopes and longings won't give up on me.

During the summer prior to my sophomore year in high school, I'm out at a ranch looking up at the grandeur of the night sky. It's so filled with stars that it seems they're stacked on top of one another. Suddenly, against all expectation, I "know" Someone is there. Someone who holds all these stars and yet has room for me. And I feel emotions stirring that I barely realize still exist.

Once back in school, things get back to normal, and this kind of intrusion seems easily dismissed. One event, however, reminds me—if only after the fact—that while I may have forgotten what I sensed in the stars, the "Someone" that I experienced there has not forgotten me.

The event is a particularly stormy encounter with my father. It is a typical confrontation: I'm owed money for working for him—which he requires me to do in order to live at home—but he won't pay me until I ask. Preceding payment is the usual diatribe in which he reminds me how useless I am and how I'm not worth the money he's now giving me.

This particular time, my rage consumes me. I throw the money back at him and head for my motorcycle, slamming the door as I leave. I race out of our driveway and within a few blocks I have maxed out my speed at over one hundred miles per hour. Weaving in and out of traffic, I have one consuming thought in my mind.

Turn the handlebars.

Just turn them and it's all over.

And yet I don't. And I don't know why. It's as though Something or Someone has a different story waiting for me. This will not be the only time I feel this re-straining force.

During this period, even my soon to be ex-girlfriend's Ouija board betrays me. In answer to the query, "What will Gary become?" without being guided by any hands it moves from letter to letter and spells out, "Pastor." I am freaked.

It reminds me of when, as a young boy, my family takes me to some meetings...quite different from the kind we are used to. A strange lady, who people describe as "prophetic," comes off of the stage to the back row, puts her hands on my head and basically says the same thing as the Ouija board has just told me.

It's getting harder to suppress these feelings of my heart being hooked by some mysterious force—the sense that there's something I'm made for. Something is expected of me. Something I can't control or would want to control. I fear it...and yet it draws me.

In a few years, things come to a head like the turning point in a classic narrative structure. My coach has lined up some basketball scholarships for me and convinced me that I should go on to college.

The assumption in my family has always been that I would go out and get a "real" job. However, having found someone who believes in me, I take the leap. After all, it will be a chance to finally leave home and find my own way.

University is the best of times and the worst of times. My basketball career is showing great promise. It's everything I've worked for since junior high school. At the same time, by the end of my second year I'm depressed, drinking heavily, and fighting off thoughts of suicide.

I'm having bizarre conversations with God, apparently confident in my belief that I can convince heaven that no one lives there. Up to now I haven't done any drugs, though I have a few joints in my pocket. (In our day athletes drink themselves to death and those in the arts faculties smoke dope. You need to know your proper tribe.)

Everything I do, though, I do to excess. I've only attended six classes by the end of the term but I am an amazing card player and I can drink most everyone under the table. But I'm playing close to a line that even I know is dangerous. Early one morning I awaken to discover that I'm in a living room that I have no memory of coming to. In the aftermath of a party, there are bodies spread around the room, seemingly paralyzed, eyes half open — it's difficult to tell if they are asleep or unconscious. I can't help staring at the guy on the floor next to me. He looks as rigid as a corpse. Could he be? I don't know who is dead and who's still alive but I know I have to get out of here.

The term is coming to an end. Somehow I've survived — I have against all odds passed the finals — but I don't quite honestly know how I'm going to navigate another year. But for now, I need to head home for the summer. At home I can live for free while I work and hopefully save up enough to do this next year.

Of course, that will mean playing the game…Pretending my life is together…Going to church.

6 Surprised By Ms. Layland

Going to church I can do. I've done it for years. You tune out. You learn to sleep with your eyes mostly open and your head upright. What I'm not ready for is the two zealots that have recently "discovered Jesus" and want to share that discovery with everyone.

Of course, I've spent my life refining ways to blow people off and let them know they are unwelcome. Yet they persist. It makes no sense. They aren't my kind of people. I don't want any kind of relationship with them. But it is just like trying to turn the handlebars.

Something is reaching for me. It's partly because of them but it is much more than that. Something—or Someone— is breathing into my heart. At least that is what it feels like. And it is inviting me.

Where? I don't have a clue and yet I inexplicably want to respond. I think it's love...and a hope of belonging.

But it's crazy. These guys are going off to a theological college in the fall in some god forsaken place in the Prairies. If I just go back to my basketball career soon all will be normal. So why is it that I want to go with them?

In the first week of September I pack up my car and head

off to the center of Canada to a school that I've recently registered for. In truth, I know virtually nothing about it. This is the most irrational thing I've ever done.

But somehow, I know that if I return to university I will miss a chance for something—a story of some sort that doesn't come around but once in a lifetime. It's like a train is going by and I jump on. Driving through the Rockies, I'm already thinking, "What have I done?"

Arriving at the school, I know I've made the biggest mistake of my life. Have I turned down one of the premier institutions in Canada to come to this? It looks like a condemned elementary school. I'm in a daze wondering how in the world I let my heart betray me like this.

Coming around a corner, I see a face. At first, I'm sure it's not true...it just looks like her.

"What are you doing here?" we both ask at once.

It's a girl I met in high school through our parents' plan to set us up on a blind date. Though we grudgingly go along with it, the relationship doesn't get off the ground. The only reason it lasts more than one date is that we can't determine who has won the arguments that dominate our first night out. She is caustic, not to be trifled with, but she is cool.

I've just taken the greatest leap of faith in my life—I feel like a novice tenuously stepping toward life in a monastery...and there she is. I soon discover that she is, on the one hand, escaping two serious boyfriends, neither of which know of the other, and on the other hand, she has given God one year to show her that he loves her. Here we are—two runaways looking for a way home.

Ironically, it isn't until almost the end of the school year that I actually take her out for coffee. (A memorable date, by the way. I buy her a cigar, which she takes back to the girls' dorm and smokes with her friends. I mean, how could that possibly go wrong in an ultra-conservative theological school?) I'm so taken by this woman that I illicitly have a key of the women's dorm made for her, so she doesn't need to be concerned about bothering the night watchmen when we return after curfew.

Her name is Joy Layland. Little do I know she will become my greatest gift while also stirring up my greatest fears.

7 We Don't Go There

Upon returning to the familiar west coast after my year in "exile," one thing is dramatically clear to me. There will be no returning to normal.

On the one hand, having run away without so much as notifying my coach has basically ended my basketball career. What I've based my entire life's goals upon has been taken away from me. There's good in that: my circle of relationships has changed and along with it, the influences that were destructive for me.

On the other hand, I'm navigating some new relationships: with Joy, and with God. Both fill me with anticipation and terror. Both are unpredictable, uncharted territories for me. Joy is in many ways my polar opposite, with very different ideas of what relationship looks like. Spiritually, while I am not ready to nominate myself for "Christian of the Year"—no matter how contrived the category—I am definitely on a new trajectory. There is an almost undefinable longing—dare I call it joy?—that is hooked into my heart and I'm being drawn to a horizon that's beyond my understanding and, seemingly, my ability to control.

It appears as though God is setting signs along a path,

inviting me to follow. Some of this is simply an awakening of my imagination—I'm beginning to see a different story for myself, one defined more by the future instead of by the past. Partly this is being ignited through people whose lives are inspiring me, who seem to be a tangible taste of what I think Jesus would be like. Something in me wants to be like them, though I don't quite know how.

And inevitably, it seems, I'm being drawn to God's book. First and most of all, it's the stories about Jesus that captivate me. There is love in those stories...and rescue. I feel like the lost sheep that Jesus has gone out after.

Ironically, despite a year studying theology, I'm little prepared to grasp what this book as a whole is all about. While my journey begins motivated by loving invitation— setting my imagination free to explore what love can do— I am quickly losing the forest for the trees, so to speak. I am becoming more a mechanic than an artist, learning how to tear the Bible apart and put it back together. Rehearsing the proper definitions and doctrines that will ensure that I won't stray from the prescribed boundaries that other, better minds have established.

Quickly, what is originally more of a love letter, becomes one more thing that I need to "get right" and master in order to prove my worth, and my right to belong. Solving some of the Bible's mysteries keep me distracted from my real issues of faith. I am simply exchanging one treadmill for another.

Nevertheless, I determine to do what seems a logical thing for a serious Christian: I'll read the Bible from beginning to end.

I think I make it to the book of Judges.

By the time I reach the story of Jephthah who sacrifices

his daughter to fulfill a vow made to God, I put the book down.[23] If I continue to read, I'll lose any faith I still hold.

I don't yet understand the internal conflict that I have with respect to God. Jesus I get. Jesus has always seemed to run after me. Jesus has hope for me. His attitude is, "Let's do this...together!"

God the Father? I guess, to be brutally honest, I expect him to say, "Turn the handlebars. You deserve it. You may fool others, but deep inside, I know who you are." I think I fear God more than love God. Of course, I know by now that God is supposedly a Trinity. But be that as it may, I can't help thinking, "Can I just deal with Jesus and let him make a connection to the others?"

I don't know the parenting story of my infancy yet, but somehow emotionally I suspect that my anxieties are of little concern to the Father. He is more interested in order and control—what is appropriate. If I dwell on it, I imagine him like an old man who has too many kids—never really liking kids in the first place—and now finds the misbehaving ones a profound irritant. What he looks forward to is punishing them one day.

The Holy Spirit? In the words of the infamous Bob Newhart sketch, "We don't go there."[24]

While I grow up in a church that gives lip service to the Holy Spirit, the only time anything is really said is to give a warning about potential undue focus upon the third member of the Trinity. Along with that caution, my first experiences as a child with God's Spirit are pro-foundly negative.

For some reason, when I'm nine or ten, I'm sent along

---

[23] Judges 11 tells the story.
[24] Bob Newhart, Stop It, https://youtu.be/Ow0lr63y4Mw

with my sister who is three years older with some neighbours to a special "prophetic" meeting. My main observation of the time is that the speaker seems excited and angry and shouts a lot.

At the end of the meeting, he invites people to come forward for prayer. I've never seen that before and it's a bit intimidating. I do remember feeling very guilty during the process—that if I really do love God I most certainly would be parading to the front. I resolutely hold back. That is, until I realize that my sister is gone—she has responded and so have my neighbours.

Terrified of being left alone in the crowd, I go to the front to look for my sister. Before I'm able to locate her, a group of men in suits surround me. Shouting out words from some strange dialect, they continually command me to "Speak it!"

In truth, I'd be happy to speak anything if any one of them would give me the words but I'm paralyzed with fear and confusion. After some time, as if on cue, they all stop shouting. One of the men says, "He's not getting it." And then they leave me.

I don't understand at all what has just happened, but I have a sense that it has something to do with God and that I haven't done very well.

Later than evening, I discover, to the joy of my neighbours, that my sister has received the *Holy Spirit*. By inference, I have not. From that day forward, the last thing I want in my life is anything that has to do with a spirit that can be so selective.

If he doesn't want me, I don't want him.

8 Do You Love Me?

It's not surprising, then, that I have some difficulty in reading the first half of the Bible—not that many of the letters are much easier, but that is another matter. First of all, Jesus seems to be nowhere around. This makes me anxious. I feel like I need somebody who is at least a bit "on my side."

So basically I park the idea of some great narrative that I can learn to live in. I do the kinds of things I've done my whole life. I perform. I study. I try to figure out what is required of me. I try to suppress the doubts that threaten to sabotage whatever faith I still have.

I do want to please Jesus, I really do. And on the outside I look like I'm well on the way. Somehow, deep inside, though, I feel like this is not going to end well.

In contrast, Joy's approach to faith is not nearly so sophisticated...or should I say, muddled. There are many things with which Joy struggles: fear of abandonment and rejection taking the front of the line. These areas of challenge will deeply impact her relationships throughout her life. She will always struggle with some depression.

However, one thing is perfectly clear to Joy. She had

asked God a question, "Do you love me?" "And in the year we were in that little school on the Prairies," she would say to anyone who ever asked from that point forward, "God showed me at least seventeen times that the answer was most certainly, 'Yes!'"

She will never doubt this; it will be the story that anchors her whole life. While there are many things Joy doesn't understand, she has a simple solution. She has a shelf in her mind labelled, "To be answered later." Those confusing things she puts on that shelf, fully confident that she can trust God to ultimately make sense of them. Instead of being paralyzed by her doubts, Joy gives herself to living in grateful response to the one God—Father, Son and Spirit—that has so unreservedly loved her.

Quite early on in our relationship, she asks me to make a backing for a decoupage of a prayer by Mother Teresa. It will be her manifesto, the dedication of her life:

Joy is prayer. Joy is strength. Joy is love. Joy is a net of love by which you can catch souls. She gives most who gives with joy.

The best way to show our gratitude to God and the people is to accept everything with joy. A joyful heart is the inevitable result of a heart burning with love.

We all long for heaven where God is but we have it in our power to be in heaven with Him right now—to be happy with Him at this very moment. But being happy with Him now means: loving as He loves, helping as He helps, giving as He gives, serving as He serves, rescuing as He rescues, being with Him for all the twenty-four hours, touching Him in his distressing disguise.

For Joy, this prayer is what the Bible is all about. And it is this story that Joy will dedicate herself to live within for the next forty-seven years...and see it as the greatest privilege.

9 The Jigsaw Puzzle

"It's a big book, full of big stories with big characters. They have big ideas (not least about themselves) and make big mistakes. It's about God and greed and grace; about life, lust, laughter, and loneliness. It's about birth, beginnings, and betrayal; about siblings, squabbles, and sex; about power and prayer and prison and passion."

"And that's only Genesis."[25]

So what is the Bible anyway?

Is it a defense of God's long story with Israel fulfilled through Jesus?

Is it the ultimate rule book that determines what God does or doesn't approve of?

Is it a text with hidden codes that unlock deep spiritual meanings?

---

[25] N.T. Wright, Simply Christian (Harper Collins, 2010), 173.

Is it the record of everything one needs to know in order to be saved?

Is it a handbook of moral and ethical teaching designed to produce personal piety?

Is it a how-to manual that is to be literally obeyed?

Is it a text that is heavily conditioned by the contexts in which it was written?

As N.T. Wright argues in his book, *The Last Word*, the Bible has been understood as all of these, at various points in history, and within various groups of people.[26]

And this is just the tip of the iceberg.

As our present world is far less controlled by ecclesiastic hierarchies, the number and extent of different frameworks for understanding the Bible just continues to multiply. Almost every Christian group thinks that the Bible is absolutely central but beyond some consensus around a small central core of what it teaches, we quite simply can't agree. In other words, we think the Bible is really important, but we don't know at all how to see it in the same way.

If the Bible is so central to my faith, why is it so difficult for me to be sure that I am even understanding it correctly?

On one level, I face the same challenge that I do with any historical document. I'm so removed from the initial context—what the first hearers would have easily understood—that no matter how hard I try to reconstruct that original setting, there is a lot of uncertainty. Add to

---

[26] N.T. Wright, The Last Word (Harper Collins, 2005). Over the next few chapters I draw heavily on Wright's thinking here.

that my significant limitations: my finite ability to know and grasp God's intentions for the Bible, and my broken state given my separation from God.

Yet there is something more than just the difficulties I face within myself. The very way in which the Bible is written ensures that there will always be some ambiguity and varying perspective. The scriptures are not simply dropped from the sky as an "untainted" revelation from God, with explicit details and instructions, ensuring no human "contamination".

Its writers are definitely human, with sometimes less than perfect motivations and less than complete perspectives. They live and write within a context which necessarily restricts their horizons—there are many things that they simply cannot envision because of their cultural framework.

It is not surprising then to find, in the earliest books of the Hebrew Scriptures, strong parallels to structures and concepts found in the surrounding culture of the Ancient Near East. Given their common cultural heritage, one would expect such things as temple layout, priestly orders, etc. to be quite similar. In a time of tribal conquest, it is not surprising that the Hebrews share with their neighbours the concept of a warrior God, fighting for their king to the exclusion of the surrounding peoples. And of course the individual writers also have their own personal agendas and concerns—sometimes which are in harmony with God's...and sometimes less so.

At the same time, there is no heavenly wringing of hands, God saying, "I knew I should have written this myself!" God is confident about the process—God's spirit moving the authors to write about the encounters they're having with God, documenting things that they believe God wants to say. God leads them in the writing within the limitations of their understanding—confident that the story needing to be communicated will shine through the human delivery system.[27]

God's decision to partner with humanity in this way in the writing of the Bible—rather than "override us"—carries over to the task of interpreting those writings, and understanding them today, both personally and together. While God's spirit is here to help guide me along the journey that the Bible lays out, I also bring my mind, emotions, longings and prejudices into the mix. That means I will often get it wrong, yet God doesn't panic— just like a good parent who knows that the freedom for a child to make mistakes is indispensable to healthy growth.

Complicating all this is the fact that the Bible, Old Testament or New, just doesn't tell me all the details I want to know in order to be absolutely sure that I have everything right with respect to God. Even more difficult than what the Bible says, is what it fails to say which makes it all the more challenging to have confidence that I'm understanding it rightly.

It's like a gigantic jigsaw puzzle without a clear picture on the box that explains what I am trying to construct. And no matter how I put it together, there always seems to be enough pieces left over that I can't make fit, that I'm left

---

[27] 2 Peter 1:20,21. I realize that I'm describing something that seems to fall short of full, plenary inspiration. While there is a significant degree of debate surrounding exactly how that 'inspiration' functioned (i.e. the exact nature of the human/divine partnership involved in the writing), at the least we can say this: that God has "authorized" what has resulted to become, taken all together, a trustworthy guide for people who are wanting to understand what God's invitation is to humankind, and how to respond appropriately.

with a certain degree of uncertainty as to whether I'm assembling the right overall picture at all.[28]

---

[28] Christian Smith, *The Bible Made Impossible: Why Biblicism Is Not a Truly Evangelical Reading of Scripture* (Brazos, 2011) 45.

10 | Misunderstood

Patience isn't one of my greatest virtues. I abhor uncertainty—it seems to go along with living in the western, developed world—and I desperately want control over the story of my life. And nothing helps me do that better than to turn the challenging narrative of the Bible into impersonal information that I can mine, analyze, and interpret—usually with the help of my chosen "experts."

For the late author, Eugene Peterson, this eliminates our need to actually *read* the Bible, since we have already figured out the scheme or summary of *what it teaches.* Which simply means we "don't have to enter the story and immerse ourselves in the odd and unflattering and uncongenial way in which this story develops...."[29]

But there is great danger in "translating" story into deposits of information. "If we mistake its form, we will almost certainly respond wrongly to its content," warns Peterson. To illustrate, here are some details from an event that took place when I was eight years old—the basic "facts":

---

[29] Eugene H. Peterson, *Eat This Book: A Conversation in the Art of Spiritual Reading* (Eerdmans,2009), 66.

1. We had finally moved into what would be our home for the next fifteen years or so.
2. My father was putting in a lawn and was pulling weeds before seeding. In front of the house were some tomato plants (his prize possession).
3. While he was working on the lawn, I took a stick and took great pride in whipping these plants until nothing was protruding from the dirt.
4. Finally seeing what I had done, my father was irate and ordered me into the house.

Here is the same situation in the language of story:

My father worked six days a week. Sunday we went to church morning and evening and in the afternoon he napped. On this particular Saturday he came home from work early in order to do some work in the yard. He was preparing the front yard for seeding grass by pulling up the weeds that were in the topsoil.

I treasured this opportunity to be with him. I imitated what I saw him doing—pulling weeds—but in a way that was a bit more exciting for me. I would whip the weeds into submission with a stick that I carried and then pull out what was left. I was being just like my Dad.

Part way through our job our neighbour came out of his house. My father called out to him, "How do you like the weeds I have growing in front of my living room window?" I took note of where he pointed, not knowing what a tomato plant looked like and not really understanding irony.

While my father continued to speak to the neighbour, I proceeded to help my dad by removing these enemy plants from in front of the window, making short work of them with my stick.

I was, of course, crestfallen when I received my father's angry rebuke. I couldn't begin to explain—the "evidence" was stacked against me.

The question is, was what I did right? Or wrong?

When I don't take time to listen to a story, what I presuppose simply takes over and defines the narrative. I like that. It gives me the feeling that I am in charge, I've taken control.

It's like wearing a pair of glasses that quickly bring everything into focus. Clarity brings confidence...but often at a cost.

11 Deductive Modelling

The one thing that helps me the most when trying to understand the Bible, is remembering that I'm always reading it through "glasses"—presupposed frameworks that I've constructed to quickly make sense of what I see. Of course, usually I haven't even constructed these lenses myself. I've inherited them from my family system, my surrounding culture and subculture and from my education—both formal and informal. Because of this I just assume that they're the way things are to be seen— which makes it all the more dangerous.

C.S. Lewis, who I mentioned previously, is one of my literary "heroes." His ability to make seemingly ob- scure theology more accessible and understandable is something I especially appreciate.

How is he viewed in theological circles? Not quite so positively. The standard criticism often focuses on his "shortcomings on scripture," likely due to the fact that he was "not a theologian but a literary critic."[30]

---

[30] Philip Ryken, The Romantic Rationalist: God, Life, and Imagination in the Work of C. S. Lewis (Crossway, 2014). Ryken's chapter can be found at: https://www.desiringgod.org/messages/inerrancy-and-the- patron-saint-of-evangelicalism-c-s-lewis-on-holy-scripture

More specifically he is characterized as being an "adoptionist"—believing that in the Bible, God has sometimes taken human stories and used them for God's own purposes—rather than wholeheartedly supporting "plenary verbal inspiration" and "inerrancy"—that all the words in the whole Bible are God's words and that they are without error in the original manuscripts.[31]

Critics will point out that Lewis has made the terrible mistake of bringing his presuppositions from the literary world into the world of the Bible, so that he has—quite sadly they say—misunderstood the nature of inspiration. They will then quote 2 Timothy 3:16 to emphasize the clarity and "rightness" of their own position: that since all of the words of the Bible are God-breathed, it can only mean that they are God's words, all of them in every way.

Of course, what they should say is that Lewis is contradicting *their* theory of inspiration—the real criticism directed toward Lewis is that he isn't wearing the same glasses as his conservative evangelical critics with respect to the system by which the scriptures are to be interpreted. And since they are certain that their presuppositions are the correct ones, Lewis must be

---

[31] All labels carry the danger of pronouncing a "verdict" on things or people in order to stop conversation and the need to continue to listen. I guess some labels are necessary, but God must weep when we use them the way we do—as weapons.

in error.[32]

N.T. Wright comments, "Anyone who has worked within biblical scholarship knows, or ought to know, that we biblical scholars come to the text with just as many interpretative strategies and expectations as anyone else...."[33]

He then goes on to emphasize that in every age since Jesus, as we have grappled with interpreting and understanding our sacred texts, the biases and perspectives of our cultural times have conditioned that process—we see, not objectively, outside of our place and time, but from within our context.

So, in every period of history, we will come to the conclusion that some previous understandings need to be adjusted, or understood in a new light—just as our present attempts will no doubt be re-evaluated in the future.

I think this, at the very least, ought to mean that I hold all "positions" regarding the Bible with great humility. I'm going to get some things right and some things wrong when trying to understand the Bible—and I often won't

---

[32] When I read something that I resonate with (which means that I am reading something I *want* to agree with), I will usually look for critiques to help me with my judgement. The first ones that I find—and usually don't do much more than skim—are the cheerleaders for the position I already want to wholeheartedly adopt. The next ones online that are relatively quick and easy to find are the *trolls*—those who are quick to condemn the writing (and writer) as worthy of whatever hell can throw at them. If I look hard and long enough, I can locate the truly helpful pieces of criticism: reviews by scholars that can—and do—see and speak out the good and then go on to identify some challenges and difficulties that will need some further conversations. These *critics* are pure gold. One of my favourites is the scholar Roger Olson. Look for some of his reviews...you won't regret it.

[33] Wright, *The Last Word*, 16.

know conclusively which is which!

But, as Wright says, I need to keep working at it, diligently, with humility, and together with others. At the end of the day, the Bible does mean something—it's not just a reflection of the meaning I bring to it—and it wants me to find that meaning.[34] Finding it will mean starting with a humble recognition that my understandings may be incomplete, followed by diligent study soaked with prayer, and continued with engaging conversations—particularly with people who have different perspectives than my own.

In this I hope for the best. I want to assume that the study of the Bible will be like Wright describes—a process in which everyone builds positively upon each new step of scholarly insight, adjusting systems and schemas appropriately. Much like the scientific method, always assuming that discovery will challenge our temporary perspectives and lead us to better ones.

Sadly, in science and in theology, the actual pattern of response too often works quite differently. As Thomas Kuhn pointed out nearly sixty years ago,[35] what actually happens, predictably plays out this way:

---

[34] This approach to scriptural interpretation is based on a system of philosophy known as *critical realism* which tries to explain how we actually know anything. It argues that there is a *knowable* world outside of us but that all of our knowledge of it is conditioned by our worldview biases. The optimism of *critical realism* lies in its belief that our prejudiced, conditioned view can be at least somewhat overcome by reflection and conversation with others. If you really want to explore this further, Alistair McGrath's *Scientific Theology* is a good place to start.
[35] Thomas Kuhn, *The Structure of Scientific Revolutions* (University of Chicago, 1962).

First, a particular *paradigm*[36] becomes established which tells us what we should expect to discover. Interestingly enough, we then tend to find what we are looking for.

However, over time, anomalies emerge, which we try to rationalize within our larger picture. Incrementally, these things that don't seem to "fit" lead to a certain degree of discontent with the overall picture—or paradigm—that has become generally accepted.

Eventually, attempts to challenge the existing framework of understanding are resisted and often ostracized— they're too threatening to the status quo.

What can happen over time, however, is that contrary evidence finally leads to so much turmoil that a revolution occurs. The old way of seeing is subsequently over-thrown—this is what happened with Newtonian physics. In its place a new paradigm—in this case quantum physics—is adopted, and a new normal is established.

Repeat process. Defend the new way of seeing at all costs. Welcome to science.

What's true in science is all too often true in theology. The theological paradigm I adopt which tells me what the story of the Bible is intending to say to me—ironically developed often with little reference to the Bible itself— far too often becomes a battlefield, ground I must defend at all costs.

Sadly, when the battle is over, the theological lens, or way of seeing scripture, which ends up dominating becomes the new persecutor—even though that position itself may have previously been resisted and opposed.

---

[36] A way of seeing things. A model or pattern that becomes a theory of how to think about things. A system that allows us to bring order to a sensory world (i.e. a mental set).

Though I might in theory expect and welcome fresh readings and perspectives, in reality when I am in the dominate majority I will always operate with the assumption that this time we got it right.[37]

---

[37] As Churchill remarked, "History will be kind to me, for I intend to write it." We always believe that we can maintain control over our narrative. To which Carol Tavris (*Mistakes Were Made But Not By Me*) responds, "History is written by the victors, but it's victims who write the memoirs." Sobering thought.

12 It's A Story

It's time for the Story to bust out of the cage and take the stage

And demand a hearing once again

It's a STORY, I tell you!

And if you allow the Story to seep into your life

So that THE STORY begins to weave into your story

That's when, at last, my friend, you're reading the Bible right.

- Brian Zahnd[38]

Most times when I find myself stalled, polarized, and myopic, I find it helpful to pull back and get a larger view of things. To once again find the thing that is most obvious—that which most of us, regardless of the

---

[38] Brian Zahnd, *Reading The Bible Right,*
https://brianzahnd.com/2013/09/reading-bible-right/

prescription of our lenses, seem to be able to see.

So what is most obvious about the Bible?

It's easy to miss, perhaps because it is constantly right in front of me.

It's a story.

Eugene Peterson writes, "The Bible is basically and overall a narrative, an immense, sprawling, capacious narrative. Stories hold pride of place in revealing God and God's way to us."[39]

I can listen to a lecture, or absorb a list of facts. But a story? A story, a good story, compels me to step in, to become part of where the story is going. It doesn't let me dispassionately, passively observe. It calls me to make a choice.

I inevitably begin to identify with the characters, become part of their thinking, their feeling, and their actions. I see parallels into my own personal life and wrestle with what I will or won't do.

A great story leaves me better or worse off. It never leaves me untouched.

The Bible isn't intending first of all to present me with a tight system of thought, commanding me to align my thinking rigidly with it. "The biblical way," says Peterson, "is to tell a story and invite us, 'Live into this—this is what it looks like to be human in this God-made and God-ruled world; this is what is involved in becoming and maturing as a human being.'"[40]

Of course, stories can be used by skillful storytellers

---

[39] Eugene Peterson, *Living into the Story of God*, 1.
[40] Peterson, *Living*, 3.

to seduce, deceive, and manipulate. They weave their spells so I will be less alive, more under their control or the mastery of the ones they serve. Others spin their tales to make me more fully alive. They are honest, yet inviting. They don't cross the line of my freedom and re-sponsibility to choose my path. The stories of the Bible are like that.

To see the Bible this way, I need to read it as it intends to be read. A story, particularly a great sweeping story like the Bible, isn't meant to be first of all examined with a microscope—studying the magnified bark of each tree in the grove. I need to pull back and open my vision: see the whole forest, including where it has been and where it will be.

The Bible is written of course over many centuries by an array of authors from within vastly different contexts and cultural realities. If I restrict myself to examining the intricacies of each detail, hoping to master the interpretive key, I can miss the obvious—what the story is about as a whole, and where it is moving. The whole shows me how to understand the parts.

By seeing the story as a whole, I'm not tempted to take early parts and hold them up in isolation to create a lens with which to judge the rest. Naturally, Abram will see God somewhat through the lens of the tribal gods with whom he is familiar. If I fail to see the movement in the story as God leads people to entire new ways of understanding, I'll miss the mercy and restraint in the "eye for eye" in the Mosaic code. That it was always intended to give way to the "mercy triumphs over judgement" in the new covenant.

In the early parts of the Hebrew story, if I just take a snapshot, nothing seems particularly noteworthy or very much different between Abram and Sarah and the world immediately around them. What I need to do is shoot a movie. If I do, I'm astonished by what begins to happen over time as God invites them on an adventure, the implications of which will go far beyond selecting new real estate.

Somehow the Jews, quite uniquely from other cultures, will break free from the cyclical concept of life, the Great Wheel—all doomed to be repeated endlessly with no ultimate purpose or direction. They will change history by literally creating history. They'll write, still using some of the concepts and frameworks with which they are familiar, but proposing previously unconsidered ways through which to see their reality. They'll envision a life that moves forward, an arc and direction to human events. All of this because of what they'll describe as a relationship with the One God.

As Thomas Cahill writes, "Most of our best words, in fact—*new, adventure, surprise; unique individual, person, vocation; time, history, future; freedom, progress, spirit; faith, hope, justice*—are the gifts of the Jews."[41] Or, I might argue, a gift from God to all of humankind through the Jews so that we might find our way home.

The understandings that begin to form about God's intention to rescue and reconcile, not only for this new, emerging people, but for all of God's creation, will take time. This is uncharted territory and in most ways,

---

[41] Thomas Cahill, *The Gifts of the Jews: How a Tribe of Desert Nomads Changed the Way Everyone Thinks and Feels* (Doubleday, 1999). Recent scholarship around culture would challenge somewhat Cahill's position. That said, even if the Jews were not entirely unique in their understanding, they were undoubtedly the most consequential culture doing so.

counter intuitive for the ancient world. Yet God will continue to breathe upon and revitalize human imagination. Not without missteps and detours, this story of God's invitation will nevertheless prepare the way for the entry of Jesus, in every way the climax and turning point of the entire narrative.

Throughout that journey, the Bible continues to highlight the manifold ways in which heaven and earth re-connect in very personal ways. In telling the rich stories of these encounters, the Bible encourages people within every period of history to be not only receptive to but actively reaching to a fully present God.

From my side, as for Abram and Sarah, I don't often know where it is all going.[42] At the same time, I see the relentless pursuit of God. Woven in and around those stories is the larger one of who I am and have been, how I have lost my way, and how God is making a new future possible for me.[43]

The scriptures are not, though, something to be worshipped themselves. The Bible doesn't present itself as the way to God. Jesus is the way, the turning point of the entire story.[44] What the Bible has been authorized to

---

[42] The story is told in Genesis 12. When the actual encounter takes place (however that does) there are no written scriptures. The event is passed along by oral tradition until which time it can be recorded and preserved.

[43] Matt Croasmun from the Yale Center For Faith And Culture has developed a wonderful course for the Vineyard Institute called The Story of the Kingdom, walking us through the Big Story of God— https://vineyardinstitute.org/usa/for-students/your-calling/disciple.

[44] Authority has clearly been given to Jesus to bring God and humanity together. The Bible simply points to that authority. As N.T. Wright makes clear, "The risen Jesus, at the end of Matthew's gospel, does not say, 'All authority in heaven and on earth is given to the books you are all going to write,' but, 'All authority in heaven and earth is given to me.'" (Wright, Scripture and the Authority of God, location 86)

do is to help me find the open door to relationship with God that Jesus has made possible.

So, the story first leads to, and then on, from Jesus.

And Jesus perfectly reveals to me who God is and always has been.[45]

The faithful and good Father who runs to meet me.[46]

---

[45] Colossians 1:18-19, Hebrews 1:1-3.

[46] The story is recorded in Luke 15. For those listening to Jesus's story, there would be at least two scandalous elements: first, that the father would willingly respond to the younger son's demand for an early inheritance, and second, that the father would run to welcome the undeserving son home. Lots of people are expected to run in the ancient Middle East—slaves run, children run, wives run—all in service to the patriarch, who would never run. It would be beneath his dignity. In this story, love overwhelms convention. The father can't hold himself back, taking up all the space between himself and the undeserving son. Powerful...and perhaps tells us the most important thing we need to know about God.

13 How To Love The Truth

Empires, be they political, intellectual, or spiritual, don't hold forever. The sun has set on the British Empire. Manifest destiny considered, the same will be true of America. The promised eschatology of the Age of Enlightenment has never materialized and the irony of post-modernism is that despite its razor-sharp critique of its predecessor, it seems ineffective at envisioning a cure.

Whatever the future of post-modernism, it's at least clear that the modern world of thought has received a staggering blow. The grip of the Enlightenment hierarchies controlling and directing our thinking is compromised. Existing systems of thought are being torn down and replaced in major segments of culture. There's a revolution taking place and we're experimenting with new ways of seeing.

We're also trying on new glasses inside the church.[47]

---

[47] Phylis Tickle, *The Great Emergence: How Christianity is Changing and Why* (Baker, 2008). Tickle's thesis is that every 500 years or so (the last time was in the 16th century) the church holds a rummage sale of sorts and decides what it wants to keep and what it wants to discard. To say it another way, it goes through a revolution or reformation. She explains that we are in the throes of this at the present time.

Church power structures are crumbling. Technology has disabled control over information and resources. We're no longer simply satisfied with rehearsed answers to what we consider lesser questions—simply tweaking the existing paradigms. We're challenging their authority. For this reason, we've gone beyond arguments over specific biblical texts within agreed upon systems of interpretation. We're challenging these systems, both for good and for ill.

Sadly, but to be expected—since we don't do uncertainty well—many of us then fight it out. Rather than entering into dialogue, listening to one another and trusting in God's ability to be fully present and to help us to find a way forward together, we stick to our tribe, stoking the fears of our base. We shout the same things louder, repeating the talking points given to us by our experts— many of which we scarcely understand, except that we know they're right.[48] After all, what is at stake is our

---

[48] Experts, of course, are inevitable. The great majority of us can't even read the Bible except through translators and scholars who do their work from within the presuppositions they bring to their task. We all have been deeply influenced by teachers who have been our guides, helping us to understand the big picture of the Bible and how it is wanting to speak to us. Of course, others with whom we disagree have their own experts as well. In both "camps" we have an array of scholars who have dedicated their lives to studying and understanding the Bible, who in most cases love Jesus with all of their heart, soul and mind... and who strongly disagree with one another. We are told that we are to judge between the experts. That is like the average person being asked to make a final decision on whether string theory or loop quantum gravity is the better route to a unified theory of physics. To expect that most of us are competent enough to make the "right" judgement is perhaps overly optimistic. We can, however, grow in our ability to choose our experts wisely and then be diligent to read sources that don't always simply confirm what we already have been told is the "right" position on every topic. In reality, most of us never read outside of our "tribe,"—the community that consistently aligns with our present beliefs—and therefore most of what we take in confirms what we already know to be true: our experts are the right ones. (See "confirmation bias" in Tavros and Aronson, *Mistakes Were Made, But Not by Me.*)

mandate to "...contend for the faith which was once for all delivered unto the saints."[49] Or so we think.

Indeed, a revolution is necessary. But it's not for the purpose of establishing a new reigning paradigm of interpretation, where theology once more rules over the Bible itself.

Perhaps by remembering that our scriptures are first of all a story may give me, and those with whom I don't agree, a little room to breathe. A story gives some room to bend, and an opportunity for people to enter it in different ways and at different times without it collapsing on itself.

It creates space to improvise.[50]

As I wrestle with the invitation to enter this story and fully live within it, may I hold my convictions of conscience, and the experts I choose with extreme humility, and respect for those with whom I disagree. Humility, knowing that I only see in part and am always suspect to self-deception. Respect, because other traditions and positions are held by people who are just as precious to

God as I am...people who love God deeply and want to know God's truth.

---

[49] Jude 1:3 NASB.
[50] While I would recommend the entirety of N.T. Wright's book *The Last Word* (or the expanded, later edition, *Scripture and the Authority of God*), especially unpack Wright's explanation of his Five Act Model of understanding improvisation within God's Story (pages 121-127). Improvisation is a central concept within that model.

The reality that there is so much disagreement among us all should humble me. It should bring me pain; it would be tragic if it didn't. It's one more piece of evidence that God's kingdom has not yet fully permeated the kingdom of this world.

Perhaps the lesser issue is my ability to read the story rightly. Could the greater concern be my willingness to allow the story to read me? Is the whole point to gain control over the narrative, to eliminate the mystery?

Or is it about surrendering that need for control?

For many years, vexed by doubts, I believe that mastering the details and systems of God's word—really knowing it—is the end goal of faith. Thankfully, my doubts eventually lead me to better questions.

Is the story trying to help me question my need for control? I begin to wonder where else this story is wanting to take me. Or more clearly, to whom this story is leading.

"If you want someone to know the truth, you tell them. If you want someone to love the truth, tell them a story."[51] It stands to reason that God, who is love, would give me a story to find my way home.

---

[51] Unknown author quoted by musician Andrew Peterson. Found in http://marshwiggle.org/if-you-want-someone-to-know-the-truth-you-tell-them-if-you-want-someone-to-love-the-truth-tell-them-a-story/

14 A Different Kind of Knowing

When the book of Acts remarks that the first disciples of Jesus after their experience at Pentecost are "filled with courage and boldness," what it means is that they have a story burning in their hearts. A story that they know will transform the world just as it has their own lives. For them, the easy part is within their shared Jewish culture— they speak the same language, have a common understanding of the story of God, and a similar way of looking at the world.

What surprises them quite early in their adventure of being heralds of the Good News, is that many of their Gentile neighbours begin to want into the story, even though at first most Jews are expecting them to be enfolded in much later chapters and in much different ways. Regardless, it doesn't take long before Gentile participation is a major part of the unfolding narrative.

I can't overstate the collision of worldviews that results. The dominant philosophy of the Greco-Roman world, while not unfamiliar with gods and revelations—including the tradition of the Hebrews—holds at its centre a firm belief that ultimate knowledge is attained through a rational process of inquiry...asking questions and thinking logically. In other words, that reality is to be found in ideas and these ideas are discovered through the questions that an inquirer forms as a result of their experience in the world.

Within this philosophy—or way of looking at the world—since the individual decides the questions that they are going to ask, to some degree the knowledge they gain is their own achievement. Of course, this understanding assumes a certain kind of dualism[52] separating the realm of the ideal—theory—and the application of that ideal—practice. In all of this process, the individual person is firmly in control—both through their logical thinking and through the action of their will, deciding which outcomes to put into practice.

That's quite different from how the Hebrew mind generally works. While Paul and other disciples of Jesus are certainly acquainted with Greek thinking—and use some elements of it to communicate the Christian story—the heart of their message, most particularly with respect to what and how we can really know, contrasts with the dualism of classical philosophy.[53] At its centre, the message of Christianity is that God has acted in human history through Jesus. The *logos*—the centre that holds everything together, enabling it to make sense—is a person, and from Jesus on, the key to ultimate reality will

---

[52] Dualism simply means dividing things into two categories. According to the Stanford Encyclopedia of Philosophy, "In the philosophy of mind, dualism is the theory that the mental and the physical—or mind and body or mind and brain—are, in some sense, radically different kinds of thing."

[53] From the time of Paul onward, Christian thinkers try to relate the message of God's action through Jesus in ways that Greek thinkers can relate to. However, they never adopt the fundamental presuppositions of Greek thought in order to "prove" the reality of God/Jesus. Of course, neither of the presuppositions behind either Christianity or classical philosophy can be proven or disproven. Both require trusting acceptance (faith) at a primary level.

only be found in relationship with him. Plato's Idea of the Good has walked into the room.[54]

This challenges head-on the two primary dualisms of Greek thought: the separation between the spiritual and the material—i.e. our soul and our body—and between being and becoming—i.e. ideas and the physical world.[55] Jesus brings everything together: God takes on human form, truth is embodied in a person. And this will demand a new way of understanding the world: one that can only come about from within relationship—a personal knowledge.[56]

Paul and others, in calling people within the Greco-Roman world to respond to the invitation of Jesus, are not asking them to work out practical applications of some new ideas. They are challenging them to trust a *real* person—one who has bridged the gap between heaven and earth, and opened a way for us to become *fully* alive. As Paul emphasizes in one of his letters, to the Greeks this seems like foolishness—it colours completely outside the lines of how they have been taught to think

---

[54] Lesslie Newbigin, Proper Confidence: Faith, Doubt, and Certainty in Christian Discipleship (Eerdmans,1995). Plato's "Idea (or Form) of the Good" is described in his dialogue The Republic, which he introduces through the character of Socrates. He argues that the inspiration and source of every good thing is a pure, eternal essence of "goodness" that exists outside of our physical world and beyond our own minds. Newbigin is arguing that the Jews believed that this core essence that Plato is describing is personal and knowable. Newbigin's thinking is central to all of my Chapters 13-15.

[55] In the most simple terms, for Plato, being represents the world of forms, or ideas. It is separate from the material, and transcendent. It is always the same, never changing and is the source of the essential nature of the physical, material world. Becoming is the physical world we perceive through our senses and in contrast to the world of being is never fixed but always in movement, always changing.

[56] Newbigin, Proper Confidence. My friend, Al Doerksen, put me onto a brilliant Christian philosophic application of Polanyi's idea of "personal knowledge" by Esther Meek entitled Longing to Know.

about things.

This process of knowing—like the bond between dear friends—doesn't prohibit you and I from asking questions. The mind is entirely involved. To experience this kind of knowing, though, I need to go far beyond what "the facts" can tell me.

I can never know another person in this way through simply studying them—they can never be reduced to the object of some kind of science experiment. No, this kind of knowledge is always a gift. I can't know someone intimately unless they want to be known. But the risk always goes both ways; both parties must embrace vulnerability because both are at risk of rejection. This knowing is not for the faint of heart.

Does this mean then that I stop asking questions, stop being curious about God's world? Exactly the opposite. Augustine said, "I believe in order to know." He realized that knowing God caused him to become more curious, not less. As I come to know God more, I also discover that God delights in my questions, that God wants to be known, and feels the same about my attempts to understand the universe around me.

What does this all mean for me? Though significantly undermined by post-modernism, the basic structures of my thinking are still by and large modern, marked by the same dualisms of Greek thought. I still think theory/practice. And I'm used to being in charge, accustomed to being at the centre. Jesus's invitation into relationship is challenging all of this.

How so? First, I recognize there will always be mystery— and with uncertainty, there will inevitably be risk and a lack of control. It means I'll have to walk by faith.

Second, my invitation into the story is one to which I can only respond with "yes" or "no." It's not an idea or theory that I can analyze and apply. Jesus didn't say, "Hey, check out my new ideas and tell me what you think." He said, "Follow me." The challenge of the Christian call was, and is, to believe and follow.

Being at peace within relationship that I can't completely understand or control isn't one of my strengths. The problem isn't unique to me, nor is it a recent phenomena. It seems to go way back, as far as the Genesis garden.

But in the first few centuries after Jesus, the church manages to keep their shared, living relationship with Jesus at the centre. The church doesn't have power or privilege. It's at the margins. Yet amazingly, there is incredible life. And it's contagious.

How do we lose it?

There are many reasons for this, some of which we'll discuss later. By the fifth century, though, it's clear that this early vibrancy is at least partially lost. The western church is powerful—Constantine has seen to that—but it's becoming so addicted to the need for control—power does that—that any dynamic of a living story is being crushed or pushed to the edges.[57]

---

[57] Both Rodney Stark, *Rise of Christianity*, and Ramsay McMullen, *Christianizing the Roman Empire*, note that after Constantine the primary reason for growth and expansion is no longer the dynamic life and presence evidenced in the first three centuries but instead favoured advantage. To use Max Weber's reflection, there is a "routinization of charisma" that has contributed to a disconnection from the previous "centre" of Christian faith. More on this later.

Over centuries, the church increasingly institutionalizes the symbols, but loses the story. The result? Given the control that the church holds over society at large, culture understandably wanes under this chokehold of power. It becomes obvious that western civilization is losing its steam.

In contrast, Islam to the south is developing a rich, sophisticated and dynamic culture greatly influenced by a revival of Aristotelian thought.[58] In a classic example of "if you can't beat them, join them," Europe attempts to re-capture its momentum by looking for ways to incorporate the way of thinking that seems to be empowering their rivals.

So, in the mid thirteenth century Thomas Aquinas, with the best of intentions, creates a new synthesis, a combining of the revived Greek thought with biblical tradition. In doing so, he does far more than he intends. He replaces the unified foundation of the Christian story with the cornerstone of Greek philosophy that Paul and others first challenged: the concept of dualism, a separation that approaches God more as an idea than as a person.

In order to bring the Christian story and Greek thinking together, Aquinas creates two categories: those things that can only be known by reason alone—including the existence of God—and those things knowable only by revelation. For Aquinas, faith/revelation is understood as the higher discipline but the door has been opened and within centuries the order is reversed. The things we can

---

[58] Of course his inductive process of rational inquiry is extremely helpful for discovering how things work and making things work in new ways. Aristotle's method gets things done. The limitations emerge when we ask, "What are things for?" and "Why should we make them?"

know for sure are arrived at by reason alone, and "Faith is what we have to fall back on when certain knowledge is not to be had."[59]

Where does all this lead? Well, we find some success in "proving" the existence of God. All good, except for one significant detail: it becomes clear that the only kind of God whose existence we can prove in this way has little resemblance to the God of the Story. The result is the distant, absent God of Deism.[60] It can be rationally explained—and it doesn't challenge our control—but it is certainly not the kind of God that would unsettle our controlled environment by actively engaging with us in any tangible way.

With the flowering of the Renaissance in the period of time that follows—and particularly with the discoveries of science that occur within it—the ways that for centuries people have looked at things are being severely challenged.[61] A growing skepticism—taking a questioning, doubting attitude toward things unless they can be empirically "proven"—is threatening to completely undermine the Church's position of dominance in western society.

Not particularly happy with this trend, and accustomed to being in a position of power, the church feels compelled to respond. Bishop Pierre de Bérulle commissions a bright young thinker named Descartes. His task? It's no small order: he is to conclusively prove the existence of God. What is proposed to Descartes is that

---

[59] Newbigin, *Proper Confidence.*
[60] Deism refers to the belief in a Deity that we can accept as a creator through a process of reason, but one that is completely uninvolved in the ongoing life of that creation.
[61] A classic example would be Galileo and his challenge of Ptolemy's description of the solar system.

he take skepticism's main weapon—doubt—and turn it on skepticism itself. The goal is to use the method of "doubting" to declare with certainty that the existence of God can't be doubted.[62]

To explain in detail the complex arguments of Descartes or to fully spell out their consequences or implications goes far beyond what I want to try to tackle here—and significantly beyond my pay grade.

What I can do, though, is point to the end result of Descartes' argument—which by our present time has largely been discarded. Rather than give us an undoubtable foundation to think from, he plants the seeds that eventually convince us of the impossibility of being certain about knowledge at all. At the end of the day, as the philosopher Nietzsche demonstrates in the nineteenth century, the ultimate conclusion of skepticism—if we are honest and consistent—leads us to doubt that we can truly know anything.[63]

When I say "anything," of course, I'm not speaking about how to understand the way things work and to learn how to use that knowledge. Putting into practice the rational thinking of the Age of Reason—the Enlightenment—has been amazingly effective in propelling technological

---

[62] Michael Buckley (*At the Origins of Modern Atheism*, 1987). While de Bérulle certainly encouraged Descartes' philosophical thinking, it's not clear whether Descartes shared the same ultimate goals. He was quite concerned about the church's reactions to new ways of thinking—mostly writing from the relative safety of Holland.

[63] As Newbigin points out, rational criticism rests on faith on the reliability of the rational method. If you eliminate faith in anything, you eliminate the possibility of knowing anything. For Nietzsche, the eternal, self-evident truths of the Age of Reason were simple products of history and a result of the desires of certain individuals to exercise power over others (a theme that Foucault expands with his concept of "regimes of power"). Ironically, the attempt to displace faith and probability with certainty has instead produced a despair and suspicion surrounding any claims to truth at all.

growth and development. It's empowered us to do things that were previously unthinkable. The work of science has enabled us to discover how to eradicate what were considered incurable diseases. It has brought a new level of mastery over the natural world.

But what hasn't it done? It hasn't answered—because in and of itself it can't answer—the deeper, bigger questions.

Why are we doing what we are doing?

Should we do everything we *can* do?

In simple terms, while we've gained the ability to know how to do almost anything, it hasn't helped us much at all in giving us the wisdom to know how any of this advancement should be used. So, ironically, the same process of discovery that has found cures for diseases and, as a result, has saved millions of lives, has also produce weapons used to kill millions. It's given us the tools to preserve our planet but also to exploit and pillage that same world, which we seem hell bent to do.[64]

How can I know the answers to the "what" and "why" questions? They come to me another way. They come through faith. The foundation of every belief shares the reality of faith.[65] The whole idea that I can found my beliefs on either faith or reason is an entirely false one. And yet that is often the way it is put to me—that I am weak in some way, having to rely on faith, unlike others who only believe what is reliable and factual.

---

[64] See Oxford economist Kate Raworth's "Doughnut Economics" diagram for a plausible alternate to our present global economy that is creating immense inequalities while destroying our planet's ecosystem.

[65] Faith being our human struggle to look for the clues that lead us to a coherent reality shaped from outside of myself.

15 Evaluated By The Game
I'm Not Playing

To use the metaphor of sport, if you question me with, "Why do you suck at football?" it will sting. More than likely I'm going to feel intimidated, somewhat of a failure. But if I stop and reflect for a moment, and then remark to myself, "Hey, I'm not even playing football. I'm playing tennis!"—then your evaluation isn't that relevant. If you're going to criticize me, then at least do so for the game that I'm actually playing rather than insinuating that I really should be playing something else.

Here's the point: you don't try to explain tennis using football terminology or meanings, as though the latter reflects a higher order of understanding. Tennis and football share the same foundation in that they are both games. The decision to play either is not made because it is the only game that makes any logical sense—all other games being somewhat illegitimate. The choice of either is one of the heart—will this game bring me joy?

As it is in games, so it is in life. Whatever we choose to believe as our starting point—whether God or ourselves—we do so, first of all because of faith and not because of reason. We all start with faith in something.

The "self-evident" truths of the Enlightenment are only self-evident to those who have put their faith in the presuppositions of humanism. The idea that I'm objective—and ever have been—simply believing what my experiments "prove" to be valid, has never been accurate.

As scientist Michael Polanyi points out, there is no such thing as truly objective inquiry—everyone, including every scientist, begins from a faith position.[66] The idea that any of us objectively follow where the "facts" lead is just a myth. All scientists experiment from within a context of truth that they have already assumed and it is not surprising then that they tend to find proofs for what they already know—i.e. their presuppositions.

The fact of the matter is that any hope of ultimately being in control of our lives through the hope of "certain" knowledge—believing something because it is "proven"—is an illusion.[67] It's supremely important to think deeply and to think well. At the same time, all of the rational thinking in the world can't create the raw materials that become the core elements of a story in which to live.

Every one of us must begin from a more mysterious, unproven place, from that part of us which is drawn to

---

[66] Michael Polanyi, *Personal Knowledge: Towards a Post-Critical Philosophy* (University of Chicago Press, 1958). Polanyi was a Nobel prize winning Hungarian scientist who demonstrated that all scientific inquiry is part of an existing tradition that informs us as to what is "self-evident." He coined the term "personal knowledge" to emphasize that any knowledge of reality requires a holistic, personal commitment on the part of the knower.

[67] As Einstein pointed out in a lecture on *Geometry and Experience*, "As far as the laws of mathematics refer to reality, they are not certain; and as far as they are certain, they do not refer to reality." We long for certainty so we can feel like we are in control. The only thing that is certain is that we won't find it.

and by a story...a story that makes sense of the longings of our heart and of the world we see around us.

Where I start has a significant impact on where I end up. When I begin with my own mind in the centre and in control of my narrative, my story always leads back to myself. In contrast to the saying, "the answer is always Jesus," when I begin by assuming that the universe is impersonal and that ultimate truth is found through my own inquiry and mastery of theoretical thinking, "the answer is never Jesus."[68]

---

[68] Phrase coined by Newbigin, *Proper Confidence.*

16 Get Back To Where You Once Belonged

So how do I then get back to the story that seems to direct the lives of the first Christians? The pathway back won't be found through removing my doubts so I'll have more confidence to fully trust God...and then apply what I learn to my practical life. It's not the way the first believers approach faith. Sometimes their answer seems too simple for me, but what radically changes their lives is that they meet Jesus—either personally or through stories about him—hear his invitation, trust it, and follow.

As Lesslie Newbigin would say—and it never gets harder or easier than this, "It is belief and obedience, and the two are but two sides of one response. It is not that we are given a vision of the new world which God purposes and then consider how we might translate this vision into practical action. We are not given a theory which we then translate into practice. Instead, we are invited to respond to a word of calling by believing and acting."[69]

There is no way forward that doesn't involve commitment *first of all*, with the promise that our demonstrated trust

---

[69] Newbigin, *Proper Confidence*, location 729

will result in the path becoming clearer.

So it's not much different than any relationship that I hope will become an intimate friendship. It begins in a somewhat mysterious way. I am drawn toward someone. There are reasons for this—common interests, etc.— but the attraction can't be fully explained by these "facts" alone.

Then I must take a risk, a step of faith. Not entirely *blind* faith, but not entirely explainable either. Something is drawing my heart. I want to know this person. But I can't do so without vulnerability, some surrendering of control, responding in some way to their invitations. And I can't say that I truly know them outside of this process.

It's terrifying and disarming, much like my marriage to Joy. Yet, after almost fifty years of journeying together within the uncertainties of life, we ultimately experience a deep knowing and trust that studying endless biographies of one another could never produce.

It's only as I trust in God's story and fully commit to it that I gain a confidence that can withstand the current of doubt and despair that rules my culture and constantly haunts me. And it must come in that order.[70]

First resolving my doubt and eliminating my risk is not the key to gaining the confidence necessary to fully surrender to God's invitation. Instead, it's the act of trusting and then stepping in to that invitation that opens the door into an ever-growing personal knowledge of God within me. And the irony of it all? This surrender then begins to relegate my doubts to a place of lesser importance.

---

[70] See the renowned Canadian philosopher Charles Taylor's *A Secular Age* for a sympathetic explanation of this tension.

How that process happens and is experienced is some-what of a mystery and is as diverse as the people who say yes to God's invitation. There is no objective way that I can "prove" in the short term that my experience and growing personal knowledge of God is indeed revelation from God and not simply a subjective manufacturing of my own imagination or desire. However diverse the pathways to a confident personal knowing of God there is always some element of risk—as there is in any relationship.[71]

Central to the confidence of the early church is the power unlocked through their simple process of believe and obey. It will be the same for me today. My confidence won't come from eliminating all intellectual doubt; my key will be to match their wholeheartedness of belief in, and obedience to Jesus. To quote Newbigin one final time:

> There is still the vast ocean of what we do not know and do not understand. But we know the way, and the way is Jesus. In the words of Dietrich Bonhoeffer..., 'Jesus Christ alone is the certainty of faith.' To look for certainty elsewhere is to head for the wasteland.[72]

---

[71] Hebrews 11:6 reminds us that the essence of our faith profession is that we believe God exists and that he rewards those who earnestly seek him. This hope acts as an anchor to our souls (Hebrews 6:19) because it's a hope that does not disappoint, as Paul reminds us (Romans 5:5). Paul also explains that the Spirit of God assures us that we are not deceived by allowing us to experience tastes of God's love (Ephesians 1:14).
[72] Newbigin, *Proper Confidence*, loc. 1193.

17 The Walls Of The Fortress

I'm not sure that the talk is going over very well. I mean, the audience is attentive—or could that be interpreted as stunned? It's hard to read what's really going on inside them. I'm giving a talk about leadership and I'm sharing very personally about my own experience and journey in it. I've just finished sharing about the emotional meltdown that happens to me in that hotel room many years ago— my "howling dog" story. I'm candidly revisiting the flashbacks I had then, from my time in the womb, all through my childhood, and to more recent experiences.

I continue on to share with the crowd my takeaways from this unnerving time. I explain how my life has been marked by a fear of rejection from the very beginning. I go on to describe how this has impacted every part of my leadership.

My ability to freely relate to people and be known by them.

My fear of letting God know me and my great struggle to trust God enough to really let go and follow.

If indeed, I continue, my life with God is—at its core— trusting and following, the essence of leadership must be as simple as the willingness to follow first or follow alone. I never move on from being a follower. I must always trust...which is why I so often struggle with the vulnerability of truly leading. It's easier to settle for adopting a leadership posture.

At the end of my talk, I invite anyone who identifies with what I'm saying, and wants to pray together about it, to respond.

Nada.

Perhaps they don't understand the invitation? So I clarify.

I'm met with even greater silence. No one dares to even look my way.

After an embarrassed silence, some five minutes or so, the inviting pastor comes up and provides a help- ful segue.

"Well everyone, let's have some coffee!"

The room comes to life and feels normal again. Within fifteen minutes my sharing will be completely swept under the rug of comfortable small talk...they may remember it but they are doing their best to pretend it doesn't exist. I decide that personal vulnerability isn't quickly going to re-enter my leadership talk repertoire.

Not too much has changed over time. I think I'm still somewhat terrified by relationship. The only way I can grow in it is through the risk of being vulnerable. That means sharing what is inside even though I'm not sure myself exactly what that inside stuff means...or how to filter it so I'm seen in the most positive light. The worst part is not knowing what the response to my disclosure will be. My greatest fear is always that it can, in fact likely will, mean rejection. Being on the outside looking in.

On the other side of the window.

I shared earlier how my Barry incident in junior high school flips a switch for me. From that point on I decide that I'll hide myself at all costs. Particularly the sensitive, emotional part of me that seems soft and ill-prepared for the war zone that surrounds me.

Since I won't physically be able to pull off a "bully" role, I determine that I'll use what I have—words. I'll use my words to hide my real nature. I'll employ them to create a barrier to protect myself by pushing others away. Even better, I'll show others through my verbal attacks that I have no feelings, no compassion, no mercy.

I'll convince the world that it can't hurt me. That I don't need anyone's acceptance. I will command their envy instead.

So I become consumed with competition. I'll be better than everyone else. I'll create a different "me." And I'll be safe from being discovered...and being excluded.

In the years following, I carefully walk out this plan by meticulously constructing a façade to hide behind. I do everything I can to prove my superiority: I'm the top academic male student throughout high school without ever being seen to do any work. In fact, I make sure everyone knows that I am drinking on the job, so to speak. I regularly have a case of beer in my locker to consume during lunch break. I can do things like this. Rules don't apply to me. There are no consequences.

I try to craft an image of being invulnerable. I abhor losing at anything. (It doesn't help that my father comes to me just as I'm beginning to dive into the world of sports and says to me, "Whatever you play, you must not lose. You need to win every time. If you ever lose at anything, even if it is the first time you've played it, you're a failure.")

During this period, to complete the picture I'm trying to cultivate, I present an image of being a huge risk-taker. I'll do what others will not risk attempting. I'll bring the things I've stolen from the previous store along with me into the next as I continue to shoplift. I'll drink more than anyone and still stay standing... and then drive home. I'll skip classes and spend the time in the main office duplicating poetry I'm writing about the teachers and selling to other students—right under the nose of the principal. These kinds of things are important steps in diverting others from seeing who I really am—a scared, sensitive kid who desperately just wants to belong.

Everything I do is calculated. I'm not naturally a risk taker at all. The fear of failure haunts me. I constantly gauge every possible outcome and manipulate every situation to create a favourable risk/reward ratio. The pressure of managing my image—making sure I won't blow my cover—is overwhelming me. It drives me to medicate. I'm more and more drinking alone.

In all this time, all my focus is on myself. I'm losing the ability to actually know anyone. They're not in my focus. Everything is about how I'm coming across, how I'm being seen.

Without understanding why, after a short time into any "relationship" with a girl, I always break it off suddenly. Actually, I just disappear. I don't call, I'm just gone. Am I afraid that they'll come to know me?

18 What Do You Want From Me?

In 1969, now safely back on the West Coast after my year of theological studies, my "relationship" with Joy continues to grow. It's a bit like a roller coaster ride, and often I'm hanging on for dear life. Though it's sometimes hard to determine what it is that holds us together—true love or pure stubbornness—we keep moving closer to a long term commitment.

Joy is quite unlike anyone I've ever met. She is so spontaneous, ready at any time to do the wildest and craziest things. One moment she laughs infectiously, the next she is in tears. She struggles with depression and a sense of abandonment—but one minute later can be enthralled by a drop of water glistening on the petal of an opening flower.

She doesn't calculate or think ahead of outcomes. She is always flirting with possible embarrassment. I love being around her, but not *too* close. She is dangerous when you want to be sure that you are fully in control of your life. Nevertheless, within two years, in June 1971, we are married.

Just to be clear, I come from an era where you married someone because they were pretty. Premarital counselling was a blood test (though in our case I don't think we ever get that done). We are woefully unprepared for marriage.

Oh, in the months prior to our wedding, we do dream and share a lot about the "team" we will be, "united" and "together." It isn't until later that I more fully recognize how easy it is for two people to use the same words and mean such different things.

It is just two weeks after our marriage that Joy seems depressed and distant. Always sure that I can fix anything, I press in.

"What's wrong? I inquire.

"Nothing."

It sure doesn't feel like nothing is wrong. So, I keep reaching out. After about two hours, Joy finally responds.

"I'm tired of being married."

This hits me like a bomb blast. What I am hearing is that our marriage is over. If these words had come from me, I would already have been to a lawyer. I am convinced Joy is telling me that our marriage is over. Two weeks! I'm in shock but scrambling to gain some control. How do I fix this? What does she want?

Over the next decades, this scenario will become a cyclical reality. Joy feels shut out and abandoned by me, so she engages her automatic protective mechanism: she attacks and criticizes. Now, I realize it as a panic response, what you expect from someone who feels like they're drowning. Having almost drowned as a child, Joy will relive that trauma whenever she is overwhelmed by life. My aloofness just intensifies those feelings.

Her emotional response is to grab onto me so that she is not alone in her fear. She believes that together, we—she—won't go under. It looks different from my vantage point. I think she is grabbing me to pull me under as well. I shake her off.

In spite of her fear, there is a deep longing in Joy to be "one." She wants me to be fully a part of her and her of me. She can't yet understand it rationally, but her soul aches for it.

The scriptures say that woman was created out of the side of man. Often it feels to me that Joy is searching my side with her fingers, looking for a way in. It feels like she wants to open me up and literally crawl right inside.

Of course, I know all the right answers to hold her off. I argue that her vision of togetherness is unhealthily enmeshed. In contrast to her idea of team being like a three-legged race where we are joined at the hip and do everything together, I know the correct answer. A marriage should be like a basketball team—we each do our part to contribute to the whole and after the game get together for a beer to celebrate.

It would be easier to relent if Joy were not so unpredictable. Inviting her inside feels like bringing a grenade into your living room. When Joy is up, it's worth entertaining the idea. But when Joy is depressed or driven by anxiety and feelings of worthlessness? Joy hurts me in those times. She attacks. I can't take that risk.

Throughout the first decades of our marriage this is a predictable pattern. Joy will sense turmoil and pain in me, but she will feel distanced and kept at arm's length. Instinctively she'll try to get inside whatever is going on within me, but to me it always will come across as judgement and criticism. Finally, there will always be a breaking point and I explode. Never toward her, of course, but what is inside erupts.

I'll hit a wall or slam the steering wheel and literally cry out in anguish. And then, exhausted from my weakness being exposed, I slump over in silence. And after this emotional explosion? Joy will feel like she got in. Like we have re-connected. That she's part of me. And she will want to be close physically again.

I'll literally be in shock for a few days. I'll find it difficult to take a deep breath. I'll feel like I'm in a bit of a dream state. The last thing I want is contact. I need to be safe. I need to be distant.

Often at this time, trying desperately to get some kind of handle with which to control and forestall these breakdowns, I ask Joy, "What do you want from me?"

"You," she replies.

The one thing I can't completely give.[73]

---

[73] If you asked me during this season, I would describe myself as an "authentic" person. Only later will I read Brené Brown: "Authenticity is a collection of choices that we have to make every day. It's about the choice to show up and be real. The choice to be honest...to let our true selves be seen. *Gifts of Imperfection.*

19 Taste And See

I think I've always believed that God is there. I mean, actually exists rather than just in a mind game that I play. Even in my darkest days post high school, when I want as little of God as possible, when I'm constructing arguments for why I don't believe in God's existence, I still debate my positions in conversations with God. And somehow I know I'm not just talking to myself.

By the end of my year away at theological college, one thing is clear to me: I'm going to be a follower of Jesus. The first thing I do is what makes most sense to me—I'll know everything I can about God so that my belief is unshakeable. My motivation isn't some kind of dispassionate intellectual search. I feel anxious about pleasing God and somehow I feel like getting all my questions answered will be the way forward to a place of greater peace.

The more I read and study though, it seems the more questions I have. I feel deeply guilty about having so many doubts. Certainly, if I were a real Christian—like Joy—I'd be able to put these things up on a high shelf and just get on with life. But I'm paralyzed. There are too many questions in my brain and I can't find a way to let them go.

What seems to make things worse, is that in contrast to Joy and other friends we begin to meet that have recently discovered Jesus, I can't manage to make any of the emotional side of this whole thing work at all. I can study all I want about the love of God, but I can't in any way feel it. There is something in me that can't let love in. It's too risky.

Thankfully, God doesn't barge in the way Joy does, but the fear is exactly the same. I have no confidence that I can trust God *with me*. I'd rather stay in control and become an expert on God…know God *that* way. I'll call that relationship.

Joy, however, won't let me keep my distance—my wife, and the suppressed longing inside me, that Lewis called "joy." With constant tugs, they invite me to take the risk to really live. Not to just dream, but to enter fully into the *real* story. They beckon to me to put away the pen and trust in the faithfulness of the true Author of the story my heart longs for.

I hear the calls of two different voices. One says I can live in the apparent safety of knowing God like a food critic who writes a glowing critique without ever sitting down to actually enjoy the food he is writing about. This option allows me to be an expert, but it still doesn't bring me out from behind the glass window.

The other choice asks me to step inside and take the risk of knowing God personally—I can enjoy an authentic relationship with the Chef. I will be vulnerable, but I will also have a chance to enjoy the meal of a lifetime.

Red pill or blue?[74]

Feeling hedged in, I bargain with God. What do you want from me?

"You."

---

[74] From the movie The Matrix. Google it to see the significance.

20 The Great Invitation

In the early stages of my own faith journey, I'm struggling to understand what I'm reading in the Bible, wishing for an owner's manual that will unpack how to fit the various parts together. In many ways, I completely lose the forest for the trees. I'm memorizing verses and cataloguing proof texts for the points of theology I'm trying to learn, but I keep wondering, "What's this all about?"

I'm really struggling with the Old Testament and all of the predictable issues within it that most readers face early on—I mean doesn't Jonah seem like a stretch to you? I'm told that these things have supposedly all been previously and neatly explained. Maybe that is the case, but the answers given still leave me at least partially unsatisfied.

I struggle with the seemingly vengeful and angry God of the Hebrew Scriptures and simply explaining it through progressive revelation isn't giving me comfort. It feels kind of like, "Look…I know I used to beat you, but now I'm going to show you a different side of my character and I'm going to be kind and forgiving."[75]

---

[75] Of course, progressive revelation is much more nuanced than the way it was originally presented to me.

Eventually, I pretty much just read the gospels and the book of Acts. It's about the only part of the Bible that seems to resonate with my experience of Jesus and my reason for even going on this journey of faith. This neglect, however, is becoming an increasing problem. With each passing year, I'm less considered a "newbie," and it feels like I'm supposed to have a lot of this stuff sorted. Yet it's not getting easier.

A major part of the problem is, of course, what I'm bringing to the text. My presuppositions—the things I have been taught growing up, either directly or indirectly—seem to create a number of conflicting narratives. They each use different parts of the Bible in different ways, and I don't know how to reconcile them.

I'm doing my best to bury doubt as I'm convinced that it's an enemy to my faith.[76] Yet everything is increasingly beginning to feel like a *zero-sum* game:[77] to believe, I need to shut down my questions. How then do I remain curious? With my emotions as broken as they are, it feels like all I've got left is my mind.

I'm not sure when I first see light at the end of this tunnel. Perhaps it's always been there but somehow I have missed it entirely.

I'm attempting once more a read-through of the Old Testament, and again I'm getting overwhelmed by the violence, brokenness and contradiction of it all. I remark to myself, how can this continued tragedy be what God

---

[76] A book which has been incredibly helpful to me in working this through is Greg Boyd's *Benefit of the Doubt: Breaking the Idol of Certainty.*

[77] The expression *zero-sum* in game theory is a situation where the win for one party equals the loss for the other. In other words cost and benefit nets out to zero.

wants or endorses? What then is the point of it all?

The idyllic garden so quickly and easily dissolves. The first love story—"bone of my bone"—shatters within a chapter as Adam basically complains, "Who is this woman?" Within generations this first family is killing each other and boasting about it. Before long, "God saw that human evil was out of control. People thought evil, imagined evil—evil, evil, evil from morning to night. God was sorry that he had made the human race in the first place; it broke his heart. God said, 'I'll get rid of my ruined creation, make a clean sweep: people, animals, snakes and bugs, birds—the works. I'm sorry I made them.'"[78]

It's not like the washing that follows cleans everything up. Noah celebrates finally getting off the boat by getting totally drunk and lying naked in his tent—I'm guessing he "just happened" to land the boat near an old vineyard. When he awakes, he somehow remembers that his youngest son, Ham saw him in the tent and so does the only reasonable thing—Noah places a lifelong curse upon Ham's son Canaan. I struggle to see the punishment fitting the crime. And, by the way, where is there any mention of culpability on Noah's part?

The next couple God chooses as participants in the rescue of humanity is Abram and Sarah. Don't get me wrong; they are amazingly courageous...most of the time. Paul later says in Romans that Abraham "never wavered." I'm guessing that Sarah would look back on the time that Abram let her be taken into Pharaoh's harem as a *slight* waver.

Of course, if you have read the Old Testament, it gets much, much worse: incest, torture, killing of innocents—

---

[78] Genesis 6:5-7, MSG.

including the sacrifice of children—and on.

And then it hits me.

God's still there. God hasn't abandoned us. Even though the association is sullying God's reputation. Why is that? Why doesn't God simply start over. This experiment is breaking bad. Shut it down and remake everything.

And yet God doesn't. I suspect that there's only one reason. I guess that's what love does. Love won't let us give up hope when the other party just doesn't get it...even though love won't—can't?—force the guilty ones to simply make the right choice. Love never gives up.

It's funny how my brain works. What I expect to see, I tend to find. Somehow, I always imagine God as being somewhat annoyed with me, frustrated because I never live up to his expectations. I believe that he blew off some of his steam by taking things out on Jesus, and for reasons only a lawyer can fully understand, it got me off the hook to a degree. Although, given my track record, I should never too fully relax.

I don't know how or when I learned this, but, to be honest, up to this point it's always been the way I suspect God must see me. In this season of my life, I know theoretically that God loves me, but to paraphrase the Princess Bride movie, I do not think that the word "love" means to God what I think it means. The way it has been explained to me is this: since God makes the rules for everybody, God does not to have to follow them the way we are expected to. I'm not sure I like that explanation.

I am taught growing up to never take more time on the telephone than absolutely necessary—I suppose the assumption being that the party on the other end of the line will not want to spend any more than the minimum required time in conversation. I feel the same about God—that somehow I shouldn't bother God with anything trivial. And certainly not when my thoughts or behaviour are not up to the expected standard. God may "love" me, but it might be a stretch to say that God "likes" me.

Some years later, I have an epiphany of sorts. The leader of our church movement, John Wimber, who at this time has significant visibility around the world, has a brief conversation with me. At the conclusion of our talk, he hands me a card. On it is a phone number. I'm fully aware that John has an unlisted number, so I'm taken aback. Stumbling over what is the appropriate thing to say in response to this, I remark, "John, I'm so honoured that you would give this to me. Please know that I will never use it unless it is to discuss something very, very important."

John takes in my timid words, smiles, and simply replies, "I gave you the number so that you would call."

I'm stunned. John actually wants to talk to me? Can this be true of my heavenly Father as well as my spiritual father here on earth? That I can with confidence approach God, knowing that I don't have to have my best foot forward...or have something really important to discuss?

For the first time in my life, I begin to come to the biblical story with different presuppositions. What if God actually *is* love? I mean love as I understand love, beyond my understanding, but consistent with what my heart *truly* longs for?

As I begin to gradually believe this might be true, the

Bible begins to read very differently than through my old glasses. One day I read, "For by one sacrifice he *has made* perfect forever those who *are being made* holy."(Italics mine)[79] Seeing the present through the future, God can already look at me and say "Perfect!" even though I'm still very much in process. If I simply stay connected to Jesus, I'm going to become like him. There is no fear on God's part that Jesus will become like me!

I'm beginning to understand that God is not anxious about me; God sees me in a way that I can't even see myself. I'm aware of where I am right now. God has the finished product in sight—how I will be once faith has had its way with me. It's taking time, but this new paradigm is starting to affect the way I'm reading the whole Bible. It's also changing how I see everyone around me.

---

[79] Hebrews 10:14, NIV.

21 The Outrage Of The Gospel

Through much of my life up to this point, I've worked at being an efficient critic—or should I say assassin, given my efforts to eliminate my competitors with judgement. I've become an expert at seeing what is wrong with everyone so that I can feel safe, coming out the winner in any comparison. For the first time, I'm beginning to see others in a whole new way—through the eyes of invitation that I'm beginning to recognize that God has for them.

While these new thoughts are stirring in my heart, I'm teaching an advanced physical education class to a co-ed group of senior high school students. (In order to take this class, you need to have achieved an A, the highest grade level possible, in the prerequisite P.E. class.) On registration day, a female student comes up to my table to sign up for the class. Instinctively, I pull the registration sheet away from her.[80]

"What are you doing?" she says.

---

[80] It's always fascinating to see how stories like this spread. I've come across it in a magazine—the author had heard the story but didn't know the source. I was also sitting in a large conference in Europe where someone re-told the story, completely unaware that the initiator of it was sitting in their audience. Every time I hear it, I still can't believe that I did it!

"What *am* I doing?" I'm thinking.

A little backstory: this girl is a straight A student, and a very good athlete. She qualifies for this course in every way, except for one thing. She's so insecure and anxious about herself, that she constantly frets about everything—every exam, every practical test, every activity! And she does so vocally...whining and complaining constantly.

And then, when the results come, she will have the highest scores in the room. Quite frankly, it exhausts my patience. I have been through it before and I don't want her ruining the class for me and everyone else.

"I've met the standards to get into this course!" she pleads.

I try to justify my actions. "You're too qualified." I'm looking for a way out, seeing that she won't be easily dissuaded. But what I do next is as much of a shock to me as it is to her.

"I'll let you into the course on one condition," I say. "You let me give you an A right now. Then, all I ask is that you attend our class, and enjoy yourself. But the pressure is off. You've got your A already."

She looks at me, stunned. Without so much as a word, she slowly picks up the pen and signs her name.

"By the way," I say as she leaves the table. "There's actually one more condition. Don't tell anyone what I've done for you."

You can imagine the outcome. Some say that to do something like this is irresponsible—that, as a result, the individual that is "freed" in this way will take advantage of the grace offered. I think most often it's the opposite.

In this case, she earned her A with one notable difference to other classes: she gave it everything she had, but with no anxiety—the result was secure—and she had the time of her life...along with the rest of the class.

This is the outrage of the gospel, as I'm starting to understand it. It's as though we're lined up at the start of a race, one that will determine whether we live or die. Of course we're filled with anxiety and apprehension. Given our track record so far, it appears unlikely that we have any chance of success at all.

Just before the gun sounds and the race begins, Jesus comes to each of us who are running and, if we allow him, puts a gold medal around our neck.

"Congratulations," he says. "You've won! Have a great race." Perfect, while being made holy.

It's this God—the one who looks just like Jesus—that I'm just beginning to be able to see. As a result, new motivations are rising up in me. I don't want to collect the medal, put it on a shelf and forget about running. I want to run my heart out in this race that is before me.

I want to say, "Yes!" to the Great Invitation.

22 What Is The Author Of This Story Like?

"I had always felt life first as a story, and if there is a story, there is a story-teller."[81] So G. K. Chesterton describes the questions that lead him first to a story worth surrendering his life to, and then to the author of that story.

What I assume about an author strongly impacts how I read their story. Sometimes, of course, if I'm really patient, I'll allow the narrative to form my conclusions as to what it means, and where it is going. Equally, if not more so, I'll tend instead to see in the story what I already expect to find because of what I already presuppose about the author.[82] As I suggested previously, these assumptions become my interpretive glasses for making sense of the whole narrative. I then argue from these lenses why my understanding of the story is the correct one. Seldom do I have the time or courage to examine

---

[81] G.K. Chesterton, *Orthodoxy*, end of chapter 4, *The Ethics of Elfland*.

[82] This is particularly true in the political arena. These days, the first thing we want to know about someone is what *camp* they are in. Once it is determined that they are not part of our *tribe*, we already know what it is they are saying, and are going to be saying...and that it is wrong.

the prescription of my glasses itself. To question what I already know may lead me where I don't want to go.

Some years ago, a close friend of mine told me a story about a conversation between two people. One is a troubled young man vexed by a conundrum that he can't seem to solve or even fully understand. He feels like his life is being stalled by this obstacle. It gives him no rest and robs him of both joy for the present and expectancy for his future.

Just at the point when he is about to give up all hope, he hears of an impending visit by a respected, aged rabbi, renowned for his depth of wisdom. "If only I can see this rabbi," the young man says to himself, "I know he will have the answer that I need."

When the rabbi arrives, the young man is able to secure an appointment. Utterly desperate to end his anguish, he lays out the reason for his visit to the wise old man.

To the delight of the anxious seeker, the rabbi agrees to hear his question. Stumbling over words in his pent-up frustration, the young man blurts out what it is that has tormented him for months. It is clear that the rabbi is listening intently and that he cares deeply for the questioner.

When finally there is a pause, the rabbi looks deeply into the eyes and soul of the young man. "Oh, my son," he says warmly, "that is such a wonderful question." Then, with compassion in his voice, he continues.

"Why would you want to exchange it for an answer?"

We seem to be terrified of unanswered questions. Perhaps it has always been so; it certainly is in our present age. I'm not entirely sure why that is, but I think that, at least for me, my fear of uncertainty and my almost addictive desire for control has something to do with it. So, partly, I respond by muting questions as they emerge in my mind. I give little time or opportunity for initial questions to give way to deeper ones. Like a politician, I ignore the awkward question by quickly inserting one of my talking points—the answer to a different query that doesn't trouble or threaten me. Conversation over. I fear that curiosity leads to risk.

The result is—though this is a generalization rather than an all-encompassing truth—a society that tends to be methodologically rich but absolutely poor. We know how to get almost anywhere; we just don't know where it is we are going. The easier questions for me to answer are the "how" questions. Answering these gives me a sense of control and functions like medication, separating me from deeper levels of pain or doubt. What I miss is wrestling with the core things essential to being fully alive: asking "what" and "why." Of course, these questions are not so easily put into containers or onto completed checklists.[83]

Is it possible that what I, and we, need today is not more answers to the easy questions—i.e. how can we get more done?—but to linger in uncertainty long enough to find better questions?

---

[83] The present pandemic we are experiencing globally serves as a powerful illustration of this. The closures and isolation could lead us to asking deep questions of ourselves, individually and collectively: "What will we want to do differently coming out of this time? Why do we actually do the things we do?" Yet, for many of us, there seems to be a panic response to the sense that we have lost ground in our materialistic pursuits. "We have to get the economy moving!" Both are, of course, important. Still, it does seem to be an *a priori* concern to find our missing steering wheel before racing ahead to supercharge our engine one more time. Just a thought....

The Ancient Greek philosopher Plato is comfortable with questions, and trusts the process of dialogue to produce answers both deep and resilient.[84]

One of Plato's most pressing questions ties in with our present conversation. In his famous dialogue involving Socrates and Euthyphro, he has the former pose the question, "Does God command a thing because it is good, or is it good because God commands it?"[85]

This question lays right at the heart of our discussion about Gods story. As theologian and historian Roger Olson emphasizes, it may be *the* basic choice in theology and perhaps the biggest difference among Christians themselves.[86]

How we answer the question will determine what we believe the author of this story is really like and therefore how we will expect the story to play out.

Is God's goodness and love only quantitatively greater than mine? By that I mean, does it go beyond what I know while still being consistent with my understanding? Or, in contrast, could it be qualitatively different as well? Does it actually mean something quite different though using

---

[84] Plato, along with his teacher Socrates, are generally considered the "fathers" of western philosophy. Their primary method involves the use of a series of questions intended to guide a small group of inquirers probing a big (universal) question—for instance, "What is goodness?"

[85] Euthyphro was an Athenian prophet—the original phrasing in Plato's dialogue is, more literally, "are the pious loved by the gods because they are pious, or are they pious because they are loved by the gods?" Enlightenment philosopher Gottfried Leibniz later applies Plato's argument to the Christian God. For background understanding of Divine Command Theory and the arguments surrounding it, see https://iep.utm.edu/divine-c/.

[86] C.S. Lewis thought that this question was perhaps the major issue of his times. For that reason, his work *The Abolition of Man* was in many ways a sustained polemic against the nominalist position— explained in the next footnote.

the same labels? In other words, while setting up certain standards of truth and morality for me, is it possible that God exists above and beyond these standards, and without reference to these values?

From the age of the apostles, through the church fathers and into the early medieval period, the answer would have been almost unanimous. What I understand as goodness or love comes first from the nature of God. In other words, I can even know what love is because God has actively loved first. This love I am to imitate. There is no discrepancy between what scripture teaches me to see as good and who God, by nature, is.

Later, in the Middle Ages, a new view begins to arise, answering Plato's question in the second way. The first hints of this are found by some in Peter Abelard, but by the time of William of Ockham, it is being clearly articulated that God isn't controlled or even guided by any eternal nature. At the core, God is a being of unlimited freedom and power.[87]

As any path chosen moves us along a trajectory, over time this perspective continues to develop and take new directions. The logical consequence of beginning with sovereignty at the center of our understanding of God

---

[87] The conflict is between two philosophic positions: Realism and Nominalism. Realism is a position taken in philosophy (quite different from our common usage of that term) that universal, abstract concepts—such as goodness—are just as real as tangible, physical things. Nominalism, along with its associated position Voluntarism, argues that there is no reality outside of our own thinking and will. So the first says we can *know* God by who God is; the latter claims we can only *know* God by what God does. For two excellent summaries of these philosophic positions see:
1. Eric Johnston: http://professorjohnston.com/a-little-philosophy-nominalism-voluntarism-and-our-spiritual-life/
2. Roger Olson: https://www.patheos.com/blogs/rogereolson/2010/12/a-much-neglected-basic-choice-in-theology/

leads us to new conclusions. To be consistent, we can't simply argue that God allows evil; God inevitably must be seen as the author of it as well. John Calvin, the 16th century reformer, leaves no doubt: "*All events* take place by God's sovereign appointment."[88]

Brad Jersak explains Calvin's ultimate position regarding the nature of God and it's implications regarding the story I am called to live within:

> ... According to Calvin, God is not only beyond good and evil, but everyone who does evil is merely acting as his instrument and at his command. When an evil person or even the devil commits evil, it is because the Lord not only permitted it—he commanded them and forced them to do it. Every act of terror, every rape and murder, every genocide or infanticide, every cancer and heart attack, every famine and plague are all in the service of God's ultimate purpose: that you would fear him and glorify his name.[89]

Of course, if I embrace this lens to help me make sense of God's story, I'll tend to see clear examples in the Bible that reinforce my view. Certainly, the Hebrew Scriptures have numbers of examples where God seems to act just as Calvin has described. And even the New Testament appears to play along: Paul in Romans 9 sounds a lot like Calvin. And the final revelation of Jesus in Revelation 19 reveals a conquering, blood-stained warrior much like

---

[88] John Calvin, *Calvin's Institutes,* quoted in Brad Jersak, *A More Christlike God: A More Beautiful Gospel* (Plain Truth Ministries, 2015). Most of the perspective taken in this section is drawn from chapter 4 of Brad's excellent book.
[89] Jersak, *A More Christlike God,* 65.

these glasses would lead me to discover.[90]

In many ways, the choice to see God this way has already been made for me—I absorbed this way of understanding the Bible in my childhood. I've grown up with it. As a result, even if my perspective is distorted, it still seems natural to me. It's the only way I've ever seen so it's easy for me to assume that it is the *right* way to view things. To defend the prescription of my glasses feels like defending "the faith" itself.

No wonder that the neo-Calvinists—strongly attached to viewpoints which dominate in the Middle Ages—treat more recent perspectives as interlopers. Even though these ideas are actually revisiting what the church thought well before Calvin, they are attacked as enemies of orthodoxy.[91]

Yet, in spite of resistance from these largely self-appointed arbiters of orthodoxy, the deeper questions keep being re-visited. I am—along with many others—re-discovering older sets of glasses that the church once used. Through them, the power of story is shaking up the familiar and causing me to see it, and its author, in new ways. Instead of doctrines formulated from outside the story becoming the interpretive keys which force the story to conform, the reverse is becoming true. I'm re-discovering the grand sweep of the astounding narrative that is the Bible, and it's *that* story, as a whole, which is providing a framework within which to grapple with the

---

[90] See Jersak, *A More Christlike* God, chapters 4, 5. What I offer here is a very minimal overview of this issue. Brad's observations and arguments will be necessary reading in order to create a foundation for the things I am suggesting.

[91] Of course, this is a label, though one that members of this network would gladly use to describe themselves. It includes a wide range of participants, including, thankfully, numbers of whom would not take a hard-line approach against all other views.

often confusing and seemingly contradictory parts.[92]

When I read the Bible this way, I realize that the entire story is pointing to a singular key—one that shows me clearly what the author is like and how to live well within the story. That key, however, isn't an assumption drawn from philosophy, or a rational concept worked through in my mind.

The guide is a person. The person of Jesus.

---

[92] I can't express strongly enough how grateful I am for a number of different authors who helped (at a critical time in my faith journey) to open my eyes and heart to recapture this way of reading God's story. Without them, I could have never found the great invitation that has become everything to me. Among many, I think of the late Clark Pinnock (we were both part of the same "Jesus People" church I referred to earlier); Greg Boyd (enabling me to embrace my doubts); Eugene Peterson (without The Message I would have stopped reading the Bible years ago); N.T. Wright (if I ever get a brain I want to be like him—but just so you know, if you write him, he responds… what famous person does that?); Brad Jersak (as a young youth pastor, he used to sneak into our early church service before going to his; what a gracious, wise man he has become).

23 It's All About...

From the perspective of the whole story, I can see that the Bible is always looking toward Jesus. Jesus is presented as, in Jersak's words, "the one true and living avatar of the transcendent God."[93] One just like me—with all of the limitations of my physical and emotional makeup, and the restrictions of being bound within the time and space of a broken creation. And yet, at the same time, perfectly revealing what God is like.

No, not a complete picture perhaps—it is God within humanity after all—but a picture free from distortion. Or, as the New Testament writers say it: an image of God that "perfectly mirrors God...stamped with God's nature." When I look at Jesus, they tell me, I "see the God who cannot be seen." And, as a result, I'm enabled to "see God's original purpose"[94]—what the story is about, where it's going and how it's inviting me to live.

What am I expecting to see when I look at this Jesus? At a time when people were beginning to be offended by how he was presenting himself, Jesus asked them this very question. "If you're looking for the usual trappings of

---

[93] Jersak, *A More Christlike* God, 83.
[94] Hebrews 1:3, Col. 1:15

royalty," he said, "you're looking in the wrong place."[95]

For me, as well as for Jesus's contemporaries, it seems counterproductive to look outside of power centers when I'm looking for a deliverer. I know how it is that empires are overthrown. It's a power game, at the end of the day—"My dad is bigger than your dad" type of thing. If indeed Satan and his evil forces are going to be destroyed once and for all, I don't just need a king. I need a KING![96] If God's promises are truly going to be fulfilled, that will mean conflict, and that means we will need someone just like king David and yet so far beyond. In fact, didn't God promise exactly that?

Maybe that's why I easily assume that power and freedom of will must be the first, most important quality of God—with love having to squeeze itself in where it can. Having studied the Middle Ages as a history major, I can understand how placing this emphasis on power would be of paramount importance. When war is as certain as death and taxes, how can you see outside the box of "who has the biggest army"?[97]

When Jesus explains why he has come, he points to his Father's love for this world—that God isn't willing that anyone would perish.[98] Naturally, to the ears of most at

---

[95]Matthew 11:7-19. Jesus is commenting on how people are trying to fit both himself and John the Baptist into their preset expectations of what a deliverer would look like.

[96] As Jersak notes, Karl Barth, the twentieth century theologian, remarked that we are always defining God as man in capital letters—assuming that the way empires are won and lost here is consistent with God and God's methods. God becomes our best conception of the powerful earthly ruler on heavenly steroids.

[97] This isn't a new problem, however. It seems that the first disciples couldn't get their heads around it either (Luke 10:18). I suppose the Anabaptists were ahead of their time in this regard, but since they seemed to "lose," the outcome appeared to confirm the power paradigm.

[98] John 3:16

the time of Jesus, that would simply be a way of saying that, as in the days of old, God has heard the cries of his people and has sent the promised deliverer. Certainly, the early works of power that Jesus displays seem to confirm the possibility that he is that promised one who will lead the nation to victory—if you can raise the dead, how long could your armies keep fighting? Yet, increasingly, Jesus rejects this option—by refusing to use the power that he seems to be able to access, for either his own benefit or for the nation's.

This paradox confuses almost everyone. One might argue that Jesus's unwillingness to add his obvious strength to Israel's nationalistic agenda—and instead to continually undermine it—is one of the reasons that the people eventually see him as unhelpful and expendable. To be clear, it isn't that Jesus is confused or hesitant about the Messiah thing. He knows who he is and why he has been sent from the Father. The problem is not that the nation has expected too much of Jesus; it is, actually, that they've expected too little.

Jesus is intending to do far more than simply solve the "Roman problem." He intends to deal once and for all with the root of all evil and oppression—to confront it at its source and to restore what was lost in the garden at the beginning of the biblical story. It's within this meek posture that he ironically embraces the role of warrior-king fighting on behalf of his people. He understands that this war—achieving victory over sin and death—can't ultimately be won through brute force.

24 Return

We are never overpowered and abducted from the Genesis garden. Our simple trust in the love and provision of our Father seems to provide all the protection we need. With the breakdown of that trust—assuming we can live freely under our authority—we soon discover the reality of our new circumstance. We are going to serve somebody, and if it's not "the Lord," then Bob Dylan poetically lets us know who it will be.[99]

Our momentous decision to step away from God creates a two-fold dilemma. First, we've been separated from the relationship that has given us life and freedom. Second, we've been overpowered and aren't free to find our way back to where we once were.[100]

The way out is the way in.

Jesus comes to reclaim us—all of us, Jews and

---

[99] Bob Dylan, "You Gotta Serve Somebody." As a lifelong Dylan fan, I had to work him in somewhere.
[100] I'm not here trying to adjudicate between the Christus Victor view of salvation and the other various atonement theories. There is much mystery surrounding exactly how we have found ourselves in our present state. What does seems clear is that we have a two-fold problem: there is a need for relational restoration and a need for rescue from the influence of dark powers. Jesus came to address both of these dilemmas.

Romans—by setting us free to choose again, and at the same time healing the breach in our severed relationship with God. That can't be done with power. Lives can be captured; hearts can only be won with loving invitation. God's love allows us to choose to leave. God will not force us to return—he doesn't make that choice for us—but God doesn't wait for us to make the first move. In Jesus, God takes up all the space between us to invite us home.[101]

"This is how we've come to understand and experience love: Christ sacrificed his life for us." According to 1 John 3:16,[102] Jesus doesn't just use the word "love"; Jesus defines it by the example of how he lives and dies. Jesus doesn't try to arbitrarily overpower evil and death by independently using God's power more effectively than the satan does. He resolutely refuses to do or say anything on his own, choosing trusting obedience to his Father in contrast to our human response in the garden story.

What has this accomplished for me?

As fully God and fully human, Jesus becomes a bridge between heaven and earth. I can't build a pathway back, so God through Jesus comes all the way to me. And from that place, having fully embraced my broken state, Jesus invites me to come home.

Yes, home to trust again. And to trust enough to choose

---

[101] To even begin to unpack how exactly this works is beyond the scope of this book. I'm not alluding to any particular theory of atonement here as much as I am describing a relational *stepping toward the other* to make restored relationship possible.

[102] The sixteenth century division of the Bible into chapters and verses has caused a host of difficulties, however the parallel of John 3:16 with 1 John 3:16 is a wonderful, serendipitous "accident."

to live within that trust—which means to obey.

To obey, not because I must, but because I can.[103]

What I, and we, fail to do, Jesus does. This, of course, seems to be the opposite of what any effective conqueror usually accomplishes. Perhaps that is why the "victories" I am familiar with in human history only serve to be the start of a new oppression...followed by another uprising.

How does Jesus overcome? He is so confident of his Father's love and care for him that he can take the lowest place without fear. Moreover, it's his trusting obedience which enables him to submit to the worst that evil can do with him—even in death God has not forsaken him.[104] Death, obviously, can't keep him.

Ironically, Jesus does become king—as the sign over his cross proclaims—just not in the way that anyone would expect. The cross, the Roman symbol of utter domination and a place of acknowledged defeat, becomes the place where Jesus is crowned. Evil has overplayed its hand. It can't keep Jesus who is still one with his Father. It has lost its grip on us as well.

Paul, the significant early leader of the first century church, describes it this way:

---

[103] "Obey" can be a trigger word for many of us, often reminding us of times when our own desires or wills were overruled by others more powerful than ourselves...usually with threats as the motivator. Instead, I'm using it as Henri Nouwen describes it in his book, *You are the Beloved*: "But none of this applies to Jesus's obedience. His obedience means a total, fearless listening to his loving Father. Between the Father and the Son there is only love."

[104] I'm indebted to university professor and good friend, Peter Fitch for helping me to see this passage in a new way. When Jesus speaks from Psalm 22 about God forsaking him, those who hear him would understand those words as *shorthand* for speaking the Psalm as a whole. Of course, the resolution of the Psalm makes clear that God has not/will not abandon either Jesus or us.

Christ Jesus...had equal status with God but didn't think so much of himself that he had to cling to the advantages of that status no matter what. Not at all. When the time came, he set aside the privileges of deity and took on the status of a slave, became human! Having become human, he stayed human. It was an incredibly humbling process. He didn't claim special privileges. Instead, he lived a selfless, obedient life and then died a selfless, obedient death—and the worst kind of death at that—a crucifixion. Because of that obedience, God lifted him high and honored him far beyond anyone or anything, ever, so that all created beings in heaven and on earth—even those long ago dead and buried—will bow in worship before this Jesus Christ, and call out in praise that he is the Master of all, to the glorious honor of God the Father.[105]

It's on the cross that I see Jesus most clearly. And in seeing Jesus there, I've most fully seen God. The sovereign God has chosen first of all to love. To love in a way that my heart can trust even if I don't fully understand. God's love is the *one* constant in all the variables of my imperfect human life. It takes up the space that separates me from both God and my deepest longings, in order to come to me where and when I need it the most.

On the cross I see such a different picture from the God constructed from philosophic conceptions. Jesus isn't distant and removed like Plato's ideals, never disengaged or expressionless. The God I find in the story laughs and weeps, rejoices and gets angry, listens and will have a change of mind. Always passionate, and

---

[105] Philippians 2:5-11, MSG.

invariably *for* me.

I am never a means to one of God's ends. God never uses me to get something done, some great victory or accomplishment that God has in mind. I, and we together, are God's end. Everything is done for one purpose—that we will fully live, flourish, at home with God.[106] Starting now.

---

[106] See John 10:10 where Jesus explains what he has come to accomplish. The concept of being at home with God is unpacked in Matt Croasman and Miroslav Volf's book, *For the Life of the World: Theology That Makes a Difference.*

25 A Glimpse From Over The Horizon

With all of these questions swirling around in my mind, I'm still new in my marriage and not even close to sorting out much of anything regarding that relationship. I'm also still very much wrestling with whether I have a legitimate faith. It will take years to gain much clarity about what God is trying to help me discover. One thing I do sense, however, is that God's grip on me is far greater than my hold on God. It's as though I'm having revelatory glimpses from over the horizon, from heaven to earth, helping me to see that the story can read much differently than I've been taught. Deep within, long suppressed desires are beginning to stir.

New glasses with new prescriptions are disorienting. I'm so used to seeing what I'm accustomed to seeing. Yet I'm living with Joy who's enamored with a God who she knows loves her more than anything. She not only keeps looking ahead, expecting the greatest story to emerge, but fully expects me to be a part of it.

I don't know exactly what happened with Abram and Sarah but I'm quite sure that whatever hooked their hearts and caused them to leave absolutely everything must have reached a pretty deep place in them. I must admit some of Joy's enthusiasm is contagious. No matter how many doubts and reservations I still have, I am beginning to sense that there's something out there for me.

Is it possible that God is not someone to run from but someone to run toward? Is God inviting me into a story that's actually worth giving my life to? A story where I'll find the joy I've longed for all my life?

I suppose that the only way I'll find out is to respond to the invitation. I can only begin by beginning. My journey feels like a combination of Lord of the Rings ("I'll take the ring but I don't know the way") and the Princess Bride ("You'll most likely die in the morning"), but there's at least a thread of anticipation.

Of course, I'm not the first to wrestle with this invitation. I can't help but wonder if the first disciples, even though they have the benefit of actually being with Jesus, feel at all anxious over the uncertainty of it all.

They, of course, are the "B" team. The truly sharp kids were long before identified and channeled into rabbinic mentoring. So, they set aside any of those dreams and settle into catching fish or collecting taxes. Someone like Jesus isn't supposed to pick them but then he in-explicably does. It must feel a bit like winning the lottery—that's at least part of the scandal of it all.

As I read the gospels, I have the strange sense that God is picking me. Do I really want the roller coaster ride that I can see defines their lives? And besides, who will pay the mortgage on the fishing boats?

They choose to trust the call to follow and risk everything. Actually, it seems like they lose everything...and still call it a privilege. Is that what joy does?

Sensing parallels between their lives and my own, I begin to immerse myself into the gospels and the book of Acts. I somehow feel that if the story can get into me, perhaps I'll be able to get into the story.

Little can I imagine...

Part 2

A Tale of Two Stories

1 Pick Me!

Second captain, first pick.

I know what happens next.

"You take *him.*"

"No *you* take him."

The two biggest, most popular kids are the self-proclaimed leaders over choosing teams to play whatever game will take up the school lunch time. It's a chance for all of us to see where we are on the pecking order.

For me, as the smallest kid in the class all the way through the ninth grade, it's a time of anxiety and humiliation. I don't know why I'm anxious. I know when I'm going to be picked. I'm not going to be picked at all.

I never have the experience of being chosen early in the process. It's part of what fuels me to practice diligently on my own for three years before trying out for my first basketball team in the ninth grade. I not only make the team, I'm a starter. I hope my dad will be proud.

I always have a deep desire to be picked...early. A

statement made that I'm important, special in some way. I've come to understand that most of us probably feel that way. What's interesting is that no matter when we're chosen in the order, most of us still feel that in some way we are ultimately on the outside looking in.

We can't help focusing on the ones chosen before us.

I often hear about the "inside group". Everyone knows about it, but almost no one feels like they're in it. Even if by some fortune we are temporarily on the "inside", we fear our place is tenuous. For those on the bubble, it will often produce a drive to find some x-factor and leverage it in the hope that it will get us inside the margin. If or when that fails, we lower our expectations, hope for a job at the mill, and buy lottery tickets.

Where I grow up, working at the mill is about all most of us hope for. We don't expect to be picked—kids from Whalley never are. But we *know* how to survive.

(Whalley is a suburb outside of Vancouver, in my day referred to as "the armpit of the city"—a place dominated by biker gangs and crime. In the tenth grade, when my friend stabs our science teacher in the back during class, we don't think it highly unusual. Doesn't everyone stab their teachers?)[107]

---

[107] By the way, this is the stereotype. I love where I grew up: the people were real, and though it was marked with a lot of hopelessness, there was always lots of light and beauty within the darkness.

2 Nazareth

Nazareth is a bit like Vancouver's Whalley. It's a backwater, less affluent, with low expectations. The big names don't tend to come from here and you can be sure that they never come through here either.

Being from Nazareth, Jesus is an outsider. His accent gives him away. He doesn't go to the "right" schools. Definitely blue collar. But can he teach! And when the talking is done, God backs up everything he's saying, with power these northerners never dreamed they would see.

It must seem surreal for the crowds that follow Jesus when he first starts travelling through the various towns and villages of the north. One thing is sure, if this was in Jerusalem, they wouldn't get a ticket—he's that good. And here they are—spellbound—in the front row and Jesus is speaking directly to them. What tops it off is that they're the overlooked ones, never considered for rabbinical school. That isn't to say that they aren't capable, or sharp, or interested. Just never considered.

I wonder how it feels for Peter, or John, or Andrew, or any of the others when Jesus is announcing the twelve key disciples that will be closest to him? They have uncharacteristically left everything to follow him. They've put it all on the line. Will they be rewarded? The significance of Jesus choosing twelve sure seems to indicate so.[108]

"For the first selection in this year's discipleship draft, Jesus selects, from Capernaum Collegiate, Simon Peter!"

I think I know what Peter is feeling inside as he stands and moves to Jesus's right side. Northern fishermen are never picked. This means he *is* special. And eventually the world will know it as well. This must be what it's like to have your ticket win the lottery.

There's no turning back now. The dye, as they say, is cast. They have gone "all in" to this story and now they are destined to be the patriarchs of a grand re-setting of Israel. Their selection can't mean anything less.

There's a reason that rebel movements begin in marginalized areas and not among the more complacent, middle class. Long term oppression with its accompanying sense of powerlessness can finally erupt into bold action. After all, what is there to lose?

Peter and the others know the risk/reward involved. What Jesus is teaching is revolutionary. It could get them all killed. But if the long-held promise is true? If God truly is raising up a Messiah to finally deliver them, how can this man not be the one? The power to which they are firsthand witnesses is undeniable. If the demons flee at

---

[108] I think that it would be fair to say that almost no one in Israel would miss the parallel between Jesus choosing twelve key followers and the twelve patriarchs. This reinforces the expectation that Jesus is inaugurating the restoration that is being eagerly expected—one that will result in the emergence of a new, liberated Israel.

his word, how will it not be the same with the Romans?

And now he's picking them.

Jesus isn't choosing them first to put them at the end of the line. No wonder they're already starting to fantasize about cabinet positions. There's much they don't understand. Jesus they barely know. But they're pretty sure they know the Messiah narrative and now they'll find out their part in it. The history books are about to be re-written.

At first, the displayed power overshadows everything else. Jesus is demonstrating again and again how he obviously has God's backing. And it's not like he's keeping the power all to himself. The twelve are being drawn into everything he's doing—they truly are his apprentices! Alright, it's a bit of a stretch when he sends them out two by two to do what he has been doing. But the result? Even the demons scatter. "Vive la révolution!"[109]

But then—just when they're quite convinced they're in control of where this story is going—Jesus starts saying some very disquieting things. Not one-off comments. More and more, Jesus drops suggestions about a different kind of revolutionary ending. A dramatically different image of coronation...cryptically involving a cross.

They hear it, but their minds can't take it in. This is not how the story is supposed to end. Cabinet titles aren't particularly helpful on a cross. Plus they're in too far now; to back out at this point may already be too late.

---

[109] "Long live the revolution"—a phrase originally referring to the French Revolution, 1789-99.

Jesus isn't unaware of the growing frustration that begins after these troubling statements, when the crowds are diminishing—impatient with his seeming hesitance to take decisive action. Finally he asks the key twelve themselves, "Do you want out as well?" Peter voices what the group all feel, "In a way, we would if we could." The decision to stay or leave has gone way beyond political calculation. Being around Jesus has begun to affect them deeply. Something mysterious is holding them, almost like a hook embedded in their hearts. They've tasted its sobering goodness, and it almost hurts. Yet they want more. They're free to leave, but if they do, will they lose whatever it is that has been breathing life into their hungry hearts?

3 The Power of Preconception

Having lost Joy, my wife of almost forty-eight years, suddenly in the spring of 2019, I understand just a little the profound sense of confusion, fear and hopelessness that the first followers of Jesus experience in the immediate aftermath of the crucifixion. Actually in fact, it seems most of the emotional response kicks in somewhat later. At first, about all you are aware of is being completely numbed, as though left concussed by a bomb blast, with every voice sounding like an echo from another place. It's a struggle to simply find your next breath. The ability to form thoughts comes later. And painfully unwelcome.

For Jesus's disciples, in the confusing hours that follow his crucifixion, one crushing thought keeps penetrating the fog. They can't shake the feeling that they've bet on the wrong horse. It seems ridiculous now. How could they imagine it would turn out any differently? In their messianic euphoria, they've believed that Jesus had access to power far beyond any of the previous pretenders and they've stayed convinced too long that the endgame will be different.

Clearly, it isn't. It's ending the way it always ends. The Romans strike the shepherd. How many more will they strike until they're convinced the sheep are sufficiently scattered?

The enduring hope that has held God's chosen people, almost more than they ever held it, now lays mostly shattered on the floor of their frayed minds. That is, if they can even stir themselves to examine it. Right now the issue is survival, hence the upper room. Strategy will come later.

I know from experience that, in the hours after deep loss, the mind plays cruel tricks. Lying beside Joy, during the time between her brain hemorrhage and final death, I can't help imagining that this is just a dream from which I will awake and all will once again be as it always has been. That she will suddenly sit up and inquire as to what we would like for breakfast. I know it's crazy, but desperate hope does crazy things.

The first reports coming to the huddled group in the upper room seem like that. Once bitten, twice shy. Like Thomas, I'd need to feel the holes.

Is all the DRC[110] dispelled the first time Jesus walks into the room? I doubt it.

By the second or third time?

Eventually, though more questions are raised than answered, one thing becomes clear. This isn't an apparition. This is Jesus. And yet it isn't. He seems equally comfortable in both realities—in their dimension, as he eats and laughs and discusses with them, and in

---

[110] Dream Reality Confusion refers to the difficulty in determining whether an event or experience occurs during one's waking state or as part of a dream.

God's, as is made clear when he periodically disappears from their sight. ("Oh, don't worry about the door, I'll be fine....")

For the disciples, this definitively answers a pressing question. Is the Messiah thing back on? Oh yes! On steroids! Having conquered death could be a definite advantage when taking on the Romans. Only gradually will the old ideas be re-framed.

Up until now, it's almost impossible for them to comprehend Jesus's messianic mission outside of the framework of understanding that they've grown up with. Of course, Jesus has tried to explain that his concept of revolution is intended to be much, much more than a return to the Maccabean golden age. God is acting to rescue the *entire* created order from exile. Still, it isn't clear that they've moved much beyond their previous arguments over such things as potential cabinet posts. Power politics are still front and centre.

The promise of vindication and renewal has kept hope alive through centuries of oppression, captivity, and servitude. They are quite sure that it was rebellion that expelled Adam and Eve from their rightful place in the garden, disobedience that sent God's chosen people into exile. Yet God had promised a deliverer, anointed by God to "restore the fortunes of Israel" and put her in her rightful place in the world—a position of preeminence relative to all the other nations.

With Jerusalem at the centre of the world's power structure, and God effectively ruling in the temple at the centre of the city, all the peoples of the earth will come in submission to be judged and presumably blessed.

The despised Pax Romana will finally be replaced with

a welcomed Pax Iudaicus.[111] Welcomed, at least, by the Jews.

"Plus ca change, plus c'est la même chose."[112]

The mission into which Jesus is inviting his disciples is a major topic of discussion over their forty days together. Jesus reminds them that he has come for a different kind of revolution, one that will begin with the house of Israel. Only by being transformed by love will she extend the merciful invitation of God to the world. Jesus has exhausted evil, triumphing on the cross to make this very witness possible. He has come to do what Israel was called to do but had failed to do—personify the mercy of God and break the endless cycle of judgement.

Still, no matter how much Jesus reinforces the very things that he had shared with them throughout the previous few years, the mystery of mercy triumphing over judgement is still counterintuitive for them and almost beyond their ability to grasp. Yes, it's clear that the cross—the seeming place of Jesus's defeat—has become oddly the place of his vindication and enthronement. His very presence with them demonstrates that he has triumphed over death. What they can't yet clearly understand is what this means going forward.

---

[111] The term for the peace that Rome brought to the ancient world was ironic in that it was imposed and maintained through oppressive force. Exchanging it with a "Jewish Peace" would work well, of course, for the Jews but no lasting peace would really have been achieved.

[112] Loosely translated from French, "the more things change, the more they stay the same." It does seem predictably true that yesterdays liberators too often become tomorrow's oppressors.

4 Grasping the Truth

Not that the roller coaster days, weeks and months that follow will give much opportunity for sustained reflection. Initially there seems to be so much to take in, let alone process. The symbolism behind Jesus disappearing into heaven—God's dimension—and the resultant words from the two unexpected angels make it clear that the two realms, heaven and earth, are now connected in a way that no evil power can ever overturn.

The implications are unbelievably exciting! What's more, the angels leave no doubt—as if Jesus hadn't—that what has begun will certainly be completed.

Yet there is to be more. Jesus promises an encounter with God's own spirit. Yes, he has already breathed that spirit into them but it doesn't seem that they are able yet to understand the full import of that simple act.

I surmise that, in that breath, they do notice something change. Perhaps they have a mysterious sense that the spirit of Jesus is now truly "in" them; maybe they began to wonder if Jeremiah's promise of a new covenant—one that will literally change their hearts—is being initiated through that symbolic breathing. Still, Jesus tells them to expect another baptism—one wild and new—that will reveal even more than this wonderful sense of unity with Jesus. A baptism of fire.

When Pentecost arrives, the flames fall.

They experience much more than a mere visitation of power: this is an overwhelming encounter with...a person. It's the Oracle of Prophecy, that same spirit which energized the prophets and the great deliverers from Israel's past. It's the same as the past, but with two notable differences. First, what was encountered by a few is now being known by all—fulfilling the prayer of Moses in Numbers 11. Second, not only has this spirit fallen "on" them, Jesus has breathed it "into" their very hearts.

This spirit—who they will come to know as God's Holy Spirit—will be their comforter and their advocate, and will go before them, authorizing their obedience to Jesus's commission given to them at his departure. There's little wonder that they are filled with courage and boldness. If God himself is not only for them but in them, how can they possibly fail to succeed in their mission?

Further theologizing can wait; there is a gospel waiting to be proclaimed. They waste no time in making that announcement. Empowered by their encounter, they spill out from the hidden room and began to boldly proclaim in the crowded streets the amazing news that God has fulfilled the promises made to Israel—even if in a totally surprising way.

The response is immediate and overwhelming. Whether we take the number given in the book of Acts (2:41) as a literal number of—likely—men or simply as an expression of a large number, the significance of even the first wave of those who accept Peter's message will mean that the disciples have work to do.

A lot of work.

The only model they've been given from Jesus and from their tradition is the rabbinic one. Model and teach; follow and imitate. What Jesus has taken almost three years with them to do, now takes on an immediacy that they have little time to prepare for. From now on, it will be "Ready, Fire, Aim."

It will be hard enough, even with receptive seekers. Soon, not all audiences will continue to prove friendly.

5 Living the Truth

Almost immediately comes political and religious opposition and threats. The religious establishment demands that they explain themselves and their actions. As an attempt to nip this neophyte movement in the bud, Peter and John are thrown in jail. Yet the story continues to capture a greater number of hearts and minds.

Upon their release, they renew their commitment to the commission that Jesus has left with them. And God re-affirms his promise to authorize their obedience, in the same way he did with Jesus. God stretches out his hand, touching them in such a way that not only their bodies but also the building they're in begins to shake—thankfully not too much given the dearth of earthquake-proof buildings, or the book of Acts might have played out differently.

What follows is an explosion of healing and transforming power: blind eyes taking in their first sunrise, demons shrieking as they run, a child restored from death into the embrace of a weeping mother. Expectancy is off the charts. How can God's promised turning of the age be far off? Now is not the time to worry about your mortgage. The believers share everything liberally; the time of abundance is right around the corner.

As the story unfolds, we see everywhere the continued presence and activity of God and God's spirit. At the same time, it's still very human—it doesn't take long to observe the first hints of insider/outsider distinctions, and dishonesty. Persecution alternates with relief and expansion. Yet in all of these realities, the story carries forward. The gospel captures hearts and changes lives. Not perfectly—it is in human hands—but relentlessly, as it continues to be empowered by God's spirit.

Throughout all of this time, one thing is clear: this is not some new story. God has not abandoned the covenants made throughout the entire history of Israel. God has not decided instead to start an entirely new narrative, disconnected with all that has brought them to this place and time. What they're experiencing is God's fulfillment of the promises. God has stepped in to do on Israel's behalf what they had failed to do and is now calling Jesus's disciples—a "new" Israel—to partner in bringing this salvation to the world. God hasn't forgotten the promise made to Abram and Sarah—that all the nations of the world would be blessed through them.

However this will be accomplished, for the disciples it means that Israel is still central, still the gatekeepers. This salvation is still Jewish. It simply makes sense that somehow the world would yet "come to Jerusalem" at least in a metaphorical sense. The promised one, the answer for the salvation of the world, is the Jewish Messiah and will be discovered in and through them and their ways.

It doesn't take them long to realize that while this is generally true, there are going to be some significant surprises in the precise way that the story will play out.

Over time, they will more deeply understand the symbolism of Jesus's judgement of the Temple—that in Jesus, and then in and through his followers, a new meeting place between heaven and earth will be established. What they don't yet recognize, however, even after Jesus breathes into them his very own spirit, is how quickly and directly this reconciling spirit will reach out into the world, taking up the space between heaven and earth.

They also will discover that this loving, inviting spirit, restless for the lowest and furthest places, wants to include them in the adventure. The ways by which that comes about, however, they could never begin to guess.

6 Breadcrumbs On The Path

Just a couple of weeks before Joy passed away from her aneurism, we were on a family ski vacation. One evening, the grandkids put on the Disney movie, *Winnie The Pooh*. All of us couldn't help but chuckle as we observed the many parallels between Pooh Bear and our beloved Joy. One line in particular seemed to perfectly describe Joy's approach to life. Winnie the Pooh is describing his strategic approach to arriving at a destination. The line, which I'm paraphrasing from memory, goes something like, "Sometimes, when I'm on my way to somewhere, I just wait...and eventually somewhere comes to me."

I've come to believe that our futures find us as much as we find them. That isn't to say that we don't make real decisions. In my case the challenge is choosing to step *toward* trust and *away* from my fears and mis-conceptions. Most times it feels like flying by in-struments, somewhat blindly stepping toward what I hope can...will be true. But every once in a while—the minority of times—a glimpse of light will flicker through, re-orienting my sense of direction, encouraging my heart.

When I reflect on my story, I tend not to be too sure how it was that I got to my present place. Each step is so predicated on the one taken previously—and that without a full understanding of its importance.

I'm not trying at all to say that God is uninvolved in our journeys. I just don't think God micro-manages. At the end of the day, I'm not merely a puppet on a stick, a marionette dancing to the tune of God's own making. At the same time I'm not abandoned to chance outcomes of my own choices. God's presence is within my reach but not so blatantly front and centre that it's impossible to tune it out—consciously or unconsciously.

Often, God's leading feels like breadcrumbs along a trail. If I keep my eyes open, I realize I'm not just on my own.

Joy and I experience this firsthand when in 1972—nine months after our marriage—we set out on a three month long, belated honeymoon in Europe. If it wasn't so tragic, it would be hilarious. We have completely different ideas of what traveling Europe is supposed to look like.

Joy wants to just take the smallest roads possible in a VW van and see where they take us. She wants total serendipity. I'm quite happy to take the train and tick off the "best sites" in the Michelin travel guide—naturally purchased in advance—and then fly home after three weeks having "done" Europe.

The only problem Joy has with her plan is that she's directionally challenged—she can't translate the markings on any map into where we really are. Of necessity, I become both the driver and navigator. Joy's primary role is to criticize my choices.

This turns out to be my saving grace because if she did know where we were she'd leave me halfway through our trip—the other saving grace is that the traveller's cheques are in my name.

We do have an auspicious start to the adventure. Originally planning to leave in early summer, in March we discover that our airline is discontinuing a youth fare that we were counting on to make our budget work. Quickly, we decide to quit our jobs and we leave within a week.

Though we haven't thought much about it, this is going to be a major shift for us. For most of the time since our wedding, we've barely seen each other—Joy has been working days and I'm working afternoons. Other than a brief kiss weekdays at one a.m. as I tumble into bed, we primarily connect on weekends. There are probably healthier patterns within which to establish a marriage relationship.

Of course, we've planned virtually nothing. Joy is convinced that God will guide us, and she doesn't want to ruin the spontaneity of our time by purchasing any guide books. Besides, they cost money…which means less time to actually travel.

Remember, all of this predates the internet, so when we get to Europe, it will be the blind leading the blind—no phones, no Google, no GPS.

All we have to do is somehow buy that VW van and then set out to see where the most insignificant roads take us. How in the world we will find that van, and insure it, is entirely up to me—still, Joy would prefer that this is done "on the fly."

A couple of days before we leave, a friend gives us a tantalizing tip. We trust him enough to assume that his source may be accurate. "Someone told me recently that you can buy refurbished VW vans from Operation Mobilization (a European missions organization)," he claims. "I think it's in Belgium—in a town called something like Sauben." His confidence sells me. At least I have an actual plan to bolster my confidence on the flight.

How hard can this be, I think? We'll simply pop over to Belgium—however it is that you do that—and then we'll zip up to Sauben and grab a van. It might have been a good idea to check on a map of Belgium, but in the seventies it's not like everyone has a European map on their coffee table.

In the middle of Easter weekend, we arrive in London without a clue of what to do next. Thankfully, international airports tend to be quite prepared for travellers like us— like cattle steered through the appropriate gates, we eventually find ourselves in front of a customs agent. Pleasant enough, she asks the obligatory questions and then...we're in England! We are clearly veteran travellers.

Somehow we find a room for the night—actually I think it's more true that the owner of the room finds us—and then we set about figuring out how to get to Belgium. The fact that we haven't calculated on arriving in the middle of Easter makes everything a bit more difficult. Every phone number I call has the same message—closed for the weekend. Joy is anxious that we are burning through our money staying in something that has walls and a ceiling. Wouldn't it be cheaper to camp in the woods?

After asking a million questions, somehow we find ourselves on a train, then a boat to Oostende, Belgium. I'm beginning to think that this Europe thing is a piece of cake. Several hours later we arrive and walk into a souvenir shop to get a map of the whole of Europe— major expenditure—and see if we can hunt down the mysterious Sauben.

We haven't counted on no one speaking our language. This ups the ante a bit. But through sign language and using the little bit of French that we know, we get our message across. Soon everyone in the shop is pouring over the map, muttering Sauben over and over. They've never heard of it. Just as they, and we, are about to give up, one of the clerks spots a small center just north of Brussels.

"Zaventem?" she suggests.[113] It's our only live option at this point, so we go with it. We run back to the station to barely catch the last train of the day into Brussels. Though tired, we are elated that we aren't stranded— wasting another day. We relax and settle in for the two-hour train ride.

We've sorted out that we'll need to transfer trains in Brussels and hopefully we'll get to Zaventem before dark. We've never really taken trains before so we're intently looking at every sign we slow down for. We jump to attention when the train pulls to a stop and we read "BRUSSELS NORD" just outside the window.

Does that mean there are other Brussels stations? We can't take that chance—the clock is ticking! As we get up to leave, we remark to one another, "I hope it's not too hard to make a connection to Zaventem." Upon hearing this, a man who's been sleeping next to us opens his eyes, says, "Next station," and nods off again.

Whew! That was close. We almost blew it. What confronts us in Brussels Centrale, however, is a nightmare. Having never been in a large train station before, it seems impossible to make sense of the massive

---

[113] By the 1970's, a national airport has been built just outside of this village, so the location is not unknown—just unknown to us.

information board which is constantly flipping from one destination to another. I'm just about ready to despair, when finally I see the word "Zaventem" followed by "Omnibus."

"We've got to find the bus station...and fast."

If I'm reading the message correctly, the bus is leaving in ten minutes! Frantically looking for signs that can direct us, I also try to ask anyone who seems like they're willing to at least try a bit of English. Finally, one person relents and helps me to understand that the Omnibus is a slow, inter-city train that is leaving from a specified track.

With seconds to spare, we race to the platform, just jumping on the car before it pulls out. It's now getting dark. We're so relieved that we once again have made it onto the last train. The alternating panic and euphoria of our adventure so far has distracted us from one major consideration—one that confronts us now. What do we do if Zaventem is a dead end?

There are only the two of us and a mother with her two young children on the train. Hearing us speaking to one another, the mom asks, "Are you from Canada?"

"Yes," we reply, "from Vancouver."

"I was just in Vancouver a couple of weeks ago visiting my sister," she said.

This is amazing! We have a Zaventem tour guide who speaks English. Excitedly we ask her, "Have you heard of Operation Mobilization?" We're assuming in a small town, everyone will know everything.

"No," comes the reply.

"Do you know of anywhere that sells used VW vans?"

"No."

"Is there anywhere to stay in Zaventem?"

"No."

As we get off the train, we are completely unprepared as to what to do next. There isn't even a suitable spot in the small train station in which to sleep. Before the young mother leaves us, however, she suggests, "There's one place we can check out. I don't know what it is, but it's worth a try."

After several minutes walking in the dark, she takes us to a door without any signage. We knock. A young woman answers the door.

"Is this Operation Mobilization?"

"Yes, it is."

"Do you sell VW vans?"

"No, I'm sorry we don't."

"Could we possibly stay for the night?"

For the next two weeks we become part of a community that literally prays for their daily bread. Actually they seem to pray for everything...all the time. They pray for their meal, then they pray during their meal—interspersed with stories about answered prayer. I don't need to mention what they do to end the mealtime.

They're in the season of preparation for their upcoming summer mission teams, and it becomes obvious that a large number of miracles will need to occur for everything to pull off—apparently it's like this every year. I'm more anxious than they are. They simply pray...joyfully expecting that God is going to come through, just like last year. It feels like we're being mentored in how to live a life of faith.

We eventually strike a deal. They're going up to Holland to buy a number of vans for their summer teams. I'll give them $300 to purchase one for us. They'll service it, insure it—which would have been a nightmare for us— and send us on our way.

As it turns out, we'll drive it on a big circuit down to Greece, returning to them halfway through our trip (at which point we pick up another couple who is joining us). To ensure that we won't have any mechanical problems, they service the van again and off we go on another circuit. Another few months later we simply drop the van off to them.

It's like breadcrumbs, or gold coins along a path. Traveling Europe isn't nearly as difficult as we thought it would be.

Once we actually get on the road, our differences confront us. Joy wants to stay in Europe as long as possible—even if that means sleeping in a damp van in the cold, spring rain rather than spending money on more elaborate accommodations. I, on the other hand, am longing to cozy under an eiderdown in the romantic pension we just passed.

Being the gentleman that I am—even though a begrudging one—I've given Joy the only air mattress we have that holds air the whole night through. Which of course means that I soon have a bladder infection due to the cold, rubber mat that my damp sleeping bag is laid upon.

I become consumed with finding public toilets. It's not an easy task in the 1970's. Since we're not generally staying in campsites that have these amenities—too costly, of course—my morning routine is a race against the clock.

Eventually, like it does in most good stories, things start looking up: the rain finally stops and the sun emerges—which means the van dries out. We get more comfortable adjusting to different languages and customs, and I get better at finding my way around and anticipating Joy's expectations. Most importantly, my bladder finally gets back to normal. Europe becomes magical, and we actually have lots of great times and bank many wonderful memories.

To be fair, doing Europe in the totally unplanned way that we are has created lots of room for adventure and surprises—and there have been many from our first arrival story onward! The seemingly divine coincidences become so frequent that even I recognize that God has joined us on the trip. I could probably write a book recounting some of the crazy outcomes of our meanderings, most of which read like a salvation narrative.

(Teaser: how about ending up on a one lane road in the mountains along the border between Yugoslavia and Albania, running out of gas in a smallpox quarantine area, and being saved by literally coasting downhill for fifteen miles into the Yugoslav city of Skopje? Why you ask? Joy doesn't want to pay extra money to buy a map that would cover the gap between what was shown on our general map of Europe and the map of Greece that we splurged on.)

As the weather—and our relationship—has improved during the trip, we've been reading the Gospels and Acts together. (I previously start on my own by once again trying to read the Old Testament, but just like my first attempt by the middle of the book of Judges I jump to the

New while I still have a semblance of faith—still too many triggers.)

Reading together is always a little delicate since we see things so differently. It's easy to get into a fight while reading the Bible. We don't think it's supposed to work that way but we haven't found a solution yet.

Nevertheless, as we persevere in reading day after day about the first followers of Jesus, a deep disquiet—dare I say, hunger—is growing within us. "Why doesn't our experience look at all like what we're reading about?" we ask. We know somehow that there could be, should be more than the things we are presently experiencing. Our faith seems so predictable, so...mundane. There is no surprise. Our God—at least to us—seems to be almost a reflection of ourselves, whereas theirs seems to have no limits. We're pretty sure that when we get back we want to live more like these people.

In contrast to our faith, the New Testament seems so wild, unpredictable, and uncontrollable. A little scary but somehow we think living our lives with God tangibly present should be a bit scary.

We're tired of being "stuck". We begin praying for God to give us a story like the ones we've been reading about. One where we can see the hand of God actually leading us and the presence of God being a daily companion.

Eventually, even on Joy's tight budget, we can see our money finally running out and know it's time to look ahead to the rest of our lives. As best we can, we sort out a set of next steps. Since I'm only a couple of years away from completing my five year secondary education degree, we decide that I'll go back to school and Joy will work. After that I'll look for a teaching job and we'll determine where we go from there.

We have a return ticket from London, so we arbitrarily pick a departure date and begin making our way from southern Europe in order to come home. (Remember, we're in 1972—before smart phones, the internet, ATM machines, or accessible credit cards.) We're trying to ensure that by the time we cash the last traveller's cheque we'll have just enough cash to get to the airport and no more—Joy definitely doesn't want to come home one day early.

How our plan is going to work once home is a mystery. By the time we get back in June, my usual summer job will be unavailable, filled by another student. All housing options near the university will have already been taken as well. Joy hasn't got a job lined up and I haven't registered for the fall semester. We aren't looking forward to returning to the same church and the same routines. As reality hits, our New Testament vision is already fading.

After dropping off our van in Belgium, we have just enough money for boat and train tickets to Heathrow. We are planning to arrive the day before so we'll spend the night in the airport. Our money is gone. Fasting is never a bad thing I guess. We're cutting it a bit tight, though.

At the airport, I get a free peak at a newspaper in one of the shops. I run back to Joy to share what I've just read. "Do you want the good news or bad?" I ask. Not waiting for a response, I blurt out the bad: the International Federation of Airline Pilots' Associations has declared Monday, June 19 as a world-wide protest strike against airplane hijacking.

What's the good news? We arbitrarily picked the day before (Sunday) as our departure date—if we hadn't chosen today, we would have been stuck for days with nowhere to go and nothing to eat. Thankfully our ticket is secure.

So we think, until we find ourselves waiting on the runway for hours. The pilot is noncommittal as to the reason and I'm getting anxious—we don't have a plan B.

Only later do we discover that a plane departing just before us (BEA 548) stalled and crashed just after takeoff at 3:45 p.m., killing all aboard. The airport is seriously considering turning us around and cancelling all flights.

Sitting on the plane, I don't know all the options being discussed in the control tower. I just know we need to get this plane off the ground and headed home. I can't help but reflect on our friends in Zaventem, and the joy with which they would face these kinds of challenges. I'm praying, but I know I don't yet have the confidence and trust that I saw in them.

The engines roar to life. Still blissfully unaware of the turmoil around me, I allow myself to relax as London fades in the distance. I'm too excited to sleep on the plane. I know as soon as we're home, there will be immediate challenges. Where will we live? Can I find work for the remainder of the summer? What about school for me and work for Joy?

The first gold coin is waiting for us as soon as we touch down in Vancouver. I find out that the city employer that I worked with every summer for five years has been—coincidentally—on strike. But, wouldn't you know that they settled over the weekend. I head in first thing in the morning and I'm working for the rest of the summer.

We're staying with Joy's parents, sleeping on a single bed—it works for relative newlyweds and sure beats the van—but we're motivated to find a place close to the university that will serve us for the next two years or so. It's a discouraging task—even more so when we see the housing options that are still available this late in the summer. It will take a miracle.[114]

Near the end of a long day of searching, we're ready to give up. There is one item on the student housing list that keeps poking at me, though it makes no sense. It's what looks like the perfect place to live—a block off the beach, one whole floor of an old house, with a spacious yard in a great neighbourhood. Why is it still available? It's listed as "summer only". Not much use for a student.

I just can't let it go. I convince Joy to drive there with me before we turn for home after a day of fruitless searching. I sheepishly knock on the door and confess that I know that the house (which exceeds our expectations from the ad) is only a summer rental and won't be available for the school year. In other words, I explain, I'm not quite sure why I'm here.

"Is that why no one has come to look?" the landlady remarks. "We want to rent it for the entire year, including the summer!"

It will be our home for the next stage of our story. We feel completely spoiled. Shortly after, a job falls into Joy's lap. I get permission to take an entire history major in one year. All together, things are starting to feel like this path is finding us as much as we are discovering it.

Where could it be leading us?

---

[114] No movie reference intended. The Princess Bride is still a twinkle in the author's eye until the following year.

7 The Hook of the Kingdom

Once we've been home for several months and the initial excitement of a new start has begun to wear off, Joy and I remember the prayers we had prayed during our travels—for a life that looks more like what we read in the stories about Jesus...for a story that is really worth giving everything for.

We're attending church again but quite frankly it's literally bringing us to tears. It isn't that there's anything wrong with it. It's just that there's nothing *right* with it. We yearn for something better than mere obligation. We desire to see life with God as pure light and privilege. In other words, we're tired of the "shoulds" and we're desperate for more.

We've been noticing that Phil—the one friend who shares our hunger and dissatisfaction—hasn't been around lately, which makes us feel even more isolated. The next time we see him, he explains why he's been absent, and strongly invites us to come along with him to witness a very strange occurrence.

It's happening at a Reformed Episcopal church composed of a smaller group of elderly people—we don't know much about this kind of church except that first, it's, of course not as good as ours, and second, that only old people go there.

"That's not what I'm trying to tell you," he says. "It's been taken over by a large number of "Jesus People"—kids our age who are coming to faith from the exploding Hippie culture in Vancouver. They pack it out every week!"

Though, like many, I've given away my Yardbirds, Doors, and Byrds albums upon returning to faith, the image that this news conjures up in my mind has to be investigated.

First of all, I've never been to any kind of church where you might need to actually come early to get a seat. Thankfully, unsure of how long it will take to arrive, we do come about thirty minutes early...barely getting in the door. Eventually not only is every seat filled but every square foot of floor space occupied as well, including the stage. There are literally people listening in through the windows. (Obviously, it's never entered a fire marshal's mind to consider monitoring a church for instances of overcrowding.) I've never witnessed anything like this before.

In addition, even though the formal service hasn't yet started, people are already literally beginning to weep, others to sing or pray. Once the directed singing starts, hands are raised, some begin to dance and others simply continue weeping. I've seen the hand raising thing previously as I went a few times in my teens to a church that we simply knew as "Pentecostal"—they had a choir that sang black gospel music which I found intriguing. I enjoyed the music, mostly mocked what I saw as the antics, and left untouched.

This, however, is different. On the one hand, everything

in me emotionally wants to moonwalk out of the building—a task more easily imagined than accomplished given the overcrowding. I feel as though a spotlight is shining on me: the outsider, obviously the one who doesn't know the secret handshake to connect with all of this—perhaps the one who really doesn't know God at all.

Yet, at the same time, nothing in me is mocking this experience of others around me. It not only strikes me as being profoundly genuine; it's at the same time impacting me personally in a powerful way. The only way I can describe my experience is that it's like an invitation from God is hooking into my heart. I can choose to simply pull away and leave, but if I do, I feel that something desperately important will be torn away. At least that's how it feels in the moment. So I stay in fear, largely because of the greater fear of walking away.

We keep coming back, week after week. As crazy as it seems, we feel like we are living in the book of Acts. People are coming off of drugs, off the streets and into a deep sense of community. We're starting community houses and living together. Before long, even though Joy and I aren't really sure we know what's going on, we find ourselves leading a house of our own.

In the next few years, Joy and I become quite closely involved with this group, and with the sparrow-like prophet of a man who pastors it. We don't know what he sees in us, but we love being included. We're serving in every way we can—often it is like the blind leading the blind, but so much is happening, so fast, we can't wait for any of us to become mature before getting involved. (We're already starting to do some marriage counselling. Our marriage isn't that good but we're not throwing things and the other couple is, so I guess that makes us mentors?)

All around me I see people having rich encounters with God's presence. I can't say that I ever fully experience the same. Why that is, I'm not sure. I've often thought that it's because of some early traumatic events in my life that have left me largely broken emotionally. What I do know is that any experience of God for me is much more of an anticipation or longing for something than the actual thing itself—like Lewis describes in *Surprised By Joy*.

Looking back later, I realize that we're living in something called "revival", although I wouldn't know to describe it that way at the time. All we understand is that God's invitation is especially near, and being heard and received with incredible impact.

On one level, I'm tremendously excited—when a building is filled to double its capacity you know something special is happening. This is the kind of thing that you read about in books. It's cutting edge stuff...and I'm right in the middle of it! Certainly this is what I've longed for my whole life; it will satisfy the deep insecurities and fear of rejection deep down inside me. How can it not?

Yet something is wrong and I know it. I'm burning the candle at both ends—isn't it because the need is so great? It seems to be working for others but, to be honest, it's not working for me. I know that I'm still on a treadmill trying to do what I think God wants me to do.

Is it so that God will finally accept me? The more I do, however, the more aware I become of my basic mistrust of God. I can't see God as a good Father. I know what I'm doing: just what I've always done—the same thing I did in theological college. I'm learning the postures and expressions that make me look like I fit in, but in reality I'm keeping my distance—from people and from God. It's turning out to be unsustainable. The more intensely I become involved, the more acute becomes the dis-ease that I have in my unhealthy understandings of God.

This all comes to a head when I am asked by Pastor Bob—as everyone simply called him—to resign my high school teaching position midway through my first year to join the pastoral staff of the church. A year or so earlier this would have been my dream, but now I am much more aware of myself. Though I feel the "right" decision is probably to go and work for God, there is no longer any joy in the thought of it, only a sense of obligation.

At the same time our home life is being strained to the breaking point: our first child, Jon, is born two and a half months premature and while he survives against the odds, caring for him is proving to be more than a full time job (beginning with daily trips to the intensive care nursery for the first two months—that turns out to be the easy part). Our marriage is in trouble, worsened by the stress. So is my faith.

Yet Joy and I have so much respect for Pastor Bob's ability to hear God's voice, that we ask him, "Did God tell you to hire us, or is this simply your own idea?" We were not sure if we would dare turn against both our pastor and God as well. Bob candidly confessed, "No, I cannot truthfully say that God has spoken to me."

We ultimately decide to tell Bob "no." Somehow we know we don't have the resilience or faith. In my heart I move on. I put my revival season aside and focus on a new family and a new career.

We move out to an old farmhouse in the countryside of

Langley, an hour out from the city of Vancouver, and join a small, rural community church. But I'm unsettled and uncomfortable around anything connected with God. My dream has dissolved. Am I crazy? I turned down an invitation into the kind of God story that I've thought is everything I need. I said no to a place to belong, and to be recognized by God and others.

But the decision has been made. I've turned away. And I don't expect I'll ever have the chance again.

Despite enduring lengthy bed rest pregnancies, we lose several babies mid-term during this season. I try to pray out of a sense of loyalty but feel a deep sense of guilt— that I rejected God's plan and probably am being punished (pretty much the stereotype of the image of God I carry forward from childhood). The God who felt so near in our early Jesus People years seems to be checking out another neighbourhood.

8 A Thaw

In this season, as my faith becomes more of a rote exercise, besieged by guilt and doubt, Joy's goes in the opposite direction. While I would hesitate to call her a "charismatic", certainly her hunger for a very present relationship with God, one in which she is learning to hear God's voice with confidence, is growing exponentially. This only increases the tension between us.

When she approaches me to share that she believes God has spoken to her about having another child, I'm less than enthusiastic. Particularly she believes that if we have the elders of our church come and pray for us, God will be faithful, we will conceive—that part has never been the problem—and God will faithfully protect and preserve that life.

She wants me to go to God to hear for myself whether that is indeed something we can rely on. I hesitate to share with her that I'm not sure God particularly wants to hear from me. I'm probably not a "member in good standing", so to speak. However, I don't want to risk any further tension in our relationship and agree to at least try. I have little confidence that God does speak; I have no confidence God will speak to me.

Not surprisingly, as I "wait" before God, all I experience is a deadening silence. Eventually, in desperation, I resort to Joy's favourite method of biblical interpretation— letting the Bible fall open. It's with some hesitation that I employ this method because I know it usually requires a fairly high level of "anointing". Usually, for me, the result highlighted will be verses like "Judas went out and hanged himself," and I'll be left pondering what the point of the message is.

This day, though, immediately my eyes are caught by the phrase, "Daughter, go in peace. Your faith has healed you." Is this luck? Coincidence? Divine direction? What- ever it is, it's enough for me to push my chips to the center of the table and trust that what Joy feels strongly about, we will hope for.

The first trimester of the resulting pregnancy draws more prayer out of me than any previous life experience. It isn't entirely what I would call faith-filled prayer. It is more like, "Oh God please be kind. I'm doing my best. I know it's probably not enough to make you happy but I've taken a risk here and I don't know how I'll ever trust again if I have to bury one more tiny body in the backyard." Each day we survive leads me to pray the same prayer again the next day. And each day I numb my heart in order to protect myself if my fears are realized.

Around four months or so into the pregnancy, after I return home from coaching a high school basketball game in the evening, I discover that Joy is losing our baby girl. At this point, we're becoming quite expert on the topic of miscarriages (having experienced several), and it is clear that she's an hour or less away from losing this life as well. I phone the doctor who confirms that it's too late to come in to the hospital. His advice is that I should simply comfort my wife as well as I can.

Joy's desire is less for comfort and more for intercession. "Go and pray!" So I pray with her awhile, trying to conjure up all the kinds of things that I think God might like to hear and/or respond to. Soon, however, I need to go to another room and tell God what I actually think.

"You set us up!" I scream. "If you want to punish me, then go ahead and do it. But if you want me to trust you? Love you? Forget it." It's at this point that a scripture reference from the Old Testament comes to my mind.

"I've had it with all that garbage as well!" I shout. "I'm sick of this whole cat and mouse thing of trying to 'hear your voice' and pretending that you actually want to know me. Why don't you just kill me and get it over with—then at least Joy can get on with her life!" At this point, I throw open a nearby Living Bible in a rage, and turn to the Isaiah reference that had come to mind. By the time I've found the page, I'm ready to lament some inane piece of information that has nothing to do with my plight. I figure that it will confirm the legitimacy of my tirade.

"I said I would do it, and I will."

The prophet's words are like a hammer to my chest. What happens next is not premeditated. It hardly seems volitional.

I begin to speak in authoritative words, demanding that whatever evil forces are behind this miscarriage immediately be removed from this time and place. I declare healing over Joy and this little life and announce that God's good plan will be accomplished. I guess, in effect, that I take the kingdom prayer of Matthew 5 and flip it from "May your kingdom come on earth as it is in heaven" to "Let it come now!" It almost feels like my words are speaking *me.*

Contrary to everything churning up in me before this surprising prayer, I now feel so peaceful I simply fall asleep—it is, after all, well after midnight. Waking up in a start several hours later, confusion gives way immediately to panic. Even as bad a husband as I am, sleeping through my wife's miscarriage is not something I am planning ("But honey, I was really tired...").

I rush into the bedroom. Joy is asleep. The contractions have subsided. Soon the bleeding will as well. Months later, our beautiful daughter Jaana is born.

This experience is the beginning of a profound healing for me in my relationship with God. None of this is earned. I haven't pulled it down from heaven. I haven't earned favour and protection because of my good behaviour. In a place where I feel furthest from God—when I most expect God's wrath—God's mercy catches me, my wife and our child.

I learn that God is good...and for no reason that I can see. Something deep within my heart begins to unthaw. I feel the stirring of an old longing. The hook is still there.

9 Stained Glass Movie

I think the line between what we might technically call a vision and what simply could be an active imagination is a somewhat blurry one. We usually assume that our conscious minds are initiating every thought, yet our actual experience at times is more like watching a movie unfolding before us. So it is for me, just a few years after the dramatic event that led to Jaana's eventual, healthy birth. I have what I believe to be an unexpected encounter with God's spirit.

During this time I am tentatively re-entering the world of church. I'm much more comfortable with God—even the Father piece—since Joy's healing gave me a new perspective, but church continues to be a struggle. I think the concept is a good one—at least it certainly seems to be in the early years after Jesus—but I am having difficulty knowing how to fit in it. Most of my perspectives and suggestions, even when I am intentionally trying to be helpful, are looked at rather quizzically as though I just arrived from another planet.

In spite of this, I'm getting more and more involved, despite some hesitation on both sides. My immediate dilemma is that the pastor has asked me to cast a vision for the idea of small "c" church in an upcoming meeting.

Needless to say, I am feeling challenged to be prepared for this talk.

Hearing from God never having been my strong suit, I am nevertheless asking God for insight, wanting to catch God's perspective on church. And then it happens. First, it is simply a memory, seemingly disconnected from my question. Quickly it becomes more and more vivid, as though I am watching a YouTube clip.

I see what I immediately assume to be Notre Dame Cathedral in Paris. Joy and I first visit it during our infamous European honeymoon adventure. I remember looking down at her from the top of one of the towers. Being afraid of heights, she has remained in the plaza— the Parvis Notre Dame—below, playing the game, "Guess which one is the gargoyle," as I wave to her. More specifically, I realize that what's in the center of my vision is the classic rose window on the west facade. Why am I seeing this?

Because my background is education, my mind quickly begins to connect the dots: a stained glass window is a wonderful example of a mosaic, which is of course a practical illustration of diversity within unity. I know enough of the Bible to connect that metaphor with Paul's use of the physical body describing the nature of the church, another example of diversity and unity, and I think, "I've got myself a talk!"

That's when my—God's?—mental picture begins to take on a life of its own. The first thing I notice is that the overall picture of the window is displaying a magnificent portrait of Jesus for all around to see. Well that makes sense. Isn't that what a cathedral is supposed to do?

It''s what happens next that completely disarms me. You

have to understand that CGI[115] is just in its infancy, so about the only thing I can use as a reference for what takes place is a kaleidoscope—and this is light years beyond that experience. The entire window begins to shift. Every piece of glass is constantly changing size, texture and colour. It's all happening at once and yet, the window remains intact. Though the picture is always in motion, to my amazement the picture is always Jesus. I am watching a stained glass movie!

At that moment, I have a strange feeling that God is trying to tell me something. I can't hear a voice, but if I could, I would know exactly what the voice is saying:

> Whenever anyone says "yes" to my invitation, a constant and dynamic process of change begins as they become more like me. Therefore my church is just like you see: always moving, always changing, always growing and learning to love. If the church even remotely expresses this, the world around it will powerfully see me and be drawn to me. You can never build this, nor maintain it, but you can trust me and ask me for it.

I feel like something hooks into my heart once again. At this point, I don't know whether I'll ever work in a church, let alone start one. But I know this much: this is what I want to be part of, to give my life to. A place where everyone is welcomed and embraced into the invitation of Jesus. I'm pretty sure that if we ever become even a fraction of what I just have seen, we'll never have to worry about evangelism.

I think of the kids that I'm now teaching and counselling

---

[115] CGI, or Computer Graphic Imagery, most commonly refers to the 3D computer graphics used to create characters, scenes and special effects in films, television and games.

—I'm working at the same high school where I graduated. They don't come from the right side of town. If they saw an offering plate, they would help themselves. They wouldn't be welcome in any church I can think of, even my own. Can there be a church for these ones? The stones that the builders have already rejected? In my eyes, these are the golden ones.

I don't really know what I'm doing, but I ask God, "Let me see something like this. I'm not asking to lead it. I'll be happy to sweep the floors. But I want to be in it."

Over the next thirty-five years, I dedicate my life to trusting God for this kind of church. It's not an easy vision to shake off. It becomes a long-term love/hate relationship. I have long seasons when I despair over the church's continued inability (not to mention my own) to embrace this reality—to the point that I wish that I'd never seen what I did. But I also have tastes, moments when it seems like, for just a brief time, Jesus shines through a unified community, one that has come together to love in spite of its profound diversity. These few glimpses are worth everything.

One thing is certain, and it will become more so as the years go by: this vision is holding me more firmly than I'm holding it.

10 What Love Can Do

It's a strange reality when your kids are young and family life is all consuming. The days are long, some delightfully and some tediously, and the years are short. Within months, it seems, the same toddler that you picked up from the ground from countless falls is now on your arm walking down an aisle. And the one worried about falling is you.

The years after Jaana's birth seem to fly by in a way. I am less defensive toward God, and Joy and I are making progress in our relationship. My father—not necessarily someone I would want to quote extensively regarding marriage or parenting—used to tell me, "The first twenty years are the hardest. After that it gets a lot easier." We've only been married a little over a decade, but already our fights aren't as frequent or dark, and we're voicing once again the dreams that we used to share about what the church can be.

We're not just dreaming; we're daring to try to put some of those dreams into practice in our local church setting. Some things are going right, it seems. The small country church that we started attending when the whole crowd numbered less than fifty is growing rapidly. A building has been built and we are racing toward five hundred. The classic success story.

Eventually, through a process marked by peaks and valleys, I become employed there. I've vowed more than once that I'll never work in a church but, not for the first time, I feel like God is overruling my corporate decisions.

I last two years. My naïveté has gotten the better of me. It's not my vision of the window, it will never be. I guess whenever people are involved, we get political. I'm probably as guilty as anyone but I can't see giving my life for this. So I quietly prepare to go back into education.

The job market is tight, but I'm extremely fortunate to secure a position through a relationship I have with a district superintendent. It will be a little unusual, and will involve a separate interview with the school board, but I've found my way out.

Almost.

Joy has been praying for God to give me a mentor. Someone who can guide me toward what she really believes is my calling. (She doesn't share, to the same degree, my conviction that education is to be my future.) And coincidentally—it's interesting how often I use that word—we get hold of a teaching tape. Our pastor has obtained it, doesn't know the name of the person that is doing the teaching, but wants our feedback.

I snap the audio cassette into my Walkman—young readers ignore as it will take too long to explain—and head out for an evening jog in the rain. Within ten minutes or so, two things happen.

First, a car drives by through a puddle and completely soaks me from head to toe. I'm sure there is a spiritual message in this but I still to this day haven't worked out what it is. (I do take down the license plate number however. I'm still looking for the car.)

Second, I stop the tape and remark, "This man is telling me my dream. It's everything I've hoped that following Jesus together can be like. Except I think they're doing it!"

At this point, a thought comes into my mind, "You'll work closely with this man." Now, if I only knew his name...

The process over the next year isn't smooth nor is it easy. The first thing that Joy and I decide is that I need to go to a conference that this man, who I later learn is named John Wimber, is hosting in California. Once we commit to this, I discover that the dates are the same as the interview I am supposed to be having with the school board.

The road not taken, which will it be? One offers security. The other keeps the dream alive. I feel like I'm back in the Jesus People church again. A door that I have been convinced was closed once and for all is ajar...and beckoning.

Whichever path we take will likely burn the bridge to the other. Do we push all our chips into the center of the table? It's not as easy a decision as it was years before, striking out in our newlywed innocence for an obscure town in Belgium. We have more to lose.

Yet once again Joy and I are in agreement. It doesn't make sense but we feel that I need to go to California. We believe our future will find us, but we need to take the steps we can take.

In the Disney version of the unfolding story, I'll go the conference invigorated, return to my church, it will immediately and fully embrace the vision, and I'll find a fruitful place within it. As we know, however, the way life unfolds is often a bit different than the fairy tale.

I return to my job in the church but the pastor no longer trusts me. The church itself is not prepared to fully embrace what has captured my and Joy's heart. Within a year, we are gone from the church.

But unexpectedly, we're wonderfully sent out—not kicked out. Some months later, our church, after a day of fasting and prayer, determines that we're to be blessed and released. We're sent out to plant a church in a church movement called *The Vineyard* that will wholeheartedly dare to pursue the dream that has been percolating in our hearts and the hearts of some of our friends.

Do we know where we're going? No, we're a bit like Abram and Sarah in that regard. But we have the New Testament. What if we dared together to live like what we read? To believe that we can experience tastes of God's future now? Like the church in Acts 4, stretching out their hands in the hope that God will do the same?

It's not like we have a clear plan. It really is "ready, fire, aim." But within a few years of our dramatic experience of God's mercy preserving our baby's life, we find ourselves "back to the future"—encountering the same kinds of revival-like experiences as in our Jesus People days.

It's not that we're looking for revival. I never have been a "revivalist," nor am I one now. Our hope, together with a small community, is to simply but wholeheartedly live out what we are coming to see as the whole point of Jesus and his coming, his death, and his resurrection—to break the power of evil, shredding the membrane separating heaven (God's home) and earth (our home) and through the loving trust and obedience of each of us begin to mend them together again.

So we step out to see what love can do.

11 God Is Closer Than We Think

I've often wondered how those who were part of the early Jerusalem church would respond if they had the opportunity to read the manuscript that we now know as the Acts of the Apostles. Somehow I imagine at first they'd be struck by how much more dramatic their story seems when packed into a few short chapters. I'm sure that upon reflection they'd agree that the stories are true. It's just that, when things take place in real time, they always seem more spread out, more mixed in with the mundane, more, well..."ordinary". It's when these individual stories are all taken up together that one begins to realize the full import of what is taking place.

So it is with us in the late eighties to early nineties. We've set out on a communal journey to discover whether God's kingdom—what this world can look like when God's desires are being realized—can really be found within our reach as Jesus proclaims in the first chapter of Mark. In simple terms we try to take the question "What would Jesus do?" into all the different parts of our lives, largely by investigating "Well, what did Jesus do?" and then attempting to do the same. If the marks that accompanied Jesus's proclamation of the breakthrough of the kingdom included sight to the blind, freedom to the captives, food multiplied to the poor, and oppression overturned then we are fully expecting the same things to occur as we "reach out our hands in the expectation that God will do the same."[116]

It might be a stretch to say that healing becomes commonplace, but it certainly is considered more as expected than unusual. Even dramatic healings. Power evangelism[117] isn't simply a theory lifted from the pages of the New Testament. We see it take place and hear the stories shared. People are being set free from addiction, relationships are being restored, and it seems obvious that lives are being transformed.

This all results in an atmosphere of palpable expectancy and awe. No one has to be persuaded to gather or to engage. Although we don't quite match the person per square foot density of our Jesus People days—fire inspectors have become somewhat more vigilant by this time—it's not uncommon for us to have over one hundred people standing during our services. We come early and stay late. We tell our friends. God is on the loose.

Similar to what I had seen with our Jesus People experience, it's common to have significant, tangible encounters with God's Spirit. Many begin to cry as soon as they come into one of our services—or even before—for no apparent reason, and often this will continue for months. Something deep within their hearts is being uncovered and, as they often describe later, healed. Increasingly when we gather and pray for one another, large numbers of people will experience God's power in

---

[116] Luke 4:18-19, Acts 4:30
[117] The thesis of *Power Evangelism* is that displays of God's power result in an increased turning of people's hearts toward Jesus.

such dramatic ways that most of them will simply be unable to stand. Sometimes up to a third or more of the packed auditorium will be impacted in this way *regardless* of how we seem to pray.

To be clear, it seems that God has an agenda for his interaction with what is by now a very large community of followers that stretches far beyond any expectations that we hold. Often we can barely understand what's going on, let alone be able to lead it. We're running as fast as we can to simply try to catch up. What we do understand, though, is that we're experiencing the kinds of things that people describe when they're writing about revival. At the height of all this wild wonder, I say to Joy one day, "If we gathered up all the stories and compressed them together, it would read much like the first chapters of Acts!"

By the end of our first decade, we're acquiring a reputation as a place where God's power can be experienced—particularly power for physical healing. It's not because we have raised up a staff of healing experts or highly "anointed" individuals; the whole community seems to have a confidence and expectation that when you pray for someone in the most simple ways, there's a very good chance something is going to happen. And it does, again and again. Eventually, people are coming to visit us from other places and other countries because of the stories that are being told.

We know of one missionary who's been healed through our prayers who regularly sends others needing healing to our services with the simple instructions, "Get anyone to pray for you—it doesn't matter who—and you'll be healed." It seems most often they are and then they tell their friends. This expectancy feeds on itself and increases an environment of great faith.

For Joy and I, one area of healing prayer where we ironically seem to see the most dramatic effect is in praying for couples that can't have children. While of course not everyone who we pray for is immediately enabled to conceive, what is notable is the percentage of those who then can—often within days or weeks. Soon after prayer they will discover they are pregnant in spite of what often has been many years of failure (though to be clear certain action is still usually required on their part).

I see it as just one example of our increased authority. After years of trying to understand and practice the ministry of Jesus, we have strong confidence in the kingdom message[118]—as we understand it—and its effectiveness. We've earned our dues, so to speak, and now it seems that God's power is authorizing our obedience. For myself, I have by now witnessed directly through my own prayers the blind see, the deaf hear, the crippled walk, cancer eliminated. And more—much, much more. All I need to check off the list is raising the dead.

I've wrestled along the way with what theologians call eschatological tension—the already/not yet of God's kingdom—but my experience of the *already* is getting bigger and bigger and I'm not looking back. Pretty soon I'll have the *not yet* part pinned to the mat. This story is getting better and better. God has made sure of that.

Still, I have always been hesitant about writing about our

---

[118] An understanding that Jesus came to make it possible for God's will and desires to be at least somewhat realized here and now. (As in the Lord's Prayer in Matt. 6:10; "May your kingdom come, your will be done.")

experiences. I have a number of reasons for this. The first shows my low level of spiritual maturity: I think it might produce the same result as a sportscaster announcing that the baseball pitcher is one out away from a no-hitter—a sure-fire curse. Will writing about our stories be the end of our stories?

The primary reason for my caution, however, is that I suspect you need to have something worth saying. Not that I don't have enough material to draw from. By the first few years of the new millennium, we have more than enough stories to easily fill out a sufficient number of pages. I also have logged enough messages to create segues between them. Yet somehow I feel enough questions lurking at the edge of any narrative I might conjure up to give me pause.

I approach my mentor, John Wimber, and ask, "When do you know you should write?" He simply says, "When you have an overwhelming number of unsolicited queries, that will be your sign." (Little do I know that he already has a clear sense of what I should be writing and that I'll indeed write it.) Interestingly enough, almost immediately after his advice, I begin to be pressed upon by a wide variety of individuals to begin a book.

The very process of writing is both exhilarating and profoundly challenging. The sheer number of stories that I begin to recall, and the dramatic nature of them, deeply encourages my sense of gratitude and faith. God is truly closer than we can imagine! Even the understated version of these narratives that make it to the final version of my resulting book read like the days of the early church. (My wife Joy has an intense conviction about the subtle enlargement associated with much pastoral storytelling and I write with her constantly over my shoulder—not surprisingly, I suppose, I can still feel her very near as I am writing these very words.)

As I write, I begin to see more clearly some of the things God has been teaching us in and through our experiences. We're joining in with God's kingdom work. The Good News is becoming much better than we have ever thought possible. Perhaps this book will inspire so many more to dare to do what we're stepping out to take hold of.

And who knows? If it goes well, just maybe I'll write a sequel.

12 Cornelius

"What was I to do? It seemed futile to try to close the barn door with the horses prancing around in the pasture—invited there by God's own spirit!"

So Peter explains his actions when visiting the home of a Roman centurion,[119] which to a number within the core group of disciples in Jerusalem seems scandalous and, well, unlawful! He seemingly has allowed, and even worse, invited Gentiles into the Messiah's family while completely ignoring the time-established gateways for such inclusion. They haven't taken on the sign— circumcision—of being set apart to God; how can they be followers of the Messiah?

"Perhaps discuss that with God's spirit," replies Peter, trying to mount a defense for his seemingly indefensible actions. "In fact, I actually didn't do anything! I had just started speaking when God's spirit did it all!" Reminding everyone of Jesus's linking of water baptism with their own baptism by the spirit, Peter argues, "On what grounds was I to withhold the outer, confirming sign of inclusion when the essential, inner sign had already been

---

[119] See Acts 10:1-11:18 for the whole story.

demonstrated?"

That, at least temporarily, quells the opposing arguments—though as time will prove, it doesn't ultimately
convince. What's clear to at least Peter, however? The
trajectory of the grand story of God hasn't simply taken
them into uncharted territory through Jesus, it will
continue to do so. While he can only begin to grasp the
concept, it seems that God is creating through Jesus a
new Israel that will go far beyond Jewish identity. The
burgeoning new creation breaking in with the resurrection of Jesus is, as part of the process, creating a new
people of God.

13 New Creation

Having dodged a bullet, at least temporarily, over the whole Cornelius issue, Peter and the fledgling church have a bit of breathing room as they try to navigate the uncharted waters moving forward.

"And I thought the Sea of Galilee was rough."

Peter is a pragmatist. What fisherman isn't? Even the way he justifies the event at the centurion's house isn't so much a deeply theologically argument as it is one of necessity—God did it, so I'm not to blame.

At any rate, God has always bent the rules a bit to welcome outsiders in, so this, in one way, isn't all that unexpected. What exactly that will mean can be left for more theological minds and for another day. We're barely keeping up as it is.

"There is one man who is up to the task," Peter muses. "That zealot Pharisee with the dramatic conversion story that stayed with us for a couple of weeks. Unbelievable knowledge of the Scriptures. Knew how to connect the dots for sure between the whole God story and Jesus."

"A hot head, though. Too bad we had to ship him back home to Tarsus, but the last thing we needed was another Stephen incident. We sure could have used the scholarly background. In fact, we could sure use it now to get our heads around all these things that God is doing."

There is also another who remembers Saul, the former persecutor. There is a major difference between this man's interest and Peter's. Barnabas, a well-known figure in the Jerusalem church has been sent to bring some order and maturity to an incredible Jesus movement happening in Antioch.

Unlike Jerusalem, it's not a solely Jewish phenomena at all. People from all sorts of backgrounds are being impacted by this contagious virus called the gospel. In many ways, they're making up their rules as they go along. It's a wonderful mess, but a mess nonetheless.

As Barnabas reflects on how overwhelming the task is, he recalls that fireball with the Phinehas T-shirt[120]. Yes, he needed to figure out when *not* to say something but maybe having to exist in his hometown for almost a decade has tempered him. If so, and if he's still there, he's exactly what we need. I wonder if I can find him?

Saul is indeed still in Tarsus. He hasn't forgotten the force of his heavenly vision or his divine call, though the family business takes up most of his time. The family is certainly hoping he will come to his senses. With his crazy ideas there isn't much chance of arranging a good marriage. It's a lonely time.

---

[120] Phinehas is a priest during the Israelite exodus wanderings. He becomes representative of Jewish zeal for God's law and for ensuring that people obey it.

Saul is not wasting these years of disapproval. At least there aren't a lot of distractions from what is consuming him. How does he reconcile what Jesus showed him on the Damascus road with the deep insight and sense of history he gained from his years with Gamaliel?[121] In spite of ultimately disagreeing with his mentor regarding how actively to seize hold of God's kingdom promises, he still holds warm respect for his wisdom and grace.

Throughout these years, Saul rehearses how he is seeing that the story he learned as a Pharisee ultimately points to Jesus. And as he does, his understanding of the mission to which God has called him keeps getting bigger and bigger.

Before his vision he fully expected God to come and deliver his people from the rule of the pagans who oppressed them. Fully restored, they then could begin to bless the world from their rightful place. Now? Saul is understanding that Jesus, God's Messiah has already defeated the evil powers that prop up Israel's oppressors. The cross, though almost no one understood its significance as it unfolded, was actually a throne. Jesus is already ruling.

And what does that mean? It's the ultimate get out of jail free card! It means that everyone, unclean or not, is free to choose—to say yes to Jesus and to walk right into full membership as one of God's family. And that means that the Temple and the Torah have fulfilled their purpose. They aren't the meeting place of heaven and earth anymore. Jesus has taken that place.

"Whew! I better sit down for a minute," thinks Saul. "No

---

[121] Gamaliel is a first century CE leading figure in the Sanhedrin, a master of the Jewish oral law, and was Saul's mentor.

one has ever thought this through before. But if it's true, it changes everything. Of course, my people the Jews aren't going to like it. Pretty much seen as blasphemy. The Romans? I don't think that will go over much better. Those authorities don't go much for reports of new rulers."

"But if it wasn't virtually impossible, why would it be worth attempting?"

Of course, this doesn't come to Saul in a weekend. It takes years of thinking, revising, clarifying. But Saul's entire life training has prepared him for just this kind of thinking.

Breaking his concentration is a knock on the door. It takes a few seconds, and then, yes, he does remember the face, from many years before...in Jerusalem.

"Sorry for being abrupt." Barnabas jumps immediately to the reason for his journey. "Are you up for an adventure?"

14 Antioch

Antioch is the perfect laboratory to test what Saul believes is the formula for the new creation that Jesus has come to make possible. What Peter prophesies, just after Pentecost, is that the promise of Jesus is, first of all, to the present hearers and their children "but also to all who are far away—whomever, in fact, our Master God invites."[122] In ways Peter couldn't have understood, that was a prophecy for this place and time. Antioch is a burgeoning but dangerous city drawing immigrants and outsiders from everywhere. Rich and poor alike. The majority, lonely and afraid.

And the invitation is being broadcast loud and clear by thankful people who are being loved and included. Their lives are being transformed. Of course, they're inviting the next ones. Jews and Gentiles, slaves and free, men and women—a community is being formed that's crossing all the usual boundaries whether ethnic, gender-based, religious, cultural, or political in a way that's literally never been done before!

Saul has been studying the arc of the whole story of God and Israel and he's absolutely convinced that this is where it has to go. And this is exactly what they're seeing

---

[122] Acts 2:38, MSG.

here in Antioch.

And he is in the center of it.

Even though they seem to be in somewhat of a bubble —the authorities aren't clamping down yet—Saul knows that this can't continue unopposed. He's ready for whatever comes. He's pushed through hardship and opposition before. He'll do it again.

Soon he'll be ready to take this message on the road. He's itching to go to some of the power centers of the newly developing emperor cult in Asia. There's something about him that loves confrontation. Part godly zeal, part in-your-face personality.

First, he decides to ensure that the message he takes to the world is validated by his Jerusalem cousins. He and Barnabas bring money to alleviate the suffering caused by a present famine. It's an opportunity to meet with the "three pillars"—Peter, James, and John—and pitch his concept of a new creation and a new people of God. But Saul can't simply leave it there. He has to take Titus, an uncircumcised Gentile, as a test for his understanding of the gospel. He fully expects the church to see Titus as an equal member of the family, with the same status as themselves.

Saul wants to make clear that this whole idea of Gentile inclusion without any preconditions other than expressing faith in Jesus is not just some side issue. Something to work on when we have time. This is right at the center of everything Saul is building. As a result of the resurrection, God's new creation is bursting through. And it won't look like the old! The litmus test will be how you treat Titus. In or out?

The pillars support him. After all, Peter's encounter with

Cornelius is still fresh. But not everyone is happy. There are seeds of suspicion. After all, Saul isn't part of the original group. He doesn't fulfill all the criteria that was established after Jesus's death to determine apostolic credentials. And he doesn't show a lot of deference.

Saul, however, has received all that he wants and needs from the key three. So he heads for Cyprus and then Galatia, taking Barnabas and the latter's young relative, John Mark. It's time to try out the gospel, as Saul understands it, in virgin territory.

Saul knows this is going to be a challenge. His message of a crucified and risen Messiah is going to be a non-starter. For a Jewish audience, this will seem a blasphemous contradiction. No Messiah will present himself this way. For the Greeks? They'll simply think he's crazy. Which might be fine, except that the implications of this gospel, that God is creating a new people, a new family that defies all the existing walls of separation— that's socially disruptive in a big way. It's not just crazy; it's dangerous crazy.

It doesn't take long and the disruption Paul[123] antici- pates, he's experiencing. But something else is happening as well. He refers to it as the "power of the gospel."[124] When Paul announces the truth about Jesus and the invitation that he has brought, people respond and believe. Not everyone, certainly, but enough people from diverse backgrounds that something takes root that's not easily uprooted.

---

[123] Moving into a territory where Greek is spoken, a slight name change is advisable because of what Saul's name sounds like in that language. Similar to why most of those with the name Richard that are still around usually go by Rick rather than the option that was more common in my time.

[124] 1 Corinthians 1:20-25.

People change. They're energized. They find each other. And they tell their friends. Paul knows he is starting something that's just going to continue to spread.

There's a second obvious pattern that emerges. God backs the message with displays of power. Paul feels it when he preaches. He knows it's breaking down strongholds in people's minds. He has power over demonic spirits—to identify them and cast them out.

Even more, people are healed in dramatic ways when Paul prays for them. Opponents can raise their voices, and throw their stones, but no one can ignore what is happening.

Returning to Antioch, Paul and Barnabas are excited to tell the stories about how their experiment at home is multiplying into the Greek world. It doesn't take long, however, for Paul to learn that not all his excitement is being equally embraced. Soon Peter comes to visit, the exact reason not specified. But less positively, he is followed by some other teachers from the Jerusalem church (obviously with some accreditation). Has word of Paul's new message been getting some air time down south? And have they come to set things straight?

The visit doesn't go well. It leads to a confrontation, not just with the teachers, but even with Peter and Barnabas as well. Barnabas, always the natural peacemaker is looking for middle ground but Paul will have none of it.

The problem doesn't go away. Eventually a council is called of all the significant leaders of the growing movement. Its purpose is to finalize the question, "What does God require from Gentiles for full participation in the family of God?"

I'm sure Barnabas is praying in tongues all the way down

to Jerusalem. What is not needed is for Paul to be combative. But God is good and Paul is restrained, at least long enough for Peter to win enough hearts and minds with his story about Cornelius. James makes the final pronouncement.

It isn't everything they could have wanted—there are some details put in to reduce offense of Jewish members—but the key element holds. There will be no required circumcision of Gentile believers. Paul's vision of one people included into the community of the Messiah through commitment to Jesus alone has been validated. Paul takes this authorization and with renewed zeal and expectation heads to city after city in the Greco-Roman world.

The first stops are all short ones, often involving turmoil, followed by beatings, next with narrow escapes—seldom without injury. But the power is there. Seeds are planted and new communities form.

Corinth brings the first big break. Yes, there is opposition but also favour at a governmental level. Paul is able to spend a year and a half, working by day, preaching by night, and seeing real fruit from his labours. He's finding a winning formula. No eloquent speechwriting, simply the basic message about the victory of God on the cross and the new creation that is unfolding through Jesus. Backed up with power, healing, deliverance, and transformation.

By the time he reaches Ephesus, the main city in the province of Asia, he knows his message and he delivers it well. By now, he anticipates the opposition he will receive, and, most of all, he has tremendous confidence in his ability to tap into the limitless power of God. He truly is God's general, one that strikes fear in every evil presence.

Predictably, the Jews respond unevenly to his interpretation of the story of God and he's forced once again to
leave the synagogue. His solution? He rents a lecture hall
and holds regular meetings, preaching and demonstrating the message of the Kingdom with power.

Able to stay for two years in Ephesus, Paul for the first
time sees impact, not just at the level of persuading some
individuals, but now to the point of influencing the entire
city. Everybody knows Paul's name, even the demons. In
a city known for its magic, practitioners are abandoning
their arts, burning their books, and joining the faith
community.

Paul is seeing unprecedented power to heal the sick.
Literally, passing around a handkerchief Paul has
touched is enough to transfer healing power for the
benefit of those who touch it.[125] Even Jesus didn't
do that!

If there is such a thing as a principality over a city, most
likely its rule will be connected to money somehow. Not
surprisingly, once the whole economy surrounding the
Artemis cult starts getting impacted, deep levels of evil
are aroused. But Paul has been here before. Paul is
God's man and he knows the kingdom of God will
advance no matter what stands against it! He'll be faithful
to the story and God will be faithful to him.

---

[125] I suspect that it is theologically significant whether the
handkerchief was new or used but we will leave that for another day.

Part 3

Slip Slidin' Away[126]

---

[126] Song by Paul Simon, Greatest Hits album, 1977.

1 Peter At The Gate

He stumbles out onto the street in the Upper City in a daze. Can this really be happening? As it slowly dawns on him that this isn't simply a dream, that the angel is real, his senses focus in on the task at hand.

"I must get to Mary's house," he thinks to himself, mentally tracing out the routes that might offer the greatest probability of avoiding any late-night patrols. If he can just get there, being in the more affluent part of town will mean at least a moment of privacy, a chance to clear his head, and to strategize his escape.

Knowing his people, undoubtedly there will be a gathering of some sort there. Outside of some kind of miraculous intervention, the rising sun is supposed to bring his end, so certainly his friends will be crying out on his behalf. As he creeps along the dark streets, he begins sketching out his plan.

Inside the compound of the wealthy widow's home, somewhat removed from both the eyes and ears of those nearby, the faithful are fervently interceding—some kneeling, some prostrate, all with arms and hands stretched out. Beyond the prayers that will mark Passover, there is a crisis at hand that demands greater than usual intensity.

Rhoda is certainly aware of the secretive meeting

happening within. As one of the lower ranking servants, it's her responsibility to monitor the outer door, both to allow entrance to all authorized guests and to help protect the privacy of the clandestine meeting within. At least with this night being the end of Passover, a meeting of some sort will be less suspect—though everyone tacitly understands that it's Mary's status that helps her neighbours turn a blind eye to what often seems to take place in her home.

"It's him!" she cries as she bursts into the meeting. Her entrance is uncharacteristic and somewhat inappropriate. It's obvious that something has happened to this young girl that has left her completely unhinged.

"It's Peter! He's at the gate."

Despite the fact that this indeed is the hoped for outcome of all the intercessory activity, what seems most obvious to the gathering is something else. They wonder if their greatest fear has come upon them: that Peter's spirit after death—still somewhat present in its transition to its new realm—is visiting them to console and encourage them that all is not lost?

Rhoda, however, can't be dissuaded. She didn't hear the voice of a spirit. It was too familiar, too...real. It's then that Rhoda realizes she has done the unthinkable. In her excitement, she has actually left Peter outside the gate!

As she rushes back to the sound of continued knocking, others follow—far enough behind to feel safe but close enough to see the outcome. The prayer meeting is now definitely disrupted, as it's obvious that there is someone determined to enter on the other side of the door.

The elation that follows betrays the anxiety that was all too present just a moment before. The group has to be reminded to get back inside before they fully wake the neighbours and attract undesired attention.

Once again in the privacy of the inner room, Peter recounts the hard-to-believe, yet true, story of the angel and his own miraculous release. To the many Jesus followers packed into the room, it brings back memories of Peter's and John's first release from the jail of the chief priest. That victory had been followed by such a season of blessing and favour.

Yes, a lot has happened in the years between that early season and where they find themselves now. But it's obvious that once again God has "stretched out his hand."[127] What other wonders will God do now?

By now the calmest one in the room, Peter shows that he's been thinking about what should come next. "Tell James and the others what has happened," he says, quickly preparing to leave. He recognizes that the time has come for a transition in leadership, since he'll need to at least leave the city, if not the country.

The departure of Peter doesn't quell the sense of jubilation in the room. They continue to recount what happened after the first prison release. They had cried out for courage and boldness, and God responded with such an overwhelming outpouring.

Surely God is with them again now! Their prayers have been answered. Certainly what lies ahead is vindication. Can this be a sign that the royal appearing of their Messiah is near? Furrowed brows give way to the widest grins. Previous stories of God's faithfulness are shared, and everyone basks in the glow of them.

---

[127] Acts 4:31, NIV.

Almost everyone, that is. There is one small cluster within the group that tries to smile along with the others and to embrace the encouragement that is so obviously present. Yet at the same time their hearts still feel deadened and they have to consciously push down the questions that are trying to steal the joy of this moment.

The family of James.

2 Finish It

"It's my baby!"

I fall to the floor. It feels like something dies within me at that moment.

It's July 2002. In the early hours of the morning we receive a call from our daughter Jaana—our "miracle" baby, the one whose story has called me back into the journey of faith. She and her husband Jeremy are planting a new campus of our church in a marginalized community where much of my childhood has been spent and where I've worked as a teacher. It was our heart for that very community which inspired us to begin a church in the first place. Jaana hasn't, however, called to share some new church planting insight. She's in danger of losing the child in her womb.

Déja vu all over again.[128]

Her first thought is to come for prayer. After all, this is what our family does. It's why she's alive and breathing in this world.

---

[128] Classic quote by New York Yankee baseball catcher Yogi Berra.

After they arrive, and the necessary questions are asked, we begin to pray. Of course I remember the prayer I prayed twenty-four years prior; the memory is so vivid it feels like I'd prayed it five minutes before. Yet I feel within me a violent mix of panic and boldness. The despair from memories of our own past losses shows me I've never really dealt with them. At the same time, I want desperately to take control. I find myself grasping to find the prayer of command I'd previously wielded.

I stall, searching for that surge of confidence I had so many years before. Failing to find it, I settle for the same authoritative words that I used the first time—"Let the kingdom come now!" Just to be sure, I pray them again...and again. I desperately try to hold on to every grain of faith, but it's betraying me—slipping out of my hand and heart.

After hours of fighting for this little life, my daughter rushes into the bathroom along with my wife. A few minutes later, I hear her cry out.

I want to be angry...angry with God most of all, though I sense somehow that to do so would be treading on somewhat dangerous ground. Appealing to justice will perhaps not be my best defense.

So instead I lay on the floor numbed by hopelessness. Are there no guarantees? No rewards for outstanding service? I've been privileged to "see what prophets had longed to see" but now what I long for more than anything has been cruelly taken away. Or, at the least, God seems to be looking the other way.

"The Kingdom of God is within your reach." Well, it isn't within my reach when I most need it to be. And I don't have an answer.

In numbed silence, my son Jon and I build a small pine box. It's helpful to do something with our hands. It seems so surreal resting this little man in his miniature coffin, fully formed yet so tiny, never having had the opportunity to run and jump, to laugh and play and love. Surreal because he looks much the same as my son next to me did, thirty years before, in the intensive care nursery of the hospital. Yet there will be no miracle for this one.

Crowding into my mind are uninvited snapshots of the other boys I have buried, one in a shoebox, another in a crude wooden box, both perfect except for the one thing that makes all the difference—the breath of life.

I've buried those mental images along with the boxes deep underground. Everyone has pain. You deal with it and move on. Now pain seems to have gained the upper hand, and exhumed the memories. I can't escape.

By far the hardest thing is to watch my daughter's anguish. My heart has always been so closely connected to hers. When she has some significant struggles during her teens, I hardly feel able to breathe. I would do anything to protect her from pain but I often feel powerless. Wonderfully, apart from any effort on my part, I watch her break through the struggles and become this courageous, young warrior, eventually spending two years in the slums of the Philippines delivering babies, while at the same time being a full-time mom to another abandoned infant.

All Jaana has ever wanted to be is a mom. Would I have to watch her experience the same devastation of loss that I have witnessed Joy grapple with again and again? What about reward for time served? What about the words we have received from "the prophets" that our children will be "hermetically sealed," that "we will not have to worry about our children, God will guard them?" Is this God's idea of guarding?

Over lunch a few weeks after her tragic loss, Jaana opens her heart to me. "Dad, you know how people speak about great difficulties and go on to describe what it was that carried them through. 'God was there,' they say. Well, I just went through the hardest thing in my life. Here's the hardest part—God wasn't there."

I have no answer. I've spent years trying to build a foundation of trust in a God who is near, who is good. I feel that foundation cracking beneath my feet. I would not abandon my daughter the way God seems to be ignoring her now. Questions I have resolutely been pushing out of sight and out of mind come marching back.

In the past years, embracing the Kingdom message of a God "within our reach" who, through Jesus, has inaugurated the beginning of God's new creation, we've given our all to reach for tangible tastes of this reality. We've gained courage from every example of God's will in heaven seemingly being done here on earth—bodies healed, minds renewed, relationships restored, spiritual captives set free.

Of course, there are some other situations where we don't see what we longed for. A few close friends die; some spiritual strongholds seem beyond our abilities to overcome; we struggle to understand the mystery of some being healed while others are seemingly overlooked.

Yet we keep our eyes on the *wins*. Surely it's just a matter of time. If the early disciples took three years to successfully replicate Jesus's success, then we will need to be patient with our learning curve and keep celebrating every breakthrough along the way.

In this moment, those temporary "losses" can't be tucked away into mystery, seen as hopefully diminishing "statistics." They are little boys in boxes.

Our little boys.

We will go through this four more times. Several times I'll receive the news of a lost baby as I'm literally stepping into a healing conference to talk about how "God is closer than we think." One time we've just finished praying for an infertile couple on another continent—who conceive their first of multiple children within weeks of our prayer—only to receive a call saying that Jaana's baby has died unexpectedly in her womb.

Whether it is spiritual warfare or an ironic sense of humour on God's part doesn't seem to make much of a difference to me. It isn't supposed to work this way.

Questions and observations that have laid either dormant or repressed push to the surface.

"God, I'm not happy with your choices. You heal and restore people that, to my view, are not particularly helpful to your cause, and those who would seem to be indispensable, you appear to ignore."

"Is all this simply arbitrary? Or am I to accept an understanding of sovereignty that puts you outside the standards with which you judge me? It feels like your 'just trust me' is a pretty big ask."

By now I've seen "miracles", I've "tasted the powers of the coming age." But I feel that if I can't choose, if I have no control over the how and when, and most particularly who, I'm not sure I want to play.

If it's all arbitrary, then at least I want to keep my distance, protect myself from the pain of caring. Seeing God's Kingdom heal and transform some, builds hope and longing for all. The pain of disappointment without under-standing is too hard for my heart. I want distance. I want to lower my expectations.

The last thing I want to do is to finish writing my book recounting all the glorious things God has been doing with us. As I stumble into my office early the morning after Jaana's first miscarriage, I am greeted by my rough draft and various notes scattered around my desk. It's then that I commit to myself, "This book will never see the light of day."

I open my computer and at the top of the string of emails is one from an old friend that I haven't heard from in years. I'm surprised he knew how to reach me.

"Greetings Gary," it says. "I don't know what it is that you are writing, but God says, 'Finish it.'"

3 Scar Tissue

They say Rome wasn't built in a day. In truth, it didn't collapse in one either. One disappointing event doesn't catapult me from being confident and faith-filled into having a crisis of faith.

Anyone who's lived with chronic back issues—something I have wrestled with for a good part of my adult life—will explain the onset of another bout of disabling pain in a consistent way. "I bent down to pick up a piece of paper and immediately collapsed in agony on the floor." We all know the weight of a bit of paper doesn't overwhelm our physical capacity. It's simply the tipping point that pushes over the edge a problem that has been quietly developing for some time.

At the time of the tenth anniversary of our first church in 1995, I have no idea that cracks are already appearing in the foundations of my life of faith. Of course, I'm not bothering to do any inspections of that sort. I'm too consumed with our present accomplishments and our future possibilities. By this time we've multiplied into five connected groups—if there are other examples of multi-campus churches in North America, I'm not aware of them—and our reach is becoming not just national but global.

Our services are marked by power; healing is common-place. Our people are stepping out in bold and confident ways. Some are selling their houses and joining together to live in communities in the more marginalized segments of our town. Our volunteers are feeding many hundreds of people every month with dignity through a small restaurant combined with a shop where they can select their own groceries. They run a free clothing store as well where clients are served just like those in estab-lished fashion outlets. We have a clear vision and we are living it.

I am so pleased that we are in a position of strength and settled in for the long haul. Joy and I love the church and the incredible team of servant leaders that we co-work with. We've been welcomed (well, that's a long story but I think I'll leave it out) onto the USA board of our movement. Though that is a mixed bag for sure, it's a marker that we're growing in influence and, at least to some extent, are being included.

Of course, this doesn't mean that everything is perfect. As the church has gotten larger, Joy has increasingly struggled with the changes that has brought. She loves the church, but she can't any longer even know who all the people are. She wants to welcome every one of them into our home and care for them personally. The idea of becoming an executive is abhorrent to her, yet it seems inevitable.

She begins to have panic attacks in our services. I learn not to look to my right when I am speaking because Joy will be on her face in the front row. I can never decide if her posture is an expression of "Oh God, save that man!" or "Oh God, save me!"

Increasingly, we find ourselves in conflict over two seemingly competing pulls. The larger organizational demands of a mega church and a growing international movement are pulling me and us away from direct day to day involvement in what we call "Kingdom ministry." The growing need to strategize and direct the actions of the many who are directly involved in it leaves little time to participate in a meaningful way ourselves.

For Joy, it conjures up images of generals, sitting in comfortable surroundings, making decisions that may send countless numbers of foot soldiers to their death. She has no confidence, nor any interest, in that scenario. So, Joy ensures that we always have some of the most traumatized and marginalized ones closely connected to us, if not living with us. In some ways, I do love it, but I don't see how it is sustainable. We can't burn the candle at both ends. And yet I know that if we disengage from touching people's lives directly, I will lose Joy.

Part of my difficulty is that I am already trying to pursue a way of living that can't be done long term and perhaps shouldn't be done at all for any length of time. Pioneering movements are seldom positive models for living sustainably. Our founder, John Wimber—a great man who is undeniably a workaholic—has set an expectation for how we are going to follow. Of course, it's never said explicitly. It's simply modelled. There's a chance to change the world, but only if we *man up* and seize the opportunity.

So I, like many others, am not only trying to lead what is now a very large church, I am also overseeing the development of our movement in parts of Europe (later it will be Asia) as well as my own country. In addition, I am doing what the key leaders in our movement have been engaged in since the early days of our existence—renewal conferences to invigorate the larger church.

As a result, I am often on the road, for many years flying over one hundred thousand air miles annually. It is not uncommon to fly home from another continent on a Saturday—sometimes arriving early the next morning—in time to do three services on Sunday. Monday is work as usual with a sense of urgency as always. My next trip is always just around the corner.

As difficult, and quite frankly unwise, as this developing pattern becomes, there is an additional factor. Quite early in my travels in Asia, I contract a parasite that's damaging my red blood cells. It's not diagnosed for almost twenty years. I feel like I have the flu every day (when less than forty percent of your blood has oxygen you tend to feel that way). Running on two cylinders is do-able but a little bit of a challenge when going uphill, which I'm doing a lot.

My ethnic heritage being German,[129] I simply suck it up and push on. It fits well with the very early image I've tried to construct for myself—the noble warrior that can do what others simply can't do. Besides, it sounds very Pauline. I may not have had multiple lashings with the physical scars to show for them, but I'll have my own version of those scars. Like Paul I'll be able to say that I held my calling to be much more important than my own life.

---

[129] We Germans are known for wanting to dot our *I*'s and cross our *T*'s. Unfortunately, we are quite fond of doing the same with yours. It has resulted in a bit of tension over some centuries.

4 Honour—Who Needs It?

There's one more detail. Something that's going to be another fork in the road. Just like my choosing of teaching over the job in the Jesus People church, or the Vineyard over a return to teaching. For a few years prior to the tenth anniversary of our church, Joy and I are together wrestling with one more really big decision. John Wimber has approached me a number of times about becoming the first national leader of our movement in Canada. (The invitation is to me, not us. While this isn't our position on the matter—as we are firmly committed to team leadership—at this point, we aren't being asked.)

This is, of course, a great honour and I'm not ungrateful. However, up to now, I've been saying, "No." I read fairly extensively about history, culture and leadership— particularly in a Canadian context—and I'm not very confident about how this story will play out.

As often happens in these kinds of things, the American movement has spilled over into Canada and, up to now, all of the structure has been based on de-centralized American oversight. The number of churches has increased rapidly across the country through this arrangement. Because it doesn't require one set of Canadians to have oversight over another, it lends itself well to rapid expansion.

There's been little effort up to now to actively build relationship and trust between the Canadian churches and I know this is going to create big problems as we proceed. The proposed solution is simply to name a Canadian leader and assume that everything will be just fine.

I've studied Canadian history as part of my major in university. Given the long tradition of regional discontent and mistrust, I'm very aware that it will not be an easy task at all to forge a common vision and culture. Relationship isn't something you can squeeze in later—at least in Canada. If it isn't the major part of the foundation, you won't have much chance of having it be part of the building at all. We Canadians—always somewhat passive-aggressive—may not oppose some-thing we don't feel included in. We will, however, subtly undermine it with non-participation.

For all their great strengths, Americans don't tend to be quick to take advice.[130] Certainly not advice from a mere Canadian. So, it will be far easier for me to stay in a place of strength—my local church—rather than risking failure within a predetermined national framework that I'm not sure can, or should succeed going forward.

I say "should succeed" because the considerable reading that I am doing is causing me to suspect that culture is shifting away from larger, centralized groupings with established hierarchies. The denominational friends that I have are all trying to figure out how to decentralize

---

[130] To all my American friends, please note that I started the sentence with the words, "all their great strengths,"—something I truly mean. The part about taking advice, of course, is just my observation. I'm not a sociologist; I could be wrong.

their organizations. Will this adventure be the classic mistake of *going up the down staircase*?[131]

In addition, there is a significant movement being formed around one of our churches in the east, in Toronto. I know the pastors well; I introduced them to our movement. They're wonderful people whom I greatly respect. But I'm quite convinced they are working from radically different presuppositions, heading down a path that, over time, will radically depart from where we're pointed.

I can see a major problem down the road and I don't want to be caught up in it. I've already tasted politics in my late teens. For a time I'm the provincial leader of the youth branch of one of our two major national political parties. My experience there has cured me of ever wanting any political involvement again. I don't like what I see looming.

So, this is going to be another major life decision. I wish I could say I've learned a great deal about making these kinds of decisions. How do we really know we have God's wisdom in these things? We walk out all the steps we've learned to take: pray lots, ask wise friends, search our hearts for hidden motives, let the Bible fall open to a verse—if you are Joy—and then you decide…and pray that it turns out to be the right choice. It's usually in retrospect that we can confidently proclaim, "Then God said…."

Largely because we now feel our church is positioned to really support and sustain a national focus, we finally assent to the new role—functionally Joy and I will do it together. And, as best as we can discern together, we

---

[131] Title of a bestselling novel by Bel Kaufman, written in 1964 about a New York school teacher. It means going against the flow.

believe we have God's blessing on the decision.

On the one hand, I'm apprehensive. It's not the safe choice for me. I don't really like going beyond what I feel I can control. On the other? Of course, it's a great honour. Our place of influence has really been stepped forward. I'm stepping ahead in the story God has prepared for me and, as long as I don't blow it, there will be greater reward—on heaven and on earth. Though, to be sure, all of it for God's glory.

The "coronation" service is held in California. Packed house. Genuinely moving, and somewhat intimidating. Yes, there are significant obstacles ahead, especially in the arena of building relationship and trust. Nevertheless, I'm confident: as I always do, I'm calculating the odds and constructing my strategies. Even better, I believe God is for me.

Then, just a week or so after the festivities, John Wimber drops a bomb.

5 Faith Of Our Fathers

John phones me to say that he believes "God has spoken to him." Now, to be clear, he's not exactly got the same stature within our movement as the Pope does in his, but it's close. When he says, "God has spoken to me," the case is pretty much closed.

I remember asking Pastor Bob, back in the Jesus People church when I was invited into a full-time position, "Did God speak to you?" If the answer had been "Yes" I would have submitted—my respect for my spiritual father at that time was so great. Now, again to quote Yogi Berra, it's Déjà vu all over again.

But I'm still to hear what it is that John believes God has said.

"I believe that you are to resign your church, release the various *campuses* as separate churches and plant a new one as you take over leadership of the country. And do all of this in the next two months."

I'm stunned.

Eventually I stammer, "Can we come down and talk about this?"

In my mind, it's insanity. The only thing that gives me confidence to take on a pioneering role in our country (with no salary) is having the secure base of our local church. A financial base and a model for the rest of the country. Reliable staff I can depend on. Already I'm fully aware of how challenging this adventure is going to be. Now I feel like an adventurer being asked to head out into the wilderness without any provision, maps, or even warm clothing.

I'm speechless. I'm sure this will be the worst possible thing for our existing church campuses. How will they survive? Second, how do you plant a church in your spare time when you can't in good conscience recruit almost any of your existing leaders to join you? It will mean walking out with no severance, no salary, starting immediately.

I can't see any way in which this will be successful. And if it isn't? I fear it will shatter my hopes and dreams to find a story that will validate me and bring me into a place of true belonging.

We go to California. Three days later, one thing is clear. John is fully convinced that God has spoken.

I'll replay this time over and over in my brain for the next thirty years. Why do we say yes? Given my father issues, along with my and Joy's great respect for our leader, I guess there's no other choice we *can* make. I feel like a member of a jury voting to condemn myself. Is it faith? Probably more loyalty. But it's now our path.

In the summer, Joy and I gather representative leaders of our newly formed movement from across the country for a few days at a lake to build communication and trust. It goes well. Everyone is trying to be nice and give one another the benefit of the doubt. But I know we're not all on the same page. (Ironically, within five years almost no one in that room will still be part of our circle.)

Right after this, we begin in the fall to tell our story—casting a vision for the new church community we've agreed to at least attempt to plant. We begin informally, opening our home on Sunday evenings to feed anyone who comes—mostly college kids—and tell stories of the Kingdom, then putting them into practice with the prayer that follows. The students are young, they are broke—a major issue given our financial need—but it's the most life-giving experience we've had for years.

Yes, we'll most likely die in the morning[132] but what a great time we're having. The encouragement I experience locally begins to give me faith for the national. But just at the time when I'm beginning to feel that we may have half a chance to make all of this work, I'm called to an emergency meeting in the U.S.

The purpose of the meeting is to determine whether or not the Toronto Airport Vineyard can remain part of the larger Vineyard organization. Ironically, I had written to our leader the year before about what we would face with them sometime in the future. "They have a different narrative," I say, "and we'll inevitably find ourselves further and further apart. We need to dialogue now!"

The letter was ignored. I never even received a response. And now, as a board, we're deciding their future. I'm fully aware of how surprising this will be to my Toronto friends and I know how significant the impact will be within our movement in Canada. We'll most likely not survive it.

---

[132] *Princess Bride* once again.

I'm part of a team of four that flies to Toronto to deliver an ultimatum: the Airport Church will need to make a choice. As John Wimber puts it in our meeting with them, "We have pastoral concerns that we strongly feel must be addressed concerning how you are handling what is a genuine work of God's Spirit. The issue is this, we can't authorize what we don't have authority over. Therefore, you'll need to decide whether you want to submit to our authority in this or whether you want to choose to be under your own authority. The choice is yours."

Of course, the advance intel that the Airport staff have received is that the leaders have come to kick them out of the Vineyard. One of their staff asks that very question. "John," he says, "can't this be undone? Is the decision already made?"

At this point, John visibly softens and replies, "Of course it can be undone. All you need to do is trust our authority in this and submit to our counsel."

While this is going on, since I too have my own "contacts," I know that they've already decided to leave. What I don't know is that their press release is ready for launch—even though we agree we'll make a joint statement. It goes out in the morning.

When I meet with the Toronto staff the next day, they're shaken by everything that's happened, just as I am. I ask them, however, a simple question.

"Right now, you and the larger movement seem to be like two railway tracks running parallel into the distance, so that people can easily jump back and forth. Ten years from now, do you see the tracks the same distance apart?"

"Not at all," they reply, "They'll be miles apart. We just

thought that you'd join us."[133]

Shortly after, Wimber, expresses his regret that he hadn't listened to me a year ago. But then, in a very matter-of-fact manner, he simply says, "Now it's your responsibility to deal with it."

Flying home, I can't help but think that I've signed my death warrant. I'm fully aware that this *divorce* is going to have a seismic impact on our fledgling movement. I wonder, "Will it be fatal?"

---

[133] I've previously mentioned *Mistakes Were Made But Not By Me* by Tavros and Aronson. Given their observations of our tendencies to self-justify, it's important that I make clear that I am writing, as best I can, my recollections of these events. I realize others can have different perspectives. I'm cautious, however, about being too zealous about defending my point of view—when all my stories have me coming out looking really good, I need to question my own self-awareness.

6 Church Growth?

Over the next two years or so, we'll "lose"[134] over a quarter of our churches and a much higher percentage of our financial contributions. The greatest impact, though, is the emotional and spiritual turmoil that seemingly dominates every gathering and conversation. The only "wisdom" that I feel might be from God is to simply take two years and listen. No decisions. Don't fix it. Trust me.

Interestingly, prior to the break-up, I've been known as a "renewal person." I'm seen as prophetic—a "power ministry" guy. I'm travelling to a lot of different parts of the world. I'm starting to travel with John Wimber a lot and with some of the key prophetic figures. But after the Airport Church's departure, I've suddenly been cast into a new identity. I'm being identified as the Holy Spirit quencher in Canada. How I got there I'm not sure. I must have taken a left turn when I should have gone right. I still feel like the same person that I was before, but somehow I'm now the enemy of all things renewal.

Thank God Facebook is still a gleam in Zuckerberg's eye

---

[134] How do you ever "lose" a church when it is never "yours"? What I mean to say is that the communities either cease to exist or leave our organization.

or I would have a thousand trolls threatening my children. I age twenty years over the next five.

I'm wondering where the stained-glass movie went. Probably just a dream. No matter what God's Spirit intends to do, it doesn't seem to be enough to override our polarized perspectives. I know Jesus's prayer in John 17 for us was unity, but I can't see how we'll ever really be one. Maybe the vision that I saw can only be experienced through CGI, not in real life.

Our Canadian group of churches does everything possible to keep reaching for the dream. Two years after the infamous "split", we stand on a common stage with the leaders of the Airport Fellowship and publicly affirm that we're not enemies, that we both want God's favour for the other, and that we'll assume the best of each other. It's a start and a healing step for the body of Christ in Canada.

Is it enough? Barely. Mistrust is still high. I don't know how to bridge the gap that exists between the Toronto church and our own movement of churches. Our differences are significant enough that I don't believe we can ever practically build things together. Yet does that have to mean that those with whom we disagree become our competitors? Is our desire for united relationships and our conscious searching for truth in actuality a zero-sum game?

I didn't sign up for this.

At this point I feel like a prizefighter that has taken a wicked blow to the gut. I'm still upright but there's no air in my lungs. When I survey the damage to our family of churches across the country after the first two years, I come to one conclusion: we will not survive.

We're like a national retail chain with almost all our stores scattered in smaller towns, and with no significant hubs. Our territory is simply too big, and we don't have the needed budget, nor enough mature leaders to build the needed structures that such a huge geography demands. If we were truly a business, we'd shut down one quarter of our remaining franchises immediately.

But we're not a business. Our small churches are led by dedicated men and women who love the people in their care. They are godly and kind—most of them—but the exceptions prove the rule. It's just that their churches may never grow significantly—which means our organization will not likely achieve success.

I'm deeply conflicted. "Big" pays the bills. Like attracts like. If we're going to succeed, we'll need churches like the one in Langley that Wimber shut down—churches that can make our organization thrive and multiply. And who will build and lead those churches? I don't have confidence that we'll find or produce them from the people we presently have. We'll need a new model and will have to attract new people.

But as I reflect on this dynamic, I see a contradiction within me—between my professed values and those my actions reveal to be what I *really* believe. I claim to value each particular pastor and hold dear the way they love and serve their people. And honestly, I do! I wasn't chosen, however, as the first National Director in our movement to just raise up a loving community of pastoral leaders who care for their people.

The assumption, of course, is that they will do that but it's also assumed that their churches will increase in size and multiply by planting new ones. In most church movements, the metrics we choose value visible success—success being defined almost always in quantitative terms.

Over the next number of years, I try every trick in my book—and lots of them completely outside it—to find a way to train and develop our leaders. Yes, they grow. And yes, we develop a wonderful community of love and support. Our churches love the poor and are centers of kindness and care. These are things to be extremely proud of.

They're just not "successful".[135]

---

[135] I hope it's understood that I'm using a very narrow definition here for the term "successful." Throughout this section I'm in no way implying that churches or leaders "failed" in some way. The wrestlings in my mind are all surrounding my personal feelings of being a failure and not in any way a judgement on others.

7 Barometer Rising

I find myself in a confused state. I love who we are. There is nothing wrong with the people we have. The only problem is that I feel I'm being seen as a failure. I want to justify myself, convince people that I have read all the literature, that I possess the skills necessary. I would love to present metrics that will show all the wonderful things that are true of us as an organization.

But these aren't the metrics my critics are interested in. How many churches? How many dollars? A good leader surmounts the obstacles facing them and makes things work. I saw the danger when I signed on. I knew what could happen. And now I'm stuck.

For a few years, I don't sleep more than a few hours a night. I have severe back pain from the years of travel and my parasitic problem is in full bloom. I'm constantly fatigued and losing weight. Most of all, I'm deeply depressed.

There is one saving grace: the church our team has planted is bringing unbelievable joy. It's filled with young people in their twenties and they make up the majority of our leaders. Many of them live in community together; they're tangibly walking out the words and works of

Jesus throughout our community and their social networks. People are coming to faith, being healed, and set free in remarkable ways.

They're wonderfully diverse. We have young professsionals, former grow-op owners, recovering addicts, and university students all in one room. You wouldn't automatically see them as a homogenous social group. But they love each other...deeply. I feel deeply humbled to be at all a part of it.

Night after night, I find myself awake, rehearsing in my mind how I can quit the national network and embrace the refuge of my local church. But I can't bring myself to do it. I'm fiercely loyal and I made a commitment to John Wimber to do this. I must see it through.

I realize though that my loyalty is primarily to John. To be sure, I've made some wonderful friends within our church movement, so there is a sense of family. But it's clear to me that I don't at all share the same loyalty to the organization and its success that most of the other national directors seem to embody. I hate the politics, the feelings of competition that rise up in me. This is not a game I can safely play—it's like inviting an alcoholic to sniff wine corks. Maybe some can and still serve Jesus, but I'm not mature enough to do so.[136]

Ironically, I feel no pressure to be successful in our

---

[136] There is no implied criticism of people's motives in these remarks. I know in almost every case, people just try to serve Jesus and do their best. We do what we do for the best of reasons (at least at the level of our conscious minds), and it is not for me to judge the motives of others. All I know is when you fill a room with mostly men much like me and tell them to make decisions? It gets political. It always has and probably always will. The challenge every organization must face as it grows out of the highly relational "movement" phase is how to overcome this tendency.

young, local community. Their age demographic is not nearly as consumed with concepts of success as mine is. And yet, ironically, successful we are becoming. We're growing rapidly, and expanding our reach—maybe the key is that we don't feel like we have to. We still have a sense of privilege that has not yet been crushed down by pervasive obligation. We feel like the church is serving us instead of us serving the church.

I'm looking for an honourable discharge from my national role, so I'm scouring our leaders looking for the potential successor. I have my eye on one couple in particular who Joy and I have tremendous respect for. A blend of passion, wisdom and tenacity.

But are they yet convinced that they need to do this?

It's at this point that I begin to have a strong sense that there will be grace for Joy and me to hold it all together until the end of the year. At that time, at least that is what I feel quite strongly, we will need to decide: loyalty to our commitment or love for our local community. We are burning out and will need to choose.

At the conclusion of this timeframe, two things take place. First, the couple we have such high hopes for announce to us that they are moving out of the country. I'm devastated, though I say nothing. In my mind there is no one else. To step out now would be to dishonour, at least in my mind, my commitment to John. Second, a totally surprising event upends my life and Joy's.

One afternoon, Joy drops something off at my elderly father's house. He's excited about his new purchase: a machine to more regularly monitor his blood pressure. When Joy walks in, he suggests, "Why don't you take your blood pressure?"

Joy runs regularly, eats very carefully, fasts once a week—in general she is extremely healthy. So why bother? To humour my Dad, she puts on the cuff.

230/130.

8 Serving Another's Vision

When my sister who is a nurse hears of this, she wants to take Joy into the emergency ward immediately as there is an immanent possibility of her having a major stroke or aneurism. We're shocked. Joy is bulletproof— at least that's what we all have thought.

Joy seems to be the calmest of us all; me the least at peace. I want to get it fixed...now. She wants to understand what God is saying to us through it.

Of course we pray and continue to pray. We seek out treatment—both traditional medical interventions and every natural strategy that seems realistic. After several years we haven't found a solution. Her condition is idiopathic and is not lifestyle related. And apparently not easily treated.

Joy does try medication, which to her ranks right up there with "kill me now." The side effects are intolerable for her and she can't imagine living this way. I am thinking, "Suck it up. I've been in constant pain for years. You get used to discomfort."

But Joy feels like it's dulling her senses, especially her spiritual sensitivity, and makes it impossible for her to feel fully present. So, she asks me to support her as she goes off medication and does everything she can naturally (diet, daily rhythms, exercise, meditation, etc.) to deal with the roots of what is causing this. She is content to leave herself in the hands of God. This becomes a central issue of faith for Joy.

It brings me great anxiety. Quite honestly, my fear is more for me than for her. She's wanted to be with Jesus her whole life. It's all I can do to keep her here most days.

"What if she dies?" I can't help thinking. "Even worse, what if she has a massive stroke and lives? It will change my entire life."

But what else can I do? I've figured out that I have one main job as a husband. It's to lay down my life—my agenda, my desires, my career, all of it—for Joy. I need to be dedicated to ensuring that she thrives first and most, and then I can think about myself. If I can't support her in this, even though I disagree with her choice, then what am I doing married?

One thing I know for sure, we have to lighten the load and reduce our stress and anxiety. The writing is on the wall, and if we need to make a decision right now, we'll need to stay with the country. There is no one prepared to step into our shoes.

It breaks my heart but we will need to step out of the local community we love so much. It's not easy to step away from leadership and still be around. I begin looking for other options, places to live that would best suit Joy's approach to life—especially with regard to pace. She's willingly joined me for so long but my world has always operated at a speed that makes her dizzy. She's laid her life down for me in so many ways and it has cost her dearly. Perhaps this is the time for me to lay down my life and live it her way.

9 Dominion Hill

It's a long story, but we eventually move across the entire country to the east coast. We purchase a historic property called Dominion Hill—a vacation estate once owned by one of the richest families in America. It's just outside of a gorgeous Victorian town on the ocean called St. Andrews-by-the-Sea.

We have a plan that is risky but exciting. A dear friend— one whom we really believe in—wants to train worship leaders from around the world. He's become associated with a small, unique university that will endorse what he is attempting to do with masters level certification. He just needs a place to host it.

What we set out to do is to create a center, like an adjunct campus of the university, that will serve as home for this masters program. I'll help create a similar program for the university in the area of leadership, operating out of this same center.

We'll augment this core emphasis by hosting round tables—bringing people from around the world to live and learn together for a short time in magnificent surroundings.

What could possibly go wrong? This should fix everything.

Over the next ten years, our friend comes to the conclusion that he needs to let go of the dream he is pursuing and he reluctantly moves back to the states. The economy of our province completely collapses. The university struggles with enrollment and barely survives.

Even still, it's hard to feel sorry for ourselves. We live on an amazing piece of land bordering the ocean. It's got historic charm and natural beauty in spades. But there's one problem with living in Disneyland. You have to maintain Disneyland. And that takes time and money. We've moved east to escape the treadmill we have been on and have jumped from a frying pan to a fire.

Meanwhile I'm continuing to be faithful within the church organization that Joy and I are leading. By now I have informed everyone that our present five-year term will be our last. A transition process needs to begin. I feel like the special grace that I've had to do this job is diminishing, and even though I theoretically was established as the founder with a lifetime appointment, integrity demands that I lead only as long as I clearly have the passion and authority for it.

At best we are treading water. For every step forward there seems to be at least one step back. The image that I try to hold of myself as a "golden boy"—everything I touch turns to gold—is looking and feeling more like the opposite. I always used to arrive at just the right place at the right time...and know just the right things to do. Now it seems like I'm always arriving a bit too late but just in time to see everything turn to dust.

What's eating away at me most is not any of the so-called

failures themselves, but the fact failure is still, after all these years, such a big issue for me. I'm supposed to be beyond that.

In the transition, less consumed now with the "how" questions, I start to dig deep into the underlying questions of life and leadership that I have thought I already answered sufficiently.

What is this all about? Has God, who I've thought was on my side, turned against me? Or have I completely misunderstood the nature of God's invitation to me in the first place?

Is it all about getting things done for God? It seems when we fall into that, people always end up being used...and hurt. Are we the means to God's end? Or are we the end?

These questions and my sense of failure are combining to torment me. I'm sleeping little and fighting depression.

Joy isn't very helpful for me during these bouts of self-doubt. She doesn't expend a lot of energy trying to convince me that I have really succeeded. She simply looks at me with that "I thought you were a Christian" look and asks, "Why does it matter? Whoever said you had to be successful?"

She is asking very different questions than I am during this season. Occasionally she will bring some of them to me.

"What would happen if we gave ninety percent of our money away and lived on ten percent?" Or, when I would whine about how we were going to keep Dominion Hill afloat, she would simply say, "That's no problem. Let's just give it away." It isn't always easy living with Mother Teresa.

During this season, because the Chairman of our board is John Wright, also the President of Leadership Development for Eagle's Flight—an international training and consulting company that specializes in experiential learning—we use a lot of their training "games/simulations" with our pastors and leaders.

The activities they create have an uncanny ability to pinpoint exactly what is needed for effective growth to take place and they do so by creating an environment where participants are caught off guard—in a game setting which leads the players to do what they really do in their real life, as opposed to what they think they should be doing in order to "pass" the training.

They have one lengthy game called *Promises, Promises.* Participants represent the governments of various fictitious nations, all of which have strengths and vulnerabilities...and past history with each other. The task of the game is to both accomplish fulfilling the promises each have made to the citizens of their countries while also becoming truly united together.

The result is consistently dramatic. I watch John do this with a large room of national non-profit CEO's. When the leader of a large non-profit dedicated to caring for the world's poor starts a world war over food, you know the game is working.

The only person ever to be forced to leave the game because they would not obey the rules is—yes, you guessed it—Joy. Joy can see where the game is going and that what we are doing is going to end in a result that is not what we ultimately want.

But here is her dilemma. She knows the problem, she can sense it, but she doesn't know the solution. Nor can she communicate what she sees well enough to convince even her own teammates that what they are doing is a mistake. So she refuses to participate and go along with the actions the entire group are quite happy to take.

This is the story of her life. Her heart is more attuned to heavenly melodies than her mind conditioned by the common sense of our natural world. As a result, people often just don't "get" Joy. Her remedies often come across as completely illogical and unworkable.

Joy is not unaware of people's responses to her and it creates great tension within her. She feels isolated, like she is marching to the beat of a very different drum. So, she tries to enlist me. I am the one who can convince others. I can figure out how to construct a path to what seems to be unknown and unknowable.

Sadly, most of what she wants me to do is way too big of a risk. I can't make sense of most of it myself. Rather than listen to her heart, and try to understand what she is seeing, I take the role of a critic, tearing down her often impractical applications. I am too consumed with my own pain to see hers. She'll have to sink or swim on her own.

On most days, Joy feels a deep tension. The intensity of her deep inner longing for a world that's put right—in harmony now with the way it will one day be—so breaks her heart that it causes her blood to boil, both spiritually and physically. Eventually it will boil over.

10 A Student Of History

The issues surrounding my downward slide only become clearer to me later, much later. At the time, all I know is that I'm caught in the vortex of decisions I've made against myself. They seem noble at the time and I'm confident I will—*God will help me?*—overcome the challenges they present and still achieve success. My story will be even greater because of them.

I've been an idealist, choosing faithfulness and loyalty over success. But while I may have won the battle in my will, I haven't won it in the arena of my emotions. I deeply want to win, and to be seen as winning. On any good day I would, of course, forcefully deny it. It's only when I feel like I'm losing that I can't avoid recognizing my true reality.

And now, my confidence that I'm in control of my story—that I can bank on God's favour—is all slipping away through my fingers. I feel powerless to stop it.

I realize, though, that there's something much more disheartening eating away at me. I've always believed that I will be able to fulfill the dream that I've seen of the mosaic. Above all else, I feel like that is a central part of my *calling*—bringing disparate, alienated parts together.

Helping people to love and trust each other and find a common vision.

The Toronto separation kicks that confidence pretty hard, but then, it's not that they're ever very close to me. We haven't really journeyed together. But something else happens, at the outset of my move east, from which I never fully recover.

One of the former campuses that have emerged from our church in Langley has been inviting me in to help and serve them. We have a lot of history together, and one leader in particular feels like a son to me, since he has been with me since a teenager. The church has been growing rapidly, and I'm glad to be a part.

They choose a new leader and ask me to mentor him. Yet quickly I begin to see this relationship is not going to function smoothly as the leader has little interest in the arrangement. It doesn't take long before both this leader's vision and style brings significant division. A nasty split is immanent. Thankfully, they call me in just in time and I give my whole heart to trying to bring the two sides together—to hear each other and find a way forward.

It's obvious that they can't remain a single group. I call them to a generous releasing and blessing of one an-other and we construct a plan to walk that out. The plan doesn't hold. Necessity trumps trust (as it usually does).[137] The division is caustic and hurtful. I see in advance how damaging this will be if not handled with grace and generosity, and yet the group who feels compelled to break away is unwilling to trust me enough

---

[137] No political comment intended.

to avoid it.

My dream dies. At least it's on life support. Looking at church history, I wonder why it is that we seem hell-bent on destroying each other, each of us wanting our pound of flesh—assuming the worst of each other. I can't say that's the motivation directing either party in this dispute, but it seems so difficult to value our relationship as much as we feel the need to defend "our" truth.

I love the theory of the body of Christ; it's the practice I can't live through. Maybe it is a zero-sum game.

11 Lifers

My big mistake has been daring to hope. Letting my gaze wander, letting the horizon catch the eyes of my heart. Joy is the problem—both of them, the one on earth and the one in heaven. My Joy is always pulling me toward her counterpart, but maybe it's time to reduce expectations and recognize how things really work down here.

I've been such an idealist. Naturally supernatural. I taught it around the world. I even wrote the book on it. And now I've lost the story.

The problem is that I don't have anything to fall back on. I've been ruined for my old ways of navigating life. This chosen path doesn't seem to be leading to my desired outcomes but it's the only one I want.

I wish my wife Joy was normal. That she wouldn't lie on the floor wailing for people in need. That she simply wouldn't care so much, long so deeply. The more you care, the more you'll be hurt. Sometimes the way she is irritates me to death. "Who is this woman you gave me?"

I want to be left alone.[138]

And yet, I love her. She's won my heart. How can you love and want to avoid someone at the same time? What's wrong with me? I think I know—my heart has been opened up and laid bare and I don't like what I see. And my drug of choice, distracting myself by getting something done, is being taken away from me. Joy won't let me settle for that diversion from my true self.

I think of Jesus when he says to his disciples at a time when many are having second thoughts and turning away from following him, "Do you want to leave too?"

Everyone in the room knows the answer is, "Yes."

Finally, Peter captures the essence of their dilemma. "Here's the problem. I, like the others, would love to go, but if I do, the hook that you've put in my heart might simply tear it out. I don't see the way forward, but there's no going back. I think we're lifers."

---

[138] C.S. Lewis makes the point that it is impossible to love without becoming vulnerable. And if we don't want the risk of our hearts being wounded and/or broken, then we simply must avoid loving at all. "Wrap it carefully round with hobbies and little luxuries; avoid all entanglements; lock it up safe in the casket or coffin of your selfishness," Lewis warns. "But in that casket—safe, dark, motionless, airless—it will change. It will not be broken; it will become unbreakable, impenetrable, irredeemable." C. S. Lewis. *The Four Loves.* (New York: Harcourt, Brace, Jovanovich, 1960), 169-170.

12 The Prototypical Paul

I often wonder what the man in the Bible we know as Paul is like as a person, a co-worker, a friend. I assume that he would wrestle just like we do with the scars and disappointments that are part of his growing up years.

Is he the shortest in his class? Does he have many friends? How does he compensate for his insecurities?

Is his Dad much of a help? Can he even talk to his Dad about his dreams, about his feelings, about anything?

Is he ever rejected by a girl?

I wonder that, because I know that people who are not only willing to lead but actually eager to do so, are often not the most well-adjusted individuals. Usually there is something that drives them toward risk and adventure, that makes them want to stand out from others. They've usually got something to prove. In contrast, the rest of us are comfortable staying home.

I'm not saying this to denigrate leaders, and certainly not to trash-talk Paul. I have great respect for people willing to be the first carving a trail through the jungle. It's easy to be second, preparing to write a best seller describing what the leader should have done. We know what is said about hindsight. The leader doesn't have the luxury of waiting for that perspective.

Leading always involves great risk because people tend to follow someone who goes first. After all, we want to go somewhere, and if we aren't willing to be at the head of the line, then we are quite motivated to get close in behind someone we think will be a hugely successful adventurer. That way we can have lots of influence without a massive amount of risk—not to mention great press interviews: "Yes, she and I are very close. Collaborate on almost everything...."

The reason I say that going first is such a great risk is that people who follow us will be greatly impacted—for good and for ill. This would be wonderful if we all were fully mature, wise, and kind. However, we aren't. Especially leaders often are not. Even Christian ones.

Encountering Jesus can radically impact us and change us at deep levels. Yet, amazingly, other parts of us can remain relatively untouched throughout our lives. The scariest thing is that we are often blind to these realities within us. We can even use the fact that God blesses every step of faith that any of us will take in life as endorsement, justification for remaining just the way we are.

Leaders are hard to discourage or dissuade. Often, when they have a vision of something and begin to invest in it, it's very difficult to convince them that it may be misguided, or even worse, pure folly. This, of course, is their greatest strength, and our salvation. Thank God for those who refuse to give up—some of our greatest inventions, scientific breakthroughs, and medical discoveries are the fruit of that perseverance.

This quality of tenacity is, at the same time, the Achilles heel of leaders. The same stubbornness that keeps them from giving up also keeps them from receiving helpful counsel and from understanding when and how their actions are harming others. All they can see is their dream; everything else is peripheral.

The young man Saul is being groomed as a leader. He is exposed to the zealous prophets, the heroes of the Hebrew Scriptures since early childhood. Saul dreams of the promises from God to Israel being at last fulfilled and is fully prepared to be the catalyst that helps bring that about. Saul isn't afraid of opposition or conflict. It's the way change comes about. He's willing to pay that price.

When Saul has his life altering experience on the Damascus road, it doesn't mute this zeal, it just re-directs it. Once he knows who Jesus is, with his already considerable knowledge of Scripture, he begins putting all the pieces of the puzzle together.

Yes, it takes some years for Saul to confidently understand what God has begun in and through Jesus— a literal launching of a new creation, a new people of God. Once Saul sees it, once it has crystallized in his mind and heart, he's ready to sacrifice anything to make that known and believed.

Saul understands completely how radical this new *gospel* is. He doesn't expect it to be received easily... either in the Jewish community or in the Roman. His— God's?—ideas are revolutionary, in a world where revolution usually equates to martyrdom.

He's not surprised at all with the persecution he faces from all sides. He's so focused on what he sees as the end goal—the marriage of heaven and earth through

Jesus—that beatings, starvation, shipwrecks, and all are simply "light and momentary troubles"[139] that he will resolutely push through.

By the time of his mission forays into the Greek speaking world, Paul has undying confidence in "the power of the gospel"—that when people hear the story of Jesus, God's Spirit will turn their hearts to belief. Not everyone, of course, but enough for a harvest of faith and faithfulness to grow up and reproduce in the lives of still others.

Paul not only has profound confidence in God's ability to produce a response of faith in human hearts, he also has great faith in God's Spirit growing and maturing that belief and growing it into vibrant faith communities. Perhaps that's why he seldom stays very long in the same place.

It's hard for us to imagine that approach being the wisest one—and of course if Eugene Peterson were alive in Paul's day, he certainly would have had something to say about Paul's methodology[140]—but Paul did it that way because of his extreme zeal for reaching the ends of the earth, and his confidence in God picking up the pieces in his wake.

This reconciling action of God—drawing all these diverse "parts" into one, united body, headed by Jesus—is absolutely central to everything Paul is doing. Jew and Gentile together. Slave and free, men and women. It's a new order. A stained glass movie. And Paul has no doubt that God will do it. He just needs to get the message out.

---

[139] 2 Corinthians 4:17. NIV.
[140] See Eugene Peterson, *A Long Obedience in the Same Direction: Discipleship in an Instant Society.* (IVP Press, Downer's Grove, IL., 1980).

God will validate it with his power. No spiritual power will be able to stand against it.

The fact that unbelievers bitterly oppose this dream doesn't phase Paul. What pierces him deeply are the arrows of those within the family of God—both Jews and Gentiles. It is hard for Paul to understand why others can't see what he sees—particularly when he's able to articulate so clearly and powerfully from the Scriptures the direction in which the story must go.

Surprisingly, genuine faith in Jesus doesn't easily overcome all of the previous prejudices and traditions that people carry into it. Even the apostles seem to respond too slowly, at least for Paul, to what is critically clear for him. It frustrates him that teachers from James are undermining his message, even though James supposedly has endorsed it earlier. Has he not understood what Paul has been patiently trying to explain to him?

Peter is even more frustrating, considering what he should have learned through the Cornelius incident. Given his place of influence, the damage he does in Antioch when he separates himself from fellowship with Gentile believers just because other Jews arrive from Jerusalem, not only angers Paul but breaks trust to a significant degree as well.

But the worst of it is to see Barnabus join Peter in this act of hypocrisy. Barnabus! Given all they have built together and all the trials they have endured as a team, this feels like an act of betrayal. Will he ever be able to trust him again?

What past experiences in Paul's life are playing into these interactions? Does he have relational issues that are making teamwork challenging? Are they—he, Barnabus, Peter, James—honestly able to talk this through and come to a place of rebuilt trust and understanding? Probably not.

For myself, I'm not sure how everyone who works with Paul really feels about him. There was a reason they shipped him off to Tarsus in the first place. I wonder what kind of turnover there is in the people who follow him around to learn from him. I'm sure he genuinely loves those that he has seen come to faith, and pay a big price for their belief. He cares for them like a father. But I wonder if he is able to relate as well with his peers? Is that more difficult?

Consistently, one of the top three reasons missionaries leave what they believe to be their calling is the simple fact that they can't get along with their co-workers. It's hard to argue convincingly that Paul has no issues in this regard after his later blowup and consequent separation from Barnabus. Yes, he finds a new partner in Silas and it seems to go well. Yet these issues don't go away.

I'm not trying to paint a picture of Paul as a relational shipwreck. Perhaps we are just seeing what happens in real life among humans—even after we have been reclaimed by Jesus.

Corinth, a place dear to his heart, where because of his extended stay he has built deep, caring relationships, is unsettled after he leaves and some of the conflict involves him. He writes a letter and it isn't received very well. He tries a quick trip and it goes even worse. He is their spiritual father but they are rejecting his authority.

These most likely candidates to be a poster for his dream of the new people of God are resisting being part of that vision. Don't they remember the powerful presence of God that authenticated the message Paul preached to them? Any struggles in the other churches Paul can put down to insufficient time and contact. But not Corinth. Paul has invested everything into them. If it hasn't connected, it's not through lack of trying.

Whatever difficulties Paul may or may not have relationally, they are easily pushed to the side by virtue of how clearly God seems to be endorsing him. Just like Jesus, his preaching of the message is invariably accompanied by power. Isn't that the best way to get through any skid? Step on the gas and steer into it. He's not trying to be teflon man, but he has supreme confidence that God will enable him to keep the mission going and not bog down around personalities or conflicts.

Then at Ephesus, it seems that Paul hits a wall, and his hopes and dreams shatter upon impact—ironically, at the place where the power of God working through him seems to be the strongest. Where it appears that principalities are crumbling in the face of his teaching and demonstrations.

To be fair, we have no direct record of what transpires. The author of Acts does reference the huge uproar that is created when the economic engine surrounding the Artemis cult is threatened. And it's clear that the backlash is not simply economic in nature but spiritual also.[141]

Acts goes on to note Paul's reaction—as we would expect, he is ready to march into the stadium and address the mob, fully confident that God's power will prove victorious. Certainly, the by-now-familiar pattern

---

[141] Acts 19:23-41.

will hold. There will be opposition, maybe a beating, perhaps a forced exit from the city but once again Paul and the gospel will emerge intact, ready for the next stage of adventure.

This time, at least, Paul is dissuaded by cooler heads. He is not simply going to power through this obstacle. Something different is taking place.

And then, Acts falls silent, leaving many to assume that Paul simply moves on. What is more probable is that Paul is imprisoned in Ephesus. Not for a day, or a week. He is likely being put on trial with his very life at stake. A collusion of forces—the Jews angry with what they see as an unholy communion with paganism and the Greeks assessing Paul as a cultural and economic threat—will prevent him from just moving on to a new center to simply repeat the process all over again.

In prison, sensing that this time things are different, the inner disappointments and doubts that, up until now, Paul has been able to keep at bay, begin to close in on him. With time to think, without the distraction of daily lectures and countless arguments and conversations, the biting rejection of his Corinthian children gnaws away at Paul's emotions. Their mocking suggestion that if he were ever to return, he should bring a letter of recommendation from someone they trusted, stings deeply. It's almost impossible not to keep replaying that last visit over and over in his mind.

Though the author of Acts (deliberately or not, it is hard to say) omits any reference to this time—it's after all out of sync with the narrative that he is trying to cast—we do have a window into this time from Paul's own later letter to the Corinthians. He writes, looking back on his experience, "The load we had to carry was far too heavy for us; it got to the point where we gave up on life itself. Yes: deep inside ourselves we received the death sentence."[142]

The timing of this last letter to Corinth is likely while he's on the road just after his eventual release. He's a free man for now, though the memory of his prison experience is still undeniably fresh:

"We are under all kinds of pressure, but we are not crushed completely; we are at a loss, but not at our wits ' end; we are persecuted, but not abandoned; we are cast down, but not destroyed."[143]

Now on the other side of the experience, Paul can rejoice in God's deliverance. But this time is different than the others. He can still describe it in the present tense. And he understands it is not just business as usual anymore. Something deep within his mind and soul has shifted.

His later reflection to the Corinthians of his experience within the prison walls lets us in on his mental, spiritual, and emotional state. This time there is no earthquake, no Roman official providing cover, no angel riding shotgun. The power that Paul has previously always seemed to be able to access, stays beyond his reach. It hasn't validated him in the eyes of the Corinthian church and it isn't making a difference in Ephesus.

Perhaps most troubling, Paul is beginning to question whether he will see the dream of a united Jew/Gentile church fulfilled. Yes, the kingdom message has come and it has brought transformation, but the barriers of mistrust and suspicion are still intact.

---

[142] 2 Corinthians 1:8-9. KNT
[143] 2 Corinthians 4:8-9. KNT

As he writes to the believers in the vicinity of Ephesus and nearby cities, probably early in his imprisonment, he appeals to these communities in his care. "The cross has torn down the barriers that previously divided us and we must not erect them again."[144] And yet, he realizes, many of these barriers have never fully been removed — his exchanges with the Corinthians seem to be demonstrating this.

How can this be? The power of the gospel is to be counted on to tear down principalities. Yes, the story that Paul has staked absolutely everything on has always existed against all odds. But what difference do odds make when God is on your side? This is what Paul has always thought.

But now, in this time of greatest need, where is God? Where is God's hand?

Paul comes to the realization that he may never see this story fulfilled in his lifetime. Will it ever be?

He can't find the power to pull through this tailspin.

Has he lost the story forever?

---

[144] See Ephesians 2.

13 Missing The Point

The already, not yet.

Theologians call it eschatological tension. I don't like that term. It sounds so clinical, so sterile, like something you can hold up and dispassionately analyze from an objective distance. In actuality, the experience is not nearly so safe. It clubs you in the side of the head when you're least expecting it—seldom with any explanation.

It's little boys in boxes.

Yet probably more than anything else, this disturbing characteristic of my experience of God's kingdom in the here and now uncovers my real motivations and heart's desires. It forces me to move beyond my first elementary attractions of the kingdom invitation—the potential power to control outcomes—and grapple with the deep seated issue that took us out of God's garden initially: the unwillingness to trust wholeheartedly without ultimately being in control.

At first I see the kingdom message of the gospels as primarily a call to embrace the things that Jesus does during his time on earth, particularly the works of power—healing, deliverance, miracles—things that seem to so clearly mark God's future breaking into the present. It feels for me like the old war-movies, when at the bleakest moment, a troop of fresh reinforcements appear on the horizon. Jesus has brought the power and he is offering it to us. We can be God's generals.

Little do I know at this time just how different God's perspective is from mine. I, of course, want more power. It seems natural within my paradigm. I want fewer surprises. Less disappointment. But now, it seems, God is graciously trying to direct me to other ways of seeing.

Initially, for me, my pressing concerns are almost exclusively, "How can God work more dynamically through me?" Only deep disappointment moves me toward the better questions:

"What needs to change for God to fully make a home within me so that I remain faithful through all the uncertainties of life's journey?"

"And not just that but expectant and faith-filled as well."

My idea of embracing God's Kingdom up to now has largely been about racking up "wins" for God's side. God is patiently working with me to adjust my paradigm—my framework needs to be enlarged. Yes, recaptured expectancy has been a good thing. But sadly, I can excel in all these "works of Jesus" and yet miss the whole point of his coming.

Power alone will never be the key to get us back in the garden, let alone beyond it. The way out has always been the way in.

14 When I Am Weak

You don't suddenly lose hope.

It seeps out slowly, incrementally. You can feel it happening in your bones. And as hope retreats it's supplanted by the usurper, regret.

Sometimes, near the end, when hope can barely be held even as a thought or concept, something deep within you may stir. Like Samson, you gather your remaining strength to grab the pillars and with one last display of power seize control of the narrative. This only signifies, however, the death throes of hope.

In the darkness of his Ephesian prison cell, Paul can feel the messengers from the satan[145] closing in on him. Their whispered accusations are like daggers, penetrating more and more deeply into his soul. Often, in the past, these enemies would flee from him as he would confidently invoke the name of Jesus. The name of Paul is recognized within the demonic community and Paul

---

[145] Using *Satan* may over-personify this character. N.T. Wright refers to *the satan* as "the quasi-personal source of evil standing behind both human wickedness and large-scale injustice, and sometimes operating through semi-independent 'demons.'" The Hebrew word for *satan* simply means "the accuser."

knows that they know and fear him.

Yet, in this prolonged time of isolation, something is different. He cries out to God repeatedly for protection and deliverance, but it doesn't come—at least not in the way that Paul expects.

Finally, an answer: "My grace is enough for you; my power comes to perfection in weakness."[146]

"Oh Paul," God lovingly explains, "The victory we are reaching for can never be achieved by being more powerful than your enemy. If that becomes your focus, you'll always be at risk. It's so easy to rely on and have faith in my power, rather than in me alone. On the other hand, when you're weak, you are desperate for me and stay close to me. And if you do that? Nothing can overcome you. After all I created power, I'm its source."

"The key to your dream, your story is not power. A lack of power never has been the center of the human dilemma. What you need—all you need—is relationship and trust. And that, I promise you."

This encounter, and the revelation Paul receives from God, no doubt prompts his sharp mind to re-visit everything he has learned about who God is.

Of course, he reasons, the spiritual battle surrounding the emerging new creation can't be, at its heart, a battle between two separate powers. This premise simply buys into the dualism that Paul has strongly rejected. If indeed God is the only creator, then power—the ability to get things done—is God's gift to humanity. We've been given access to use it—to duplicate it or create our own is

---

[146] 2 Corinthians 12:9, KNT.

beyond our ability.

Without God as our source, we simply can't even exist. As Paul himself has said to the Athenians, "For in him we live and move and have our being."[147] Yet, at the same time, while a gift freely given, this life force is never intended to be possessed or manipulated on our own. Rather, it's something to be enjoyed *with* God.

What's true of us is true of every created thing—including the devil. Even evil entities can't create their own power to use in opposition to God's. Instead they seize hold of God's gift of power and use it in unauthorized ways, without reference to God's desires and to the purposes for which it was created—they seek not to build life but to destroy it.[148]

Paul knows that judgement will eventually come to the devil's empire. To be sure, while justice may be delayed it's not thwarted. The pseudo-kingdom of the satan will ultimately be held to account for every misuse of God's gracious gift. But if God is to hold open the door of invitation, and give humanity the freedom to step into that opportunity for reconciliation, the full judgement of evil will necessarily have to be delayed. And as long as there is choice, there will ultimately be the consequences of

---

[147] Acts 17:28, NIV.

[148] While there is danger of oversimplifying how this has become possible, it does seem that one way the dark powers have gained access to this power is through us. In creation, God authorized humanity to steward this created world and granted power to be able to accomplish it. As the Genesis story illustrates, we stepped away from using this power from within relationship with God, intending to exercise it autonomously. As it turns out, we were deceived—independence being a myth—and we became enslaved in various ways to the satan's dark forces. Consequently, wittingly or unwittingly, we, along with the power made available to us, can be used for evil ends.

choosing badly.

For now, the satan still fights and powerfully so—usurping God's power and using it in a variety of ways. Sometimes it is wielded as a threat to intimidate and ultimately enslave us. At other times, power is employed to entice us—promising to let us control the outcomes of our own stories...as though he/it has authority to grant that wish or the trustworthiness to follow through on it.

This is no different from the way in which the devil confronts and tempts Jesus in their encounter in the wilderness. The satan uses the same voice that was so successful in the first garden—whispering the temptation of independence. But Jesus knows his Father and can't be lured away from the moment by moment dependence that characterizes his relationship with God—the very foundation of his authority.

This is the plan that was so effective in the original garden.[149] Be your own authority. Seize control of your own story. But there's nothing in Jesus that's vulnerable to this kind of temptation. Jesus isn't seeking power or desirous of independence; he has relationship with the Powerful One and knows that's all he needs.

As Paul reflects on these things, something settles in his own heart. Not too long after he will write, "So I will be all the more pleased to boast of my weaknesses, so that the Messiah's power may rest upon me. So I'm delighted when I'm weak, insulted, in difficulties, persecuted, and facing disasters, for the Messiah's sake. When I'm weak,

---

[149] Someone has shared with me that my description of what takes place in the first garden somewhat parallels that of Bonhoeffer in the first section of his *Ethics*. I need to brush up on my Bonhoeffer.

you see, then I am strong."[150]

Paul from this point on, will be content to be God's ambassador rather than God's general. He doesn't waste his sorrows. The depression and despair he suffers in his prison cell give way to a deep settledness and confidence in God's strength working through his weakness.

We can see the difference even in his writing style—for example, between the first letter to the Corinthians and the second. Later, in relating how he almost lost his dear friend Epaphroditus, the emotion he conveys is much less brash confidence as it is profound gratitude for God's mercy. Less a bold general and more a thankful ambassador.

Yes, for Paul, the gospel is still powerful. It embodies the living Jesus, who is now—using the Jewish imagery Paul is so familiar with— at the right hand of the Father. But power isn't something Paul feels any need to grasp. Having God's authorization is enough for him—whether visibly the power seems present or absent.

---

[150] 2 Corinthians 12:9,10, NIV.

15 A New Way To Live And Lead

It's early 1995—a full decade before I finally arrive at the conclusion that I've squandered the special opportunity that God provided me. After many months of listening, prayer, and dialogue, we have decided upon and executed a plan to multiply the Langley Vineyard into five different communities—spread out over various parts of the valley surrounding Vancouver.

This move is radical enough to catch John Wimber's attention: he schedules a visit to come and evaluate first hand what it is that we are doing. In all honesty, he's prepared to reign me in, fearing that I'm going to "mess with a good thing"—his words—rather than simply continue to build and grow what is by now one of the larger churches in Canada.

In spite of a few wrinkles, the visit comes off without a hitch.[151] Upon leaving, after having visited virtually all of our groups and conversing with a number of our leaders,

---

[151] Well almost. Since John is going to be staying at our home, my PA, Heidi—who is also a close personal friend and presently the CEO of an HR company—helps Joy clean the house in preparation for his arrival. (Note to reader: Heidi has never seen a practical joke that she didn't like.) Part of her *helping* us includes putting a bottle of rum on the fireplace mantle. Thankfully I spot it just before his arrival or this story could have a different outcome.

John tells me that he has been deeply moved by his time. What he has seen is everything he has hoped for in beginning the movement of Vineyard churches: strong community, a humble receptivity to God's Spirit, and a servant heart in our various leaders.

Our motivations in bringing about this decentralization go far beyond change for change's sake. Nor, quite frankly, is it related to a desire for numerical growth. A failure to gather people has never been a problem; the primary difficulty seems to be gathering people too quickly and too easily.

As we are becoming a popular destination—both for visitors from around the world and from others looking for a church home—I'm becoming more and more disturbed by the trends that I see within our church community.

Intensity of worship is still an amazing strength—we have gifted, experienced worship leaders along with the dynamic of large, densely packed services. There's regular evidence of God's power visibly seen in our various gatherings. We're establishing extensive, effecttive and creative ministries to extend the reach and mission of our church.

What's missing? To be frank, the measurements I really care about are going in the opposite direction. Every year, as we become more and more famous, the real numbers measuring the engagement of our people in reaching for spiritual growth, their participation in our surrounding community—especially with the marginalized—and their commitment to forming authentic community...are all going down relative to our overall size.

It's not that the red warning light is buzzing yet, but the outcomes we dreamed for in planting the church are not being caught and embodied at a pace that can match the numeric growth of our church. Almost everyone thinks we're better than we've ever been, but I know it's not the truth. The many are beginning to be content with living vicariously off of the few.

So we break up the show. Now our people are meeting week to week in groupings within which they can really, not metaphorically, be known and loved. We've created an opportunity for an entire new group of leaders to emerge and begin to grow.

Once every two or three months we rent a large auditorium and have a blowout party—big band, big prayer, inspiration. And then we get back to the business of real life and growth together.

Wimber has backed us, and I love what we're doing. For Joy and I, our church has shrunk down to the individual pastors leading these communities and to the centralized staff that empower and train each center. We love pouring ourselves into these amazing people and believe in what God is doing through them. In spite of the physical challenges I'm facing and the apprehension I feel about larger national and international challenges, at least at our local setting I'm in the best possible place ever. A place of strength.

There is a hint of storm clouds on the horizon but given my track record, I'm quite sure they will pass another way.

It's at this time that I have a strange, re-occurring sense that God is trying to say something to me. I've never been very good at the "hearing from God" thing. Maybe I ask too many questions? Or maybe I simply keep score? But it is always somewhat obscure to me. And I'm never entirely sure if I've mastered the discernment process in determining the difference between God's speaking, my imagination, and the indigestion caused by pizza.

It's usually in retrospect that I'm able to conclude that God has "spoken" to me. In this instance, over the space of a few months, what I become more and more clear about is that God is extending an invitation to me.

"Are you willing to learn a whole new way to live and lead?"

Within the context I'm now in, this seems like an exciting proposition. Will it mean much greater power? Will the numerous prophetic promises that always seem to swirl around large churches be further realized and fulfilled? Will I have an even larger sphere of influence?

Of course, this sense of God speaking to me doesn't just spring out of a vacuum. I've been wrestling with some questions about Jesus and how it is that we are to follow him. I have a sense that grappling with these will necessarily have an impact on my leadership in the future.

Looking back, I can see that God has already been starting to prepare me for a new paradigm of leadership, even though I haven't yet fully said "yes" to the invitation to embrace it. There are a few different threads to this, but at this point in time I haven't fully made a connection between them.

First, I've been looking at Jesus as the leader that I want to emulate. But what I'm seeing is challenging both my present practice and what it might look like in the future. I'm understanding that Jesus has clearly come to restore his people from exile as their rightful king, and that this is, in fact, just the first step in a plan to restore and unite the whole world. To any reasonable mind, this all necessitates power, especially the power to subdue all the enemies of this plan. So what I'm looking for originally is how Jesus uses his power.

What do I find? Over time, I'm struck by all the ways he *doesn't* use it. Eventually his very resistance to be a powerful king in the way most have cast him results in the nation ultimately rejecting him. Yet, in this, it seems clear that Jesus is doing exactly what the Father has sent him to do. What does that mean for me and for my leadership?

Second, for some time I've been fascinated by the peculiar interplay I see in Jesus's life between authority and power. I've often used the words interchangeably — when speaking or writing it helps to use synonyms rather than repeating the same word. But increasingly I'm realizing their significant difference.

I'm struck by the way that Jesus seems to contrast power and authority—a clear example is seen in the conversation he has with a group of his disciples upon their return from a fantastically successful ministry trip.

He's sent them out two by two, and has "authorized" them to do the very things they have seen him doing.[152] And it works! When they return they are enthusiastically describing the impact of their prayers and actions. They're most excited about their success in commanding demons to relinquish control over the lives of people.

Jesus acknowledges that these wild encounters haven't

---

[152] Luke 10:1-19.

been merely products of their imagination—he has seen in his spirit the spiritual victory and the impact that their actions have had. The plan is working! They are overcoming the power of the enemy. What he says next, at first glance, seems strange.

"But..."

16 Do We Really Need Another General?

"Wonderful, but don't get too excited."

That's what this word "but" usually means—there's a correction about to follow. In what Jesus says next, it's almost as though he opens the heavens and rains on their parade.

"But—don't celebrate having spirits under your authority. Celebrate this, that your names are written in heaven."[153]

Yes, Jesus has received heartbreaking news about the death of his cousin John while they've been gone. Is he just depressed about that? Certainly he can't be jealous that the disciples have been as successful as they have? This ministry trip was his idea all along.

In trying to understand Jesus's response, I keep being drawn back to the previous verse, specifically his words, "Look: I've given you authority to tread on snakes and scorpions, and over every power of the enemy."[154]

"Authority over power." I begin to question my previous

---

[153] Luke 10:20, KNT.
[154] Luke 10:19, KNT

habit of seeing them as one and the same, and over time I begin to see their significant difference. Power, of course, is simply the ability to get something done, the capacity to direct or influence. Authority is something different again. It is the *right*—the authorization—to use the power that you have the ability to access.

Authority doesn't ask, "Can I do something?" It asks, "Should I do it? Have I been authorized to do it?"

To illustrate the significance of this, we can use the example of generals and ambassadors of any national government or ruler. Both carry authority—they are authorized by the ruling body of that nation. It means that the nation "backs" what they do in the name of that country.

There's a significant difference between generals and ambassadors, however. The former have an army; the latter may only have a small staff and a few soldiers to protect them. In a very real way, the generals have power in addition to having the authority to use it. Ambassadors have authority alone.

Theoretically, generals can only use the power at their disposal for purposes authorized by the commander in chief/ultimate ruling body in the nation. Soldiers pledge allegiance first to their nation, and not to their general, in order to ensure that military officers can't use power for their own means.

That's the theory. In practice military coups happen—and have happened—over and over. When power is within our reach to grasp, very often the temptation to do so can't be resisted.

The Satan is the archetype of the renegade general... one

who has taken God's power[155] illicitly to use it for purposes other than for what God has intended. Jesus is cautioning his disciples not to be caught up in a contest of power against power with an adversary who has been at this game for a very long time.

"I've got something better for you," Jesus says, "and that's the safety of authority over power. Choose to continue serving as an ambassador. As long as you're committed to embrace wholeheartedly the things I've sent you to do, you'll have my authorization. Our enemy will never overwhelm you because I'll aways be with you. I've got your back!"

"So, don't celebrate because you have won a spiritual battle. Celebrate your relationship with me. It's what safeguards every success, every time."

I realize that this is exactly what God is saying to Paul in his prison cell in Ephesus. Power isn't the issue. The issue is authorization. By this time, Paul is familiar with spiritual power and almost certainly knows how to use it—as does anyone who has spent time around it.[156] He could take things into his own hands and try to go "Mano

---

[155] The only power that there is. As I have previously mentioned, the satan is not a creator but relies upon God for breath itself—just like every created being. In that sense, he/it is, after all—as Luther said—God's devil.

[156] I could write a book about this one issue. I believe that you become familiar with spiritual power and can learn to employ it. When traveling in the late eighties and early nineties, I became more and more aware that if I did certain things, I would see certain results. It was easy to convince myself that the end justified the means—if people saw a display of God's power, it must be the right thing to do. The fact that it would make me look powerful was beside the point. Of course, it was anything but—the fact that I was tremendously drawn to this power, and desired to use it, was exactly the point. Eventually I came to realize that I could not trust myself to "only do what I saw the Father doing" and pulled myself off of the road. I knew that to take God's power and use it in an unauthorized way—even ostensibly for the sake of God's name—was in very real terms practicing witchcraft.

a Mano," and power his way forward.

But this is precisely what Jesus doesn't do when confronted by the devil in the wilderness. He doesn't grasp at the power which he knows he can exercise. He refuses to face the temptations alone; each one he confronts in complete unity *with* his Father. He trusts in God to wield the power necessary to deal with his adversary.

When the soldiers surround Jesus in Gethsemane, his response stands in such contrast to that of Peter, who immediately takes out his sword and starts swinging. "'Put your sword back where it belongs!' said Jesus to him. 'People who use the sword die by the sword! Don't you realize that I could call on my father and have him send me more than twelve legions of angels, just like that?'"[157]

Just like Peter, Paul might win a battle or two, but eventually most who try the "power over power" game discover that the satan has become very good at it. When our focus is first on power, and second on authorization, it's very difficult to keep a sharpened sense of discernment over time. Yesterday's revolutionary usually becomes tomorrow's oppressor, controlled by the same lust for power that they set out to overthrow.

In his prison cell, Paul re-affirms his decision; he'll rejoice in what at first seems the weaker choice—that of an ambassador.[158] It's not that he has no expectation of God powerfully acting on his behalf, authorizing his

---

[157] Matthew 26:52-53, KNT.
[158] "Seems like" is the important expression here. At a deeper level, as Brené Brown notes, "Vulnerability sounds like truth and feels like courage. Truth and courage aren't always comfortable, but they're never weakness." *Daring Greatly.* (Penguin Books, 2012)

obedience. He fully expects God to do just that.

But his posture will be the same of the early disciples after the release of Peter and John from prison. They lift up their voices in prayer to ask two things. First, that God will give them courage and boldness to do nothing less than what Jesus has commanded them to do—preach and embody the gospel. And second, they pray that as they step into this, God's hand will be stretched out to perform mighty signs and wonders.[159]

God is the sovereign; they are simply God's humble ambassadors.

It's not surprising that in the same letter where Paul describes this exchange with God, he makes a powerful statement about the Corinthian believers, contrasting who they once were with who they are now. "You are a new creation!" he exclaims, as he goes on to explain who they—including himself—have now become.

"So we are ambassadors, speaking on behalf of the Messiah, as though God were making his appeal through us. We implore people on the Messiah's behalf to be reconciled to God."[160]

Not generals—we never find that expression or concept in Paul's writings—but ambassadors who rest in the security of God's backing.

---

[159] Acts 4:30.
[160] 2 Corinthians 12:20, MSG.

17 A Life That Others Write About

This becomes a critical passage for me. It's not an objective Bible study that I can hold at arms' length. I realize God is asking me to surrender what has been the core concern of my entire life: keeping control of my narrative. Wanting to win, and be seen as winning.

Taking selfies with my army.

"Will you let me show you a whole new way to live and lead?"

There's something in the question that stirs the deep, still mysterious longings in my heart. Another crossroad with a decision required. I can stay with what I know and turn away from the path before me, but will I leave my heart behind?

I know that God is asking me whether I'm willing to learn how to lead out of weakness rather than from a position of strength. I suspect the invitation will not be a victory procession—leading from one success to another—but I know somehow that I must say "yes."

On one level, the years that follow as I attempt to lead from within this new paradigm, become the most satisfying and fruitful years of my leadership life.

Faithfulness rather than success begins to become the most important metric for me. I become more and more aware that people are never the means for some great work of God to be accomplished.

They are the great work of God.

Throughout this period, Joy and I continue to see the faithfulness of God to heal, save and deliver—one person at a time. We discover that he *is* the same yesterday, today, and forever.

But at the same time, I become so disappointed in myself that this still doesn't seem to be enough for me. After all, isn't this what I signed up for? I realize I'm still counting on visible success to validate me and it isn't happening. The choices I've made have worked against me. On one hand, I know they've been the right ones, but on the other, I still can't let go of my compulsive desire to be successful.

I'm facing my greatest fear. The words from my father haunt me, "If you ever play anything, you must win. If you lose, you are a failure."

I remember years prior, when my friend asked me about writing a book and I replied, "I'm not so sure. I think instead I want to live a life that others write about." Now, as I examine my life, I think, "No one should want to write about me." I feel like I have no other choice than to admit that I've failed. I had a chance for a story like those in the Bible or church history where great people do great things—a story with lots of adversity but with big wins shining through at the end, validated by a powerful conclusion. It was in my grasp...but I let it slip away.

18 Starting Over

There's a hidden blessing when the phone stops ringing, and the invitations dry up, and when like Elijah after Carmel you find yourself removed and alone. You can hear the quiet. And it's in that still place that the voice of God can best be heard.

It doesn't feel like a blessing at first. Even with the outer noise stilled, I'm still bombarded by my disparaging self-talk, lecturing me for irretrievably losing the story to which my entire hope for belonging is tethered. But even self-condemnation gets exhausted and needs to catch its breath. When it does, in that moment of disquieting silence, revelation from "the unforced rhythms of grace"[161] begins to form in my mind. It's almost imperceptible at first, but unmistakable.

I recall a memory from more than a decade before—something deeply significant at the time that somehow has been buried under the agendas, anxieties, and distractions of life. As I replay the memory, I am overwhelmed by the realization that God, many years ago, was already preparing me for the place within which

---

[161] Matthew 11:29, MSG.

I now find myself.

What I remember is an experience from my first years as a pastor in the heady, early days of our movement. Opportunity seems to be everywhere, if you can seize it before someone else does. I see the open doors but I am having difficulty mastering what seems to be the necessary criteria. Our message is all around the presence and power of God but I can't seem to really "get" it. My emotional side seems to be wired into a different frequency and I'm not having the same experiences that appear to come so easily to others. I don't feel spiritually gifted and am struggling to believe that I can say, "Come Holy Spirit" and expect it to make much difference.

Once again, I feel like the short kid in class, the one last picked.

I complain to God about it. I've volunteered and giving it my best shot—now I need God to supply what I lack. And then, something seems to take over in my brain. I have a sense of a picture in which I am right at the center.

I see God in the distance. I don't know exactly how I know that, but it's absolutely clear to me—dreams, whether experienced sleeping or awake are always a little hard to explain. As I begin to move toward this presence, I realize that I'm not the only one. There are countless others and we are all in competition with each other, anxiously trying to reach God before everyone else has filled every possible point of access.

This realization brings back to me all my unsettled fears of arriving late, of being the one left out. I realize I've always suspected this of God—that God will allow others to take the place I am hoping for. As I get closer still, my worst fears seem to be confirmed. God is surrounded by seekers and there seem to be no spaces left.

Somehow, in this waking dream, I am pressed to continue rather than turn away in discouragement—even though my anxiety is rising. And as I do, the picture I see is radically altered. Coming closer, I begin to see that God is more expansive than I've expected. There's still room.

Closer still, I not only recognize that there are empty spaces, I see that each of them has a sign...with someone's name on it.

It is then that I have a sense of a voice speaking to me— not out loud of course—but nevertheless, crystal clear and understandable.

"Gary, there's a place in my heart that has your name on it. In that place is everything you need, the fulfillment of your deepest longings. No one else can take it; it's reserved for you. If you turn away, it will remain vacant, for it's yours alone."

"You don't need to strive or compete. In fact, you can take your time and help others who are anxious to see what you now see. You can assist them to find the place reserved for them. For all you hope for—all you long deeply for—is waiting just for you. Your story begins and ends in me."

The impact of this memory holds my heart as my brain tries to catch up. I've always wanted to belong. I guess we all do—I suppose it's a consequence of the cosmic tearing that's taken place as a result of leaving the garden. But somehow I've thought that the way back will come through great victories of faith, accomplishing wonderful things to further God's kingdom, becoming one of God's heroes.

And yet, I know that we were never overpowered in the garden, seized and kidnapped from the presence of God. We succumbed to seeds of doubt and mistrust and decided we could/should make it on our own. I'm beginning to really understand—though I've preached it for years—that my whole life story isn't about what God wants from me. God has always been simply wanting me.

"In repentance and rest is your salvation, in quietness and trust is your strength, but you would have none of it."[162]

The way back is on the same path upon which we left. It's always been about trust.

This path, to the degree that I have found enough courage to follow it, has led me to a powerless place. I've lost hope of capturing the narrative that I've believed will fill the aching void within me. And in that place, where I feel like I've lost the story that seemed within my reach, a revelation comes to me.

"Perhaps you haven't lost the story at all. Maybe you are only now beginning to understand it. Now, let's give you your 'A' and get you enrolled."

It takes several years for me to put this revelation in quotation marks, and really believe that they reflect God's perspective. But I'm beginning a new journey. God has given me a guide, a Joy here on earth to keep me from losing sight of the joy that is set before me. To help me stay connected with the deepest longings of my heart and God's.

Yet so soon, she is lost to me. As Joni Mitchell sang, "You

---

[162] Isaiah 30:15, NIV.

don't know what you've got 'til it's gone."[163] On one hand, life now seems more clouded than I would like, but it's never felt less muddled.

Eugene Peterson's writings become a helpful and timely guide to me. Writing about faith and clarity, he assures me that they are not in conflict with one another. It's just that the clarities that faith brings are starkly opposed to the certainties that my mind wants to impose on my life, striving to bring some semblance of security and control.

Instead, Peterson writes, they come from within, they are "organic and personal, not mechanical and institutional...Faith invades the muddle; it does not eliminate it. Peace develops in the midst of chaos. Harmony is achieved slowly, quietly, unobtrusively—like the effects of salt and light."[164]

The confidence that faith brings, emerges from commitment, not from control...or being controlled. It comes from "...adventuring deep into the mysteries of God's will and love, not by cautiously managing and moralizing in ways that minimize risk and guarantee self-importance."[165]

Years ago, I have a dream in which I'm sitting in a classroom with my knees around my ears. Why? I'm in a kindergarten class with its child-sized desks and am feeling quite awkward. Another student, a child of the appropriate age, calls out, "What's he doing here?"

---

[163] Joni Mitchell song, *Big Yellow Taxi*.
[164] Eugene H. Peterson, *Run with the Horses: The Quest for Life at Its Best* (IVP, 1983), 194.
[165] Peterson, *Run*, 194.

Quickly comes the response, "Starting over."

I'm not that far along, but I feel like a yoke has been cut away from around my neck. I still sense Joy's presence with me and it encourages me. Now I just need to figure how to live. "Perfect while being made holy." (Hebrews 10:14 NIV.)

Part 4

The Road Less Travelled

1 From The Edge To The Center

In the fourth decade of the Common Era, the smart money is not on the fledgling church. Yes, there is some marked, early acceptance and favour within Jerusalem—though it's possible that the numbers of new followers noted in the book of Acts aren't intended to be taken literally.[166] At the same time, persecution doesn't take long to become somewhat the new normal.

Paul's experiment of creating previously unheard of communities—founded neither on ethnicity nor on family ties but simply on allegiance to the Messiah Jesus—constantly offends the Jews and threatens the established order of the Roman cities within which they are founded.

Assuming, as sociologist Rodney Stark does,[167] that there are little more than one thousand "believers" in the decade after the remarkable Pentecost visitation, the

---

[166] For historians in the first century, statistical accuracy was less a concern than it is now...though, hang on: we are seeing the emergence of *alternate facts*. Back to the Future...

[167] Stark reaches his conclusion based on an estimate of the population of the city of Jerusalem being close to 20,000. Depending on the source, estimates for the city of Jerusalem during this vary widely, but if the numbers in Acts are intended to be viewed literally Jerusalem would be virtually a Christian city.

miracle seems to be that this early church is still present a century later. But present it is—though for a very long time, extremely fragile.

Even by the end of the second century there are probably not many more than two hundred thousand followers, meeting in homes largely located in the various urban centers of the Roman Empire—which at its peak population will approach sixty to seventy million.

In this period after Paul and the other apostles, we have no record of any mass conversions nor any large-scale events that dramatically increase their numbers. We don't even have any indication that there are other travelling itinerants like Paul stimulating and inspiring further growth. They have no central bureaucracy, no established training processes, no money—they don't generally even have specialized buildings!

We would expect them to increasingly become insular, wagons circled, their best stories all in the past—trying to endure the constant suspicion that occasionally boils over into overt persecution.[168]

How long O Lord? No doubt the early Christians utilize the language of the Psalms to express their anxiety, confusion, and yes, disappointment over the apparent delay in Jesus's return. Certainly the apostle Peter, when writing generally to churches in Asia Minor who are experiencing one of these periods of active persecution,[169] seems to acknowledge the expectation fatigue and the questions that come out of it.

---

[168] Although there were a few universal movements of Roman persecution in the first three centuries, some parts for the empire allowed the nascent Christian church to grow and flourish for significant periods. This gave room for Christianity to take root.
[169] 2 Peter 3:1-11.

Peter encourages the churches to be patient, understanding that this delay is not coming out of indecision or weakness on God's part. There isn't a heavenly conference going on, wondering how to land this Jesus project and bring it all home. When it's time, he says, there will be no hesitation from God.

Instead, Peter centers his readers on the real issue behind the unexpected time gap—it's all about mercy. God keeps holding the door open; heaven doesn't yet feel full. There are still more who may respond to the invitation that has begun through the death and resurrection of Jesus.

What can we do to hasten the final, expected day when God acts to bring heaven and earth finally together? Be that invitation, says Peter. We need to be Jesus in tangible and reachable form today. It is so important that our response to delay is to embody God's heart of mercy and live our lives in purity and peace—building conscious bridges of peace toward the hope of the reconciliation of all things.

And amazingly, it works. Not perfectly, of course—the church is, after all, filled with people like you and me. But within the humanness of it all is a spark of the divine. The invitational heart of Jesus sufficiently captures the imagination of this early church so that God's heart of compassion is seen in them. Not just words, or abstract ideas. What we read about Jesus doing, they do, and they keep on doing...for two hundred and fifty years!

At first the effect of living this way is hardly noticed, but by the time Christianity is officially recognized as a legitimate religion in 313 C.E.,[170] its property restored, and persecution halted, incredible changes have taken root.

We are sometimes led to believe that the key event that precipitates Christianity coming into center stage in the empire is a dream or vision that Constantine has just before going to battle with Maxentius for control of the Western Roman Empire at the Milvian bridge in 312 C.E.. This vision assures Constantine victory if he will fight under the banner of the Christian God. His resulting success, it is supposed, is what brings about the change in fortune for Christianity, moving it in a relatively short period of time from the margins of society to a place of favoured advantage.

This indeed may be somewhat true. There is, however, an additional, rather important factor in Constantine's decision-making process. He is likely aware that at this time up to seventy percent of the population of the city of Rome is already Christian. They have permeated every part of society and hold many key positions.

Within the empire as a whole, they comprise over ten percent of the entire population and are rapidly increasing—and this after almost a decade of accelerated persecution begun by the emperor Diocletian. Is at least part of Constantine's enthusiasm a case of "if you can't beat them, join them"?

---

[170] In the Edict of Milan, which is notable in that it wasn't really an edict and it didn't happen in Milan. It is most likely a regional letter that expanded on an earlier legal decision by Galerius. This isn't a particularly important point unless you want to have a clever thing to say the next time the Edict of Milan comes up in conversation at a party.

Obviously something dramatic has been taking place for a long time, and it's sustained over such a lengthy period that exponential effects are now being realized.

2 Radical Response

The real question isn't, however, whether or not this almost incredible transformation has taken place—that fact is undisputed. The pressing matter to explore is, "*How* has this thing taken place?" Without power, without privilege... without any of the things we now would think essential for any church to survive, let alone thrive?

As the website *catholicity.com* puts the question, "How did a tiny and obscure messianic movement from the edge of the Roman Empire dislodge classical paganism and become the dominant faith of western civilization?" Over time, historians have examined this question from a wide variety of perspectives. Using the tools available to them at the time, they've identified certain factors as being influential.

The traditionally quoted reason for this dramatic, sustained growth originates as early as Tertullian's *Apologeticum*—"the blood of the martyrs is the seed of the church." His view, echoed through the centuries by many others, is that the impact of how martyrs voluntarily face their deaths with peace and faith results in even greater numbers turning to follow Jesus as well. Through a period where dissatisfaction with paganism is growing, and much attachment to the cults is nominal at best, the authenticity of Christian belief is arresting.

A second, long held explanation for this transformation over time is the prevalence of miraculous works. Even Edward Gibbons—hardly a fan of Christianity—in his classic work, *The Rise and Fall of the Roman Empire*, is forced to admit, somewhat begrudgingly, that the miracles that keep happening as Christians simply continue to try and do what Jesus had done, are an indispensable factor in its continued growth.

Ramsay McMullen, the esteemed Yale University historian, in his book, *Christianizing the Roman Empire,* says much the same—in essence, the first Christians demonstrate authority over the spiritual powers of paganism by healing the sick, setting people free from spiritual strongholds, breaking curses and exercising what are seen as miraculous powers.

This doesn't mean that these early Christians are holding constant crusades or special events. Most of what we see happens within the context of their everyday, ordinary lives, lived out within extended family networks and crowded neighbourhoods where our present concept of privacy wouldn't be known.

Now, at first glance, this can seem like a negation of everything we've been talking about so far. Are these Christians a prototype of God's "men and women of power for this hour" that we seem to be so desirous of today? Is this sustained faith over a significant period of time simply due to early stage anointing, or lingering effects of Pentecost? Are they God's generals killing it on the battlefield? Given their context, it's hard to imagine them seeing themselves in this way.

I think there is something deeper going on, that Paul's framing of their role—as Christ's ambassadors—has stuck with them. If that's so, what we see in generation after generation is people simply living their real, daily lives believing that everything they do matters, and that God can and will "authorize" in powerful ways their attempts to live just like Jesus did. For two centuries they re-enact the Acts 4 prayer: asking for courage and boldness from a powerful and present God, with the confidence that God's hand will be stretched out as they stretch out theirs in imitation of the model of Jesus.

Examining this period from another perspective, sociologist Rodney Stark in *The Rise of Christianity* sees many other powerful, if less visible, factors for this continued, steady growth. One of the most significant is their profound sense of community. Community is an almost overused word today, though one with wide application and acceptance, but in the first centuries the communities of Jesus followers cut across all the boundaries of what is deemed acceptable or possible. There's simply nothing else like what the Christians are modelling.

The followers of Jesus, particularly in the early stages of this time period, are at the least misunderstood, slandered, and marginalized. The trolls are out against them. This exclusion has its blessings, however. There aren't a lot of "free riders" among Christians. You aren't hanging with them because of possible business connections or because it's what everyone does. If you identify as a follower of Jesus you're prepared to pay a price.

In many ways Christians are easy targets: they don't make the customary sacrifices to the emperor which is a reassuring sign of loyalty, they don't participate in the frequent festivals, and their somewhat "closed" gatherings are ripe for criticism. With life in the ancient world always insecure and unstable, you either avoid the outliers or join in with throwing stones.

They're odd, they stand out. Who wants to identify with them? Well, it turns out, many do.

Ancient cities are incredibly inhospitable and unsafe places. You don't go out carelessly at night and you think twice about it during the day. Cities are filled with displaced people—slaves, migrants, dispossessed, fugitives, and more—all trying to scratch out a place to exist and hopefully advance. Virtually no one considers anyone outside of their tribe or family. You don't get invited out for lunch.

Except by Christians. Their hospitality is legendary. They don't seem to avoid strangers, they seek them out. They welcome them in. They understand family in a way that no one else does. That kind of news travels quickly among the unwanted and excluded.

There is a second factor that sheds light on how Christianity works its way into the more influential segments of society. Women in the Roman world are, by and large, not a privileged lot. They are, in many ways, simply chattel property. That is, except among Christians, where they're seen as equal heirs of God's grace along with men. They take visible and prominent leadership within church communities in a way that's virtually unknown within Greco-Roman culture.

It's no accident that a disproportionate number of women find a way into faith in Jesus and thrive there. This is occurring in a period of history where, due to infanticide, maternal mortality, and several other factors, there's an acute shortage of marriageable women within society. The end result is like leaven within the loaf, so to speak, as Christian women become wives to a wide variety of men—some with very privileged positions within the culture. Like a very positive virus being introduced into a host culture, the faith of these wives is "caught" by an ever-increasing number.

Finally, there's one more factor that must be mentioned to understand the "miracle" that takes place in the status of the Christian church. While life in ancient times is never very predictable and, in fact, fraught with every kind of uncertainty—whether social, or political, or religious— something happens in the mid-second century and then again in the third which is absolutely a game changer. In fact it is one of the primary causes of the eventual decline and collapse of the entire empire.

Plague.

Even one year ago, we all would have a different reaction to that word than we do now with the COVID pandemic seemingly in charge of our lives. Already after only less than one year in, the world-wide casualties are continuing to climb, economies are devastated, and health care systems are in danger of being overwhelmed. The mental health cost is immense—and we are only in the beginning stages with no clear solutions that we can bank on.

In 165 C.E., during the rule of Marcus Aurelius, returning Roman soldiers bring back a disease along with the plunder from one of their campaigns—likely smallpox. It is little understood and there seems to be no defense. The manner of death is gruesome; the fear of that death inescapable.

Over the next fifteen years, this plague will take the lives of almost thirty percent of the population of the Roman Empire. Almost nothing is untouched by it. Rome suffers military reversals because of the simple lack of soldiers. Farms are left abandoned because of the absence of workers. Every part of societal and economic life is devastated. Family systems are destroyed with un-counted numbers of people simply having to fend for themselves.

In this prolonged period, anyone who can, simply es-capes and isolates—leaving the dead to bury their dead. Even then, there is no immunity. Aurelius himself dies in the final year of the plague.

It takes, of course, a century to heal from something as horrific as this, though the scars go far deeper yet. And then, less than seventy years later...it happens again. This time almost twenty five percent of the population will be erased. At its height, almost five thousand people a day are dying in the city of Rome and it will last for thirteen years. To some degree the empire never recovers.

In these two situations there is one group that stands out, distinct from almost everyone else—the Christians. When all who can are fleeing, the Christians are present, caring not only for their own, but also caring for their neighbours.

And dying doing so.

There is no health care system in the ancient world for the common person. If you don't have connections or family support you are truly abandoned. And yet even the most simple form of primary health care can often mean the difference between life and death. And this is exactly what these Christians do—they see caring for others as the core essence of following Jesus and of the entire story of God. It's God's unconditional love for us which calls us to love our neighbour in the same way.

But here is what rocks the entire society. These Christians don't just nurse their own, they also care for the very people who have been previously part of the persecution against them. Who does that? And it's not just during year one. They consistently show up year after year—and it doesn't go unnoticed. By the time the plague is finally over, Christians are viewed in an entirely new light.

Something more results from their response beyond increased social standing. Having a greater survival rate, there are now more of them. Their relationship with their neighbours continues of course even now that the crisis has past. For most of these people, their family networks are shattered and they are looking for a place to belong. The ranks of Jesus followers continue to swell.

When you add all these things together and apply them to our previous question of how the church transforms the empire the way it does, one summary seems to describe it best: they taste like Jesus tasted. They believe that God's spirit working in them can empower them to imitate Jesus, with the same kind of heavenly backing that was seen in all that he did. And just like what happened when Jesus walked this earth, his living presence in these followers produces hunger and thirst within so many that touch them.

It's never dramatic really. Stark computes that the average growth rate is two to three percent a year—most pastors today would be worried about their job security with that kind of result. It's just that it never stops. It's not a church program; it's who they are.

Paul's life and his teaching have made a difference after all. "So we are ambassadors," they recall Paul pleading with them, "speaking on behalf of the Messiah, as though God were making his appeal through us. We implore people on the Messiah's behalf to be reconciled to God."[171]

This they do, through their words and their actions, as though Jesus himself was making the invitation. Their motivation is simply the outcome of being loved and included. They are not in control but they don't need to be—they have a loving Father who always keeps them in view.

Amazingly, a significant portion of this faithful group is composed of Jews. It's unclear how effectively the Jews and Gentile have integrated; there is still undoubtedly work to do. But Paul's dream—the dream of New Creation and a New People of God—is not dead. It is God's dream and God will never give up on it.[172]

In the beginning of the fourth century, sadly, the power they lack is given to this burgeoning church. It then continues to grow, but increasingly the reason for that growth is favoured advantage. They win their neighbour by coercing their neighbour. It isn't long before the once persecuted church becomes the persecutor.

Once power is firmly in their grasp, their message begins to change until eventually they are treating the pagans in

---

[171] 2 Corinthians 5:20, KNT. I love the way Peterson expresses it in The Message: "We're speaking for Christ now: Become friends with God; he's already a friend with you."

[172] Pope Clement, writing very possibly around C.E.96 to the church in Corinth indicates that Paul's later reconciliation with them had tremendous impact and that they were to become a leading and vibrant church for a period of 20-40 years—what Paul poured into them was not lost.

the same way they were previously treated. Eventually they turn to killing one another to ensure continued control—all for the glory of God, of course. They become God's generals... and Inquisitors.

And God quietly surveys the margins and moves into those neighbourhoods. Perhaps from there, outside of the power centers, the church can regain what it once had...and failed to value.

3 Storm Chasers

It's a long journey from Mount Carmel in the north of Israel to the southern border of Judah and then beyond. Though the location of the mountain where Moses received the law isn't entirely clear to us now, undoubtedly it is for Elijah. A five-hundred-kilometer walk isn't out of the question for people who basically always walk everywhere, but it's still a hike.

Who knows if Elijah takes the fastest route—where is Google when you need it—because this journey is designed for escape, not for vacation. He's trying to get as far away as possible, at least out of the jurisdiction of Queen Jezebel. He's cancelled his phone plan so he can't be traced.

It's ironic how sometimes the darkest times in our lives are immediately after what seem to be great triumphs. He has single-handedly outgunned the prophets of Baal and proved that Yahweh is the preeminent deity, controlling even the elements. This is who Elijah is; confrontation is what he is all about.

Yet something has caused him to bolt. It's unclear exactly what it is. Does he feel that he's overplayed his hand killing all the pagan prophets? Does he think that his actions are going to result in retribution against whatever prophets of Yahweh that still remain? Whatever the reason, Elijah has hit bottom. He leaves his servant and heads for the desert to die.

It's there that God's angel tries to rouse him. Not an easy task. Even with some miraculous provision of food and water, Elijah seems beyond hope. Not giving up easily, the angel somehow gets him mobilized for a long journey to Mount Horeb.[173]

Once there, Elijah has the enthusiasm of a teenager—he immediately crawls into a cave to sleep. He isn't exactly pressing in to receive his next prophetic instructions. Nevertheless a messenger from God manages to get his attention, and calls him to the mouth of the cave, where he's assured God will speak to him in person.

Then comes the progression that Elijah would expect—a godly version of "shock and awe". First a hurricane wind. What better medium could there be for God's presence? Nope, God's not in it.

Then an earthquake. Still no God. Finally fire—God just used that medium for a powerful head to head up on Mount Carmel. Certainly God's voice will be heard in that? Not yet.

Then God speaks...in a whisper.

ॐ

We're conditioned to paying attention to the loudest voices, the most powerful encounters, the highly visible people. Do we assume that whoever shouts the loudest

---

[173] Forty days and nights is probably a way of saying it's a big hike. For someone in a reasonable state of fitness it would probably be around 11 days.

must have the most important, or godly, thing to say? That God only speaks from power?

Is it possible that God is trying to interject something important through the Anabaptists during the period of the Reformation, when so much formative theology is being formulated and written?[174] Do we discard what comes from the margins at our peril?

I remember years ago, listening to John Stackhouse, a professor at Regent College in Vancouver, speaking to the Evangelical Fellowship of Canada annual meeting. John has been invited to comment on a recent report indicating that evangelicalism in our country is taking a bit of a beating. The concern is that we are losing our privileged place within the nation. So, John is asked how we are to view this—with the implication being that we need to figure out how to fix it.

John's response is striking. He encourages us to first of all be very careful in the assumptions we make. He then goes on to illustrate how throughout the history of the church we have often got our analysis wrong in the short to medium present.

Often the things we think are the glory of the church turn out to be the opposite, he said. And the things that cause us to wring our hands, are the very things God especially uses to strengthen and advance it.

Are we missing the whispers, storm chasers that we are?

---

[174] It is hard not to wonder how different the next several centuries of church history might have looked if instead of baptizing them for the long count, we had taken the time to listen to what they actually had to say.

4 Effectual Doubt

It's interesting how, when I am no longer "in demand", I begin to find time and space to listen at a completely different level than has been the rule during my "ministry" years. I'm free enough from distraction to dare to look within. Up until this time, my most pressing decisions revolve around what to do...or not do. Now, post retirement, when not many care what I do, my mind is drawn to seek out another, very different question.

Who am I? I guess it's another way of echoing David's "search me, O God." Having spent the major part of my days building a container for my life, I'm trying to "fall upwards" and in Richard Rohrian fashion take stock of what is actually in it.[175] In a refreshing way, it's a bit late to fully salvage the image of myself I've wanted to present, and, quite honestly, one does wear out some-what from the effort. It seems counterintuitive, but is it possible that the best way to actually find my worth will be to stop trying to prove it?

---

[175] Richard Rohr, *Falling Upwards*. I realize that by some people's calculations, Richard Rohr is a heretic. Whether that's true or not, I don't feel particularly prepared to cast the final vote. I suppose most of those that I have referenced in this book will be heretics on at least someone's list so I am doing my best to be consistent.

Certainly, without a position to defend, there's less pressure in acknowledging the many questions I have about things. Ironically, it seems the more honest I'm able to be about my doubts and uncertainties, the more grounded and rooted is my faith. Even when I don't know exactly "what" I believe, I am completely convinced in "whom" I believe. Questions, even very important ones, that previously have threatened me—I have needed to have *the* answer—are almost becoming like surface noise. I know at the end of the day, I'm at home with God.[176]

---

[176] Or to state it more poetically with a line from Brian Thiessen's song, "At the end of the day, love covers me." I realize I have said this same thing numerous times throughout the book. That must mean 1) that I think it's important and 2) that I want to be sure that nobody misses this fact.

5 One By One

In 2012, when Joy and I retire from our national role, we really have a bit of a dilemma. We have virtually no retirement income—ah, the joy of pioneering movements—and our main investment has been generously giving our money away. (Thank God for healthy compromise in a marriage or, in our case, literally all our money would have already been dispersed.) The expected primary source of business that we expected to generate through our leadership center, as I've previously explained, has pretty much evaporated—along with the economy of the province we are located in.

As beautiful as Dominion Hill is, we can see the writing on the wall. We begin to look for a transition—first hoping to sell the property as a women's treatment center and then, after a number of possibilities fall through, eventually recognizing we will simply need to list it. As a temporary stop gap to provide a bit more income, we decide to register the property on Airbnb.

Even this is not so simple as it seems. Joy almost wants a resume from every potential guest to ensure that God is leading them to stay with us. I point out to her that there are some challenges to this business model but she's still very cautious. At the end of the day, Joy cares not at all about finances. She knows that God will take care of us. I wish I could have her optimism.

So tentatively we begin hosting, little aware of how important and healing this side venture will be. One thing I begin to discover is that when people are not a necessary component for the accomplishment of some pressing task, it's possible to see them in very new ways—not through the lens of *what they can do* but instead through *who they are*.

The former is kind of like looking toward the evening sky, scouring the horizon for an airplane that you hope is arriving on time, all the while completely missing the sunset. Having the weight of expectation to make things happen lifted off of our shoulders is like a breath of fresh air to both of us. Rather than seeing our guests as commodities, we welcome them as stories waiting to be shared and savoured.

Joy and I have always claimed that our dream job in the church is that of a small group leader. Now, through our Airbnb experience, what we do every day becomes all about people again—one by one, seeing their face, and asking God for each individual, "Lord what is your incredible invitation for this special one in your created world?"

Each day we make an over-the-top breakfast which we serve ourselves, and then we walk the fine line between "hovering" and "attentiveness"—asking questions that flow out of genuine interest. Inevitably, conversation continues, eventually turns to prophetic encouragement, and then prayer, usually finishing with hugs all around. Seldom does anyone leave before noon.

Our "conversations" range from prayer for physical healing, to marriage counselling, to deep journeys into the soul. No wonder hospitality has been considered a preeminent spiritual gift throughout history! In many ways, this is what we signed up for...and now, in this later season of our lives, we are reminded again of the model of Jesus. He doesn't start a healing ministry—he heals people. He doesn't begin a school of prophets—he speaks life-giving words into real lives. It's always about people...one by one.

6 No Other Hand

During this season, a good friend, David Ruis encourages me to explore the biblical concept of Shalom. I'm confident I already know what needs to be known—it's the Hebrew word, of course, for peace. What more is there to understand?

A great deal it turns out. As is often the case, much is lost in translation. I begin to discover that while Shalom embodies the concept of peace it embraces so much more. It calls to and speaks from my deepest longing—to be back in the garden again, the world put right, as somehow my heart knows it should be.

Shalom is the flourishing that results when heaven and earth come together. It is the deep sense of healing and rest that comes when the disparate, broken strands that have unraveled the tapestry of my life are re-woven, the original masterpiece restored.

At best, I have brief tastes of this deep, inner rest. They're gifts from God's spirit, keeping my hope and expectancy alive while my soul, and the soul of all creation "groans" for restoration.[177] The tastes are needed, as I find that the

---

[177] See Romans 8:18-28, MSG.

deep yearning that keeps me reaching is like the voice in Elijah's cave—it's easily drowned out by the distractions and preoccupations of anxiety.

Joy and I begin to gather young people from around the world to live together for a week and explore how to understand and seek Shalom as our defining center. I'm more of a co-learner than an instructor. I feel often like mathematician John Nash, the subject of the movie *A Beautiful Mind*, who suffers from schizophrenia through much of his life. His eventual freedom comes from learning which voices inside his head to trust and to follow.

I realize that through much of my life, my so-called leadership has been more driven by anxiety, than invited by Shalom. It's not that God's peaceful presence is absent; it's just that, like Nash, I need to learn how to tune into a different frequency. I wonder if I'm not the only one.

Our new setting in life is making that task much more reachable. It's amazing how different things feel when the pressure of having to accomplish is relieved. The change in pace is therapeutic for Joy and I. What we originally signed up to do, we now have time to do.

Looking back, I can see how easy it is to get on a treadmill. In the beginning I simply want to say yes to imitating Jesus and doing the things Jesus did. Far too soon, I find myself on stages, training others to do what I have only begun doing myself. Soon it seems like there is very little time to take what I am training others in and work it into my own life—I'm too busy inspiring and training. I'm constantly trying to squeeze in enough "practice" so that I can have fresh examples to share. I at least need enough to validate my integrity.

The treadmill is never a temptation for Joy. She's focused instead on bringing a timely gift to the next person who needs to be encouraged. She's holding someone's baby as though it's her own. She's either on the floor wailing for the delay of the world being put right, or she's celebrating its coming—whether spellbound watching a bead of water glistening on the petal of a flower, or enraptured by the miraculous entry of a new life into this world.

These years are a wonderful time for us. In many ways, I'm now more settling into the pace of Joy's world rather than our previous pattern of Joy breathlessly trying to keep pace in mine. As a result, we're both more able to truly see the gift that each of us are to the other. I've always *loved* Joy; more and more I'm beginning to *like* her.

With the gift of time restored to us, we live each day trying to live in harmony with "the unforced rhythms of God's grace."[178] In many ways, Joy does most of the heavy lifting, initiating daily practices of worship, prayer, affirmation, rest, and practical care for those within our reach. Even if a little along for the ride, I can sense that I'm becoming more fully alive...more connected with the horizon. And more connected with myself. I'm so looking forward to our next season of life together, convinced it will be by far the best yet.

"You never know how much you really believe anything until its truth or falsehood becomes a matter of life and death to you," writes C.S. Lewis in *A Grief Observed*.

---

[178] Matt. 11:28-30: "Are you tired? Worn out? Burned out on religion? Come to me. Get away with me and you'll recover your life. I'll show you how to take a real rest. Walk with me and work with me—watch how I do it. Learn the unforced rhythms of grace. I won't lay anything heavy or ill-fitting on you. Keep company with me and you'll learn to live freely and lightly."

After Joy's sudden death, I have to come to grips with what *I* really believe as opposed to what I have simply absorbed vicariously from Joy.

Is God still good? Do I want to stay on this journey of actually knowing God more and more—regardless of the risk and uncertainty? Am I willing to believe that the best part of my story is yet ahead of me?

It's not actually a wholehearted wrestle. By this stage, I realize that like Tevye in *The Fiddler On The Roof*, there is, in this case, "no other hand." I *do* know one thing. I *do* believe and trust. God *is* good and I choose to believe that the best days of my life are still to come.

Now I just have to learn how to walk it out.

Breathe deeply.

Shalom.

7 The Naïve Hook

"If you're not a liberal when you're twenty-five, you have no heart. If you're not a conservative by the time you're thirty-five, you have no brain."

Though most of us have understood this to be another of Winston Churchill's witty quotes, it actually pre-dates him by a lot of years.[179] The point still stands, irrespective of the author. Life has a way of changing our perspectives.

Zeal and youth go hand in hand. When I'm young, I have dreams and visions—and I'm not often able to distinguish between them. I have difficulty discerning my own motivations. Is the fire burning inside evidence of a noble calling? Or am I simply being driven by my own brokenness?

Earlier in life, I really don't have enough life experience to know the folly or difficulty of what I'm attempting to do—and that's a good thing. If we knew at twenty what we do

---

[179] One of the likely candidates for originating this statement is the French Prime Minister in the late 1800's, Aristide Briand (he was formerly a socialist). His quote went something like this, "The man who is not a socialist at twenty has no heart, but if he is still a socialist at forty he has no head."

at forty, very little risk would be entertained and very little reward realized.

The young man Saul grows up on the tales of the early Israelite heroes—Phinehas,[180] Gideon, Elijah. He re-enacts in his imagination their zealous feats of bravery and savours their victories. His own sense of destiny, before and after his dramatic encounter with Jesus, is shaped within the framework of their lives.

There's no question but that the early Saul is filled with faith. He's ready to take on all opposition, he doesn't hold back from confronting head-on any obstacle. It's admirable, but not always helpful. There is a reason why Peter, James and the others pack him off to Tarsus.

Much later, likely in a Roman prison, writing to his disciple Timothy at the end stages of his life, Paul—being the name he now goes by in this part of the world—is and isn't the same man. The passion isn't gone but it's tempered. The faith-filled quality of Paul's life is still there...that's good news. It hasn't been eliminated by the complexities, disappointments and confusion of life. It has, though, been changed.

I don't hear the bravado of one of God's generals. He's not simply shouting the same things louder. There's now a humility that only pain can bring about. The pain of betrayal, though the sting is always somewhat double edged—What could I have done differently? The broken-heartedness from continued rejection by people he loves and has invested his life in. The sad realization that his dreams for new creation are likely not going to be fulfilled in his lifetime.

---

[180] You can read his story in Numbers 25.

Yes, his understanding of the message has changed but he hasn't given up, nor simply doubled down on his earliest postures and positions. He has let the message change him. He has become comfortable with leaving power and control in God's hands. He has been faithful.

"I have fought the good fight; I have completed the course; I have kept the faith."[181] Writing what might very well be his last letter, the gratitude that he has for God's grace throughout his journey is obvious. He's going to finish well. He's still a faithful ambassador. He's not simply putting in time until his retirement. The fire still burns within him, even though so much has changed in the way that he understands it, and he's been obedient to the vision that he had so many years before.

And now, joy awaits. The longing, the "hook" of God's call long ago, is still drawing his heart. "All that's left now," Paul writes, "is the shouting—God's applause!" Like Jesus, for the joy set before him, he's endured the cross, the shame, the disappointment and the finish line is within sight.

---

[181] 2 Timothy 4:7, KNT.

8 Faithful And Faith-filled

Faith-filled can never hold its edge without being tempered by the process of faithfulness. A vision worthy of giving my life for, requires giving my life.

The road is a long one, filled with deep potholes of discouragement and disappointment. Beginning a new quest stirs excitement but only continued commitment brings the fulfillment my soul longs for.

The vision that inspires my heart can only continue to do so if I give it space and time to form my heart. In this, revelation from "over the horizon" functions somewhat like prayer. I pray, not to convince God to do things that God would otherwise be reluctant to do; I pray to become more fully part of the answer to my own prayers. So I reach for a heavenly vision, aware that in some mysterious way, my mind and my heart will become more aligned with heaven through not only the dreaming, but the hard, hard work of trying to turn these dreams into reality.

It seems far easier, and considerably more exciting, to simply find a new vision. Unfortunately, there is a law of diminishing returns I can't avoid when constantly trading in old visions for new, hoping to keep the previous magic alive. Eventually, always reaching for a new dream simply becomes another form of medication, or diversion, designed to delay the inevitable—when I no longer dream at all. In that vacuum, cynicism soon moves in.[182]

The remedy, though, is not to abandon my dreams, or—alternately—to turn them into codes or creeds to which I faithfully submit. Faith-filled and faithful can only separately sustain when working in harmony together. Faithfulness can never replace being filled with faith—it can, however, preserve it.

Divorced from my revelatory longings—and the zeal that they produce—seemingly "faithful" practices can appear godly, but simply become a way for me to retain a sense of control over my life and destiny. They quite easily become detached from the untamed God—revelations from whom disarm me. Over time it becomes quite easy to profess a deep faith in God when in reality what I really have is "faith in faith." It is in the system that I have constructed around faith that my confidence is rooted—"If I do this, then God will grant me that..."

Dallas Willard, in the paper I refer to in my introduction,[183] comments on how, in his observation, it's almost impossible for organizations/movements to finish with the same quality of vision and faith that marks their early stages. According to Willard, what happens is this:

> What, then, is the general pattern? Intense devotion to God by the individual or group brings substantial

---

[182] One challenge of the revolutionary sixties was the relative inability to keep the vision alive against the contrary tide of consumeristic mainstream culture. By the end of the 70's, most of the original "revolutionaries" had simply been absorbed, their dreams seemingly forgotten.

[183] Willard, *Living In The Vision Of God*. The article can be viewed at: https://dwillard.org/articles/living-in-the-vision-of-god

outward success. Outward success brings a sense of accomplishment and a sense of responsibility for what has been achieved—and for further achievement. For onlookers the outward success is the whole thing. The sense of accomplishment and responsibility reorient vision away from God to what "we" are doing and are to do—usually to the applause and support of sympathetic people. The mission increasingly becomes the vision. It becomes what we are focused upon. The mission and ministry is what we spend our thoughts, feelings and strength upon. Goals occupy the place of the vision of God in the inward life, and we find ourselves caught up in a visionless pursuit of various goals. Grinding it out.

Once the fire has gone, Willard remarks, things almost always end with the selling of memorabilia.

I'm very aware that the art of living out my days fully alive requires these two perspectives functioning in full unity, one with the other—like pedals on a bicycle. I must treasure what God has spoken in the past and yet realize that God still speaks today, and often in new ways not previously understood or grasped. This means I must hold equally a deep respect for the past along with the courage to explore new perspectives and understandings.

I can't be afraid to re-visit old questions, lingering there in the hope of discovering yet better ones. I need to do so with the great humility of knowing that I'm constantly looking through lenses, seeing through "clouded glass" as Paul describes it in his second letter to the Corinthians. Interestingly, as I try to live in this space, I find I'm much less certain than I was, yet, mysteriously, I feel much more confident. I still have considerable doubts, but they don't frighten me nearly as much as they once did.

Do I still have the same zeal? I hope so. But I do know that it presents differently today than it did many years ago. I'm so grateful for all I've been privileged to see in my life—I've observed undeniable outworkings of God's presence and power. I'm so thankful that I've been able to participate, even in a small way, in God's kingdom tangibly impacting the lives of real people. I always want to look at those experiences with a mixture of awe and humility.

What then has changed? For one, I'm much more suspect of seeking after power in any way. While in the past I would have cultivated it as something that would stir up faith, I now will almost bend over backwards trying to avoid drawing attention to it. Everything God does in a person's life is powerful, even when what is taking place is almost invisible to others. Often God intends for it to remain that way. I'm happy to let God make that decision.

In earlier seasons, my reasoning has been that if people see power, they'll be attracted to God's work. It appears that Jesus understood it differently: if people are enticed by power, they will be attracted to power. There is a reason, after all, that he told people continually, "Don't tell anyone."

When zeal has been rescued from a fixation upon power, and been brought into the safe harbour of authority, it undergoes a dramatic shift in motivation. Leadership that is at its core driven by anxiety, no matter how well inten- tioned or directed toward worthy ends it might be, always produces the fruit of anxiety. Like begets like. When I embrace my role as an ambassador my focus is not on my own dis-ease—trying to overcome it. It is on the heart and intention of the One who has authorized me.

This isn't something that requires hard work on my part. It's quite simple. When I give myself to relationship with God—even if I'm not entirely clear on how to best do that—somehow I seem to become more like God. My heart begins to care about the things that God's heart cares for. I increasingly see the world around me through the same lens of cruciform love I see so powerfully illustrated through Jesus on the cross.

With that love as the glasses through which I see the world, outcomes seem less important. It's enough to simply love—loving is its own reward. And once I am released from needing certain outcomes to validate me? Then I am free.

Numerous times in the last years before my retirement, I feel like I am painted into a corner from which there is no escape. Like the Psalmists, I pray for deliverance. When no quick answer comes, I inevitably find my mind returning to a question—one I believe God is presenting to me.

"Can you trust me for any outcome?" When it comes to the insecurity surrounding Joy's life expectancy, it takes me years to be able to finally say, "Yes." When I finally say it—and mean it—I realize that I am free.

Only when I'm liberated from the anxiety that keeps my constant focus on myself and my needs, can I begin at all to live in love. Love requires seeing the other first... and most.

Love isn't a strategic means to an end that either I or God want accomplished. Love is the end.

It isn't a reward for the worthy; it is an unreserved gift for those in need of it.

9 What Love Does

For Paul, the question, "What drives you?" could be answered in a number of different ways earlier in his missionary efforts. By the time he writes the Corinthians the last time, his answer is much more focused. After his prison experience in Ephesus, and the deep encounter with God he has in that cell, Paul's answer is crystal clear.

"Christ's love has moved me to such extremes," he explains, "His love has the first and last word in everything [I] do."[184] Paul isn't driven anymore, but he is compelled. The same love that moves Jesus to willingly choose the cross is Paul's core motivation.

All these "sacrifices" I have made, Paul says, are not a hardship. They're a privilege. They're simply what love does. Paul knows[185] the reality of trusting in God's love that can only be fully known by experience and never totally captured by reason. And he understands the intention of this love from God. It wants to win our hearts...to call us into its story.

---

[184] 2 Corinthians 5:13, MSG.
[185] It's the Greek word for relational knowledge that Paul would use in this conversation with those in Corinth—as almost always is the case when Paul talks about knowing.

The prophet Ezekiel[186] tries to paint a picture of the nature of this love—which is synonymous with the presence of the God who is first of all love. He describes a scene with the temple in the center. Water is flowing out from it toward the east. This is the love and presence of God on the move.

And where is it going? It is headed for the desert—one stream from a single source. As Ezekiel measures the river it keeps getting deeper as he walks away from the Temple. And then it continues all the way through the desert to the Dead Sea where it literally rejuvenates everything! The lowest, most dead place on earth becomes filled with life.

Here's where the analogy seems to break down. Any source of water will be subject to loss over time and distance—particularly involving a journey through a desert. And what does this mean? It's clear—what Ezekiel experiences can't happen. A river gets wider and deeper over time for only one reason: the addition of other sources of water that join it in its journey. The addition of new sources is greater than the loss to evaporation and absorption along the way.

What's impossible in the natural world is the reality when I let God's love penetrate my heart. Human nature would lead me to construct a pool around the vicinity of God's presence so that I can give myself to swimming in the river of God's love. (Of course, this seems to be the primary purpose of most renewal movements.)

What I see in Ezekiel's picture mirrors my own experience—this love of God is not at all content to stay comfortably within the vicinity of God's temple. Love

---

[186] Chapter 47.

soon becomes restless there as it does within me. There's simply too much of it. It isn't satisfied having reached me—though it delights that it has. It now wants to continue to flow, just like water does, to the lowest and the furthest place.

In the case of water, what stops it is its own capacity— when the amount of water used exceeds the amount supplied. With love there are no limits. There is an endless supply so there is nowhere that love cannot reach.

And it wants me to come along for the ride.

My fear, of course, causes me to hesitate. If I trust in this love it will take me away from the source. It, and I, likely won't survive the desert, let alone make any difference to the Dead Sea. And yet it beckons me to trust.

What am I discovering, even in my limited steps taken toward this trust?

I discover what seems to make no sense: the further I let this love take me from the safe place of God's presence, the deeper, the more real and full is my experience of it.

It's the upside-down kingdom once more. I save my life by losing it. I receive by giving away. I experience the highest place by going to the lowest.

There's no other way to explain the Moravians than by this compelling presence of love. They're the followers of Jan Hus, one of the earliest reformers. Following Jesus in a very practical way is at the center of their faith. They choose *Unitas Fratrum—Unity of Brethren*—as their descriptor.

During the upheaval of the religious wars in the

seventeenth century,[187] they're scattered and often severely persecuted. About one hundred years later, a pietist named von Zinzendorf gives a small remnant of them refuge within his lands in Saxony.

Sad to say, unity seems to be the last thing on their minds. Within five years, von Zinzendorf is at his wits end—he never intended to save them from their adversaries so that they could become enemies of one another. In desperation, on August 13, 1727, he gathers them in their large wooden chapel and they wait for God's presence.

They're not disappointed. One participant later remarks, "It was like unto Pentecost." Another says simply, "We learned to love that day." God's love penetrates their hearts.

They're so moved by their experience, that some stay and pray all night. And then the next day and night....

For one hundred years.

But it isn't long before this love begins to stir within them. It, and they, can't stay where they are. God's love is seeking the lowest place. It leads them to, among other places, the West Indies, where they even offer to sell themselves as slaves to be able to reach the enslaved plantation workers.

We can make people do a lot of things through guilt or coercion. Only one thing can move people to entertain selling themselves into slavery, while considering it a privilege. It's what love does.

Over the following centuries, love sends this small group

---

[187] Known as the Thirty Years' War, it more than decimated the Germanic countries—killing almost one third of the entire population.

to almost every corner of the globe, for no other reason than this—"they understand their distinct calling as bringing the good news of God's infinite love to the poorest and most despised people of the world."[188]

Faithful...and faith-filled.

Love is the key to carrying zeal and passion through the greatest opposition without it becoming either hardened or disillusioned. I don't work at love; I rest in it. I trust the process of love by lifting my feet and letting it take me where it wants to go.

---

[188] From *Moravian.org*, the official website of the Moravian church.

10 Never Quit

When we first discover Joy's astronomically high levels of blood pressure, we pursue a variety of tests to try and discern its cause. In one of these appointments, we're shown an analysis of Joy's blood. As it is explained to us, the tension that she experiences can be clearly seen on the slide.

At one point, the discerning analyst turns to her and says, "Do you personally try to care for every person on this earth?"

Joy pauses, and then with all seriousness, replies, "I don't know everyone on the earth. But if I did, I guess the answer would be, 'Yes.'"

As Joy will readily admit, she struggles—as most caring people do to some extent—with a need to be needed. But far beyond that, Joy constantly feels the restlessness of the water of God's love within her, wanting to reach the lowest and the farthest places. Like Paul, "it's God's love that moves her to such extremes."

Her heart is big enough to love the whole world. Actually, to be more accurate, Joy always understands that God's heart is big enough to love the whole world. She knows that on her own she can never begin to touch the needs she sees even in her own neighbourhood. So she reaches moment by moment for tastes of God's love to share generously with everyone she sees throughout the day.

Back in the season when we have national responsibilities, it is almost impossible for Joy to stay "on task". Though she may understand on one level that it's important for her to organize an event or program, or to make a series of phone calls, those activities always take a back seat to the person that comes to the door, panhandles by the storefront, or calls in distress.

This is often a significant tension between us. When we meet a homeless person, Joy's first response is to take them home with us—or at the very least, to lunch. I hesitate, my mind bombarded with strategic questions.

If we do this, how will it affect other promises that we have made? What is it that God is asking us to do right now? What *is* the best way to help this person? Will our efforts possibly become the "good" standing in the way of the "best"?

By the time I'm halfway through my list of questions, Joy has already tucked her arm around our new friend, introducing them to the people we are scheduled to meet for lunch. The fact that our lunch meeting is supposed to be a strategic planning session will have to wait. Something more important has intervened.

For Joy, there is no buffer between her and the pain of the world. This weight is beyond what she can carry, so like a child, she comes to her Father again and again throughout the day. She asks God for everything. She believes that God, being loving and good, cares for the people she loves much more than she does. So she lives in full expectancy that God will supply everything that is beyond what she can do.

Joy is notorious—as anyone who knows her will attest—for her practice of praying for absolutely everything. She even prays for weather—it's one of her specialties. She prays for machinery to be fixed, for parking spaces, for every human ailment. There is no human dilemma that will not evoke a response from Joy, "Let's pray about that right now!"

Though Joy often struggles to get her facts straight, it doesn't seem to have much impact on the effectiveness of her prayers. When, Natasha, one of our key young leaders from our church plant in North Langley, undergoes two different kidney transplants—both of which her body rejects—Joy tirelessly prays for protection and healing for...her liver.

No matter how many times our friend clarifies for Joy what the need is, it simply doesn't seem to register. Years later, after far too many years of dialysis—and countless corrections—Joy still will not give up on the liver.

Just this last week, I am brought up to speed on a fascinating twist to this story. In the last couple of years, Natasha is brought into a highly experimental treatment process for Hepatitis C—she contracted it twenty years or so ago through tainted blood given to her during one of her transplants. The uniqueness of this treatment is that it does not place any extra burden on the kidneys, so she takes the risk.[189]

---

[189] Natasha, by the way, against all odds, has been given a third kidney. Though it has been an unbelievably challenging journey—and her present kidney is functioning at a very low level—Natasha is thriving...even training for a marathon!

The amazing outcome is that it has worked! She appears to be free of Hep C. An ironic secondary discovery? Though the long term chronic presence of this virus badly scars the liver, testing in preparation for the treatment shows a very unusual anomaly. Natasha's liver shows no sign of damage. Joy's prayers are more prophetic than we know!

I try to tell Joy that, while prayer is of course extremely important, there are some things even God expects us to take personal responsibility for. There is a difference between childlike and childish. My appeals seem to fall on deaf ears—Joy seems designed to live in the present and simply can't account for possible outcomes when making decisions in the moment.

Having no sense of direction, she will strike out on adventures, getting hopelessly lost every time. She will lose her keys and driver's license in the worst parts of town. She will leave our house doors unlocked, even when we are out of town. (Her response? What if someone wants to come and leave us a present when we are gone—how will they get in?)

She is so irresponsible that I suggest to God that she be allowed to experience in a small way the consequences of her decisions. The purpose, of course, so she will understand that we live in a broken, separated world which isn't heaven yet.

God's response? Someone always shows up when she is lost or runs out of gas. The wallet is returned by a stranger. People leave gifts.

She finds the perfect parking space. The sun breaks through just in time for the birthday party.

God seems to keep enabling her.

"Always pray and never give up," Jesus tells his disciples. When an answer doesn't come in the way Joy hopes, she simply digs in deeper. If Joy says she will pray for you, you can take it to the bank. She will pray all through the night for a mother in the middle of childbirth. She will fast sugar for a year to help a friend break through an addiction. Almost every morning when I awake, her hand is laid on me, already praying for me during the previous hour.

For about twenty years, partly because of all the travel, I have constant and excruciating back pain. Ironically, since throughout that period I am doing healing conferences, I see numerous people experiencing complete and instantaneous relief from pain due to a variety of back conditions. In one conference I remember a half dozen people claiming to be free of all the symptoms of herniated discs. At the same time, I am popping muscle relaxants and doing everything I can do to cope with the pain.

Of course, I then have others pray for my back—with Joy's urging of course. After repeating this scenario over and over, I receive prayer with my post-prayer response already prepared—thanking everyone for their efforts and assuring them that I have felt peace even though nothing has changed physically.

As the years go by, "faithful" has completely replaced "faith-filled" with regard to my physical condition. I will persevere through the pain for the glory of God. Joy, however, will simply not let it go. Everywhere, every time, she solicits people to pray for my back. It gets to the point where it's irritating. I don't even want to hope anymore. It's easier to simply cope with what is.

A few years ago, at Easter, Joy decides to gather a

number of friends to sing over me and pray again for my healing. I reluctantly submit—it's often just easier to go along with Joy's ideas than to argue. So we worship together and Joy has everyone gather around to pray for me.

I do appreciate it. I'm grateful for people who care. But, of course, I have my speech prepared for the end, "Thanks so much everyone for coming. Nothing has happened physically but...." And that's exactly how it plays out.

We are leaving the next day to fly to Chicago for a week and then on to Toronto. We are staying in homes, which is always a challenge for my back, given unpredictable beds. Flying won't help either.

A couple of days in, I noticed that I've slept strangely well. I'm thankful. A few days later, arriving in Toronto on a wonderful spring day, our host asks me if I want to join him in a round of golf.

"If only," I reply, and then go on to imitate the motion of a golf swing that I can no longer do. Except I can.

Surprised, I suggest that perhaps we try it. If I simply can't pull it off, I can always walk the course with him and maybe confine my involvement to hitting a few putts on each green. I play without pain, driving the ball farther than I have in years.

Within two weeks, I'm probably eighty percent better. Within a month, ninety. Within several months I'm pain free with full mobility and returning strength. Still today, I can run, cycle, ski, golf, work out. I think it qualifies as a healing.

Always pray and never give up.

Still, watching Joy live the roller coaster ride of emotions while giving herself to what love does, is extremely difficult for me. I don't want to be that vulnerable. I don't want to dare to keep hoping. I'm afraid that the disappointment of it all will crush me.

I can see that in every sad and hopeless moment, Joy runs to God. I tend, like a wounded cat, to disappear from God and others for a few days. I curl up into a fetal position, deciding to wait it out until I either feel better or die. I know that I'm supposed to, like a child, simply go to my Father with my pain. I'm not as far along the journey of trust as I profess.

The way Joy explains it—and I know that she's right—if I'm not willing to embrace the disappointment and pain, then I will not be able to experience the joy as well.

"Faithful" seems like my safe place, but I know that it's an illusion. It's a way of cutting my losses but at the expense of quenching the longings that keep my soul alive. As the familiar saying from my previous basketball life goes, "You miss one hundred percent of the shots you don't take."

Where is that basketball? I think it's time to resurrect my shooting stroke.

11 Open Your Eyes

On Joy's last day, we take advantage of the almost balmy spring morning and head for the forested Trans-Canada trail. It's a place that Joy and I love to go together for a run. "Together" is a bit of a stretch in that only Joy really loves running—for me it's a necessary evil that keeps me at the weight and level of fitness that I desire.

Because of that reality, we run at a very different pace. I charge ahead and get it over with as soon as possible: making sure that I have hit my target heart rate, lowering my times and increasing my VO2 max.[190] Joy jogs along, from flower to fern, view to vista—savouring every sensory experience on her way through the forest.

I've tried for years to explain to Joy how running actually works, but she's hopelessly unteachable. Somehow she thinks that the key to really living is to breathe in deeply the beauty of the natural world and God's presence in it—God speaks to her there. Whatever physical benefit accrues from within that experience, she is happy with.

---

[190] Maximal oxygen uptake—it is the measurement of the maximum amount of oxygen a person can utilize during intense exercise. It is a common measurement used to establish the aerobic endurance of an athlete.

When Joy arrives back at the car, she's unusually intense. "Look at me," she says. It's still early in the day. I wonder, what can I have done already to make her upset? She's been somewhat like this over the last month or so and I'm beginning to wonder what's going on inside her head...or heart.

Whatever is happening, I first notice it with a slightly strange idea she has a month prior. She brings a book into the car to read to me whenever we drive—*Tuesdays With Morrie.* This account of a series of meetings between a university professor dying of ALS and his student is all about preparing for death. Why does she so specifically want to cover this ground now?

In the last two weeks, she's strongly asked me—and our kids—to promise her that I won't marry for two years after her death. In this same period, she has also been prolifically sending out actual hand written letters. Many of these will arrive to their recipients after her death.

Not too long before, she gives me a card for my seventieth birthday, depicting a single tree, standing alone, surviving in the middle of a desert. In the card, she praises me for my ability to endure alone.

Somehow I've missed all these cues, and on this day, she wants to make sure she has my full attention.

"Look at me."

"First, in a very short time, the water from the river we've jogged by will empty into the sea and will be no more. It's identity will seem to be lost, but it will become part of the ocean—a symbol for our lives being found in the immensity of God's love."

"Second, God is saying to you, 'Open your eyes! I have provision everywhere.'"

This is Joy's last encouragement to me.

There are at least a dozen or so of these kinds of "clues" that indicate that Joy, at least on some level, knows that her time is short. Somehow, even with that, I don't really piece it all together until a week or so after she is gone. The trigger, ironically is a toilet brush.

Sometime in the previous months, I suggest to Joy—just trying to be helpful of course—that I've noticed a lot of houses have these implements in their bathrooms. Her tried and true method that she inherited from her mother is hand washing the toilet with a rag. "They must work or everyone wouldn't be using them," I suggest, but before I can go any further she makes it clear no change is about to be made. "When I'm gone," she asserts, "You can buy a toilet brush. Until then, this is how we do it."

Of course, almost immediately the conversation slips out of my mind—that is, until I'm starting to go through our closet in the aftermath of her death and discover, just inside the door...a brand new toilet brush still in its wrapper.[191]

"Open your eyes. I have provision everywhere."

---

[191] Just after writing this, my friend Miriam reminded me of the birthday book Joy made for me just a few months prior—for my seventieth birthday. Joy, God bless her, solicited a large group of people from around the world to send me greetings, but given her relative lack of technical ability, didn't know how to print them. So she wrote them all out long-hand. At the end, she wrote a lovely note to me. Just a few months ago, I pulled out the book and re-read her words to me. It was then that I noticed what I had missed in the first read through. She signed the note, "From Joy...your first wife."

12 Filtering Out God

The promise that God will be enough for us is something Joy has never taken for granted. For as long as she can remember she's struggled with intense fears of abandonment. In the early years of our marriage, she's terrified that I am going to die and that she and her children will be left alone. She constantly struggles with feelings of inadequacy; panic attacks court her.

She's watched her mom for well over a decade immobilized by severe depression and anxiety and knows she can be just like her.

Like the portrayal of John Nash in the movie *The Beautiful Mind*, Joy deals every day with two seeming realities vying for her attention: one in which she is utterly abandoned and another in which she belongs, and is in the care of a loving Father.

Joy's response is to dedicate herself to strengthening her will and desire to choose the latter picture as her reality. She probably reads Brother Lawrence's *The Practice of the Presence of God*, at least fifty times in her life—I think it's almost always on her bedside cabinet, and usually open. On every jog, every walk, she'll want to share what she hears God saying to her through creation. She lights a candle at every meal, to stop, pause, and remember that Jesus is the light of the world.

Her weakness—fear that she will be separated from God's love—becomes a driving force for her to press in and find what will become her greatest strength. By the time of her departure, she can see...and discover God everywhere. Something has happened to the focal length of her eyes.

Not her physical eyes of course—though that sight has actually improved as she's gotten older. But the most significant thing is that her spiritual sight is now more attuned to the long range vision necessary to see over the heavenly horizon than it is adjusted to the short-sightedness required to fit into life as we generally live it in our modern world.[192]

In this, of course, Joy is uncovering one key reason that makes faith today as weak as it often seems to be. Especially in the parts of the church that identify with the label "charismatic", we speak constantly about the "presence" of God. But could it be true, in spite of all of our words, what we actually presume is God's absence?

For years, I've had all the right answers about God being fully engaged with this world. Yet, if I'm truly honest, I realize that in most ways, day to day, I function as though God is, if not actually absent, at least disinterested. I'm

---

[192] There's no question that materialism and consumerism have severely impacted our ability to focus on much outside of ourselves. Billions of dollars are spent to manipulate us into feeling deprived and needy—to which the antidote can only be having more stuff. We are deliberately maneuvered into wearing glasses that are focused in such a way as to see only a thin version of ourselves, the image of God distorted. Out of this place of dis-ease, we become addicted to a solution that only worsens the problem. This poverty of soul keeps us from seeing one another in a healthy way and seals us off from heavenly perspectives.

sure I'm like many of us—the prescription of the lenses through which I tend to view reality is strongly conditioned by the dominant worldview that tries to influence me every day.

Every moment I take into my mind a massive amount of data—things I see, hear, experience in some sensory way. How do I interpret all this and make sense of it? Thankfully over time my brain helps me to sort it all out. It creates shorthand interpretations so that when I note certain combinations, my brain is able to quickly say, "Hey, I know what that is. Here is what to do in response."

It's an efficient process and I really couldn't function very well in this world without it. At the same time, the algorithms my mind sets up can be very limiting. Often the same data can be seen, understood, or organized in very diverse ways—the classic illustration of the old woman/young woman used in most Psychology 100 classes demonstrates how dramatically different interpretations can be.[193] The problem of already knowing what the picture is going to be is this: I see what I'm expecting to see.

Our presuppositions, or mental set, filters out what I don't expect, in order to make it easier for me to navigate life and to feel that I'm in control of our reality. Once I know what I should see, I seem to find it easily and every-where.[194] If I expect God to be nowhere to be seen, very likely I'll take no notice of anything that doesn't fit within

---

[193] These kinds of pictures were very popular in the early twentieth century. See as an example:
https://www.researchgate.net/figure/The-optical-illusion-The-Young-Girl-Old-Woman_fig1_233626368
[194] See again "confirmation bias" in *Mistakes Were Made*.

that established paradigm.

Sometimes to illustrate this, I'll have someone who is wearing an "old style" watch hand it to their neighbour. I then instruct the one now holding the watch to ask its owner questions about what is on the face of the owner's watch. Amazingly, in spite of the fact that the said owner looks at that watch face numerous times a day, they usually can't recall very many details.

Everyone finds it amusing. I then ask for the watch to be returned, and follow by asking the previous questioner a query of my own. "What time is it, by the way?" Usually the person has no idea. They were looking right past the obvious, which they couldn't see because they were searching for different details.

If the paradigm that I have *actually* accepted—as opposed to what I *say* I believe—is that God is functionally absent in the "real" affairs of my life, then I'll have great difficulty seeing that involvement. This, then, functions like a self-fulfilling prophecy and reinforces the paradigm I already hold.

Once separated from any hope for or responsibility to a future with God, I'm tempted to throw away any restrictions that might hinder either my pursuit of power or pleasure in the here and now. Proverbs 29:18, contrary to what we might think, was not written to provide a tag line for missionary posters: "without vision, people perish." A better translation is the NIV: "where there is no revelation, people cast off restraint." When I lose all connection with my future hope, I become a shadow of whom I'm intended to be.

One of my heroes is Viktor Frankl, a Jewish psychologist, who survives four different death camps in the Second

World War, including Auschwitz. In 1946, he writes a powerful psychological memoir, *Man's Search For Meaning*,[195] in which he describes—among other things—what seems to be the key factor in determining whether people are able to survive the horrors of the camp.

Frankl writes, "Woe to him who saw no more sense in his life, no aim, no purpose, and therefore no point in carrying on. He was soon lost." He explains why this is: "With his loss of belief in the future he also lost his spiritual hold; he let himself decline and became subject to mental and physical decay."[196]

What Frankl realizes is that it isn't necessarily the physically strongest who survive. It is the people who quest for some meaning in what they are experiencing who endure—most specifically, those who ask what life yet expects from them, what they still need to do. What it is that life yet requires of any person can be a wide variety of things; it's the act of taking responsibility for that future that unlocks something deep and powerful within them.

This, Frankl believes, has a revelatory quality far beyond the power of positive thinking. We're connecting with something outside of ourselves. He relates a powerful story where, at the break of dawn, digging a trench in frozen ground, light from heaven breaks into his darkness. He has an overwhelming sense that heaven has broken through and, at the same time, experiences a real

---

[195] Frank's approach to psychotherapy based on meaning stands in strong contrast, and in direct opposition, to the other two Viennese schools of psychotherapy—that of Freud, who saw pleasure as our controlling impulse, and Adler, who focused on the drive for power.
[196] Viktor E. Frankl, *Man's Search For Meaning* (Beacon Press, 1992 edition), 76,74.

sense of his wife's presence—that she is truly with him. There is something still to come.

Quoting Nietzsche, Frankl emphasizes, "He who has a why to live for can bear almost any how." That "why" is not found in our circumstances, our achievements—or lack thereof—or in the odds for or against us. It's found when we open our eyes and see that we are not alone. There is One who is with us, and is calling us to something greater than ourselves.

Of course, I know all this! I believe, through Jesus, that the future has broken into the present. The problem is that on one level I know that God is powerfully present but on another level often my senses are too dulled to see it. Like the Laodiceans, I need "medicine for my eyes."[197]

I do know the first step to healing is awareness—as Jesus points out to the Pharisees, their biggest problem is that they're convinced there is nothing wrong with their vision. Just behind is the step of prayer, crying out to God for a living encounter with Jesus. Over the last forty years, I have witnessed thousands of such encounters, and I've seen the transformative effect that the grace working through these visitations of God can have. Certainly, Paul's encounter on the Damascus road is something he refers to again and again throughout his life. It changes his paradigms in a heartbeat.

Having said this, I've also seen the impact of these revelations fade in the lives of the recipients to the extent that there is almost no continuing presence. Their eyes simply close off again.

---

[197] Rev. 3:18, MSG.

How can this be? Simply stated, God's relationship with me always involves partnership. God isn't interested in puppets on a stick—passive objects who don't make real choices or consequential decisions. God's grace is always looking for a partner—in my case, my response of faith.

13 The Peril Of Perfunctory Practice

All spiritual gifts work this way. They're gifts of grace that only are unlocked when I respond and receive them through an act of faith—in other words, I trust the grace that's given and step out into it. Of course, in the way Paul structures how he writes about this in his letter to the Corinthians, he makes clear that there aren't just a few "special" gifts that operate this way. He's trying to tell them that almost everything they do is a result of this kind of partnership.

God is actively involved in everything I do—even the things I think are quite "natural". Reinforcing this same thought to the believers in Philippi, Paul emphasizes that this should give us great confidence. We can work with all of our zeal and strength, because we know God is also at work.[198] With this partnership how can we fail?

As this last thought clarifies, let's make one thing clear: having faith is a breeze; getting faith takes discipline and work. Once I really believe—really trust—faith is effortless. My challenge is when I know that what I need is faith...but I'm not quite there yet. Beyond praying for a fresh encounter with God/Jesus so that my vision will get

---

[198] Phil. 2:12,13.

sorted out for at least a while, is there something I can do longer term? Is there medicine I can take for my eyes, so to speak?

Jesus speaks to this in one of his dialogues with his disciples—though at first, I must admit, I don't see the connection. Here's what he says:

> Don't hoard treasure down here where it gets eaten by moths and corroded by rust or—worse!—stolen by burglars. Stockpile treasure in heaven, where it's safe from moth and rust and burglars. It's obvious, isn't it? The place where your treasure is, is the place you will most want to be, and end up being.[199]

Imagining I am one of the disciples, what is Jesus saying to me in a nutshell? Obviously, in the first part of the quote, he's saying, "Don't store here; store there." But why? Jesus goes on to explain that first, I will want to be where my treasure is and second, my desire will likely be realized—where I put my treasure will ultimately steal my heart.

James K. A. Smith, the Canadian philosopher, unpacks this in his book, *You Are What You Love: The Spiritual Power Of Habit.* First of all, he helps me see that what I treasure tells me a whole lot more about me than do the things I "know." Smith writes, "Jesus doesn't encounter Matthew and John—or you and me—and ask, 'What do you know?' He doesn't even ask, 'What do you believe?' He asks, 'What do you want?'"[200]

Why is this significant? Precisely because I am what I want. As Smith states it, "[My] wants and longings and

---

[199] Matthew 6:19-21, *The Message.*
[200] James K. A. Smith, *You Are What You Love* (Brazos, 2016), 1.

desires are at the core of [my] identity, the wellspring from which [my] actions and behavior flow."

Maybe this is why the Proverbs warn me to "above all else, guard [my] heart, for everything [I] do flows from it."[201]

I am much more than a "thinking thing," Smith tells me; I am a lover with deep longings—C.S. Lewis would smile at that. Saying "yes" to Jesus before anything else means re-orienting my loves—what I treasure.

How do I really know what I treasure? Well it's not necessarily what I profess it to be...I know that much. What it is, quite simply, is revealed by what I repeatedly do. That's what I really value. My treasure is found in the habits of my everyday routine more than in the theoretical ideas bouncing around in my mind. And, even more, these habits keep reinforcing my "loves"—securing their place in my value system.

Most of this reinforcement and training happens virtually unconsciously. My desires are, in the first place "more caught than taught" from the desires modeled all around me every day. A classic example is materialism: I see it, I practice it, and eventually it simply becomes a habit. The more stuff I keep buying, the more entrenched my habit becomes. And once it is engrained deeply enough, these desires produce behaviour that is virtually unconscious—I don't even think about it. I just assume it's the "right" way to behave.

When I come to think about it—of course, the problem is that most times, I don't think about it—I don't live in a neutral environment. All around are everyday "liturgies,"

---

[201] Proverbs 4:23.

or love-shaping practices that are forming my heart to desire what my culture wants me to want.

I can understand where this goes: if I'm not intentionally forming my heart through conscious practice in a different direction, or within a different paradigm—I'm simply going to go with the current. This is simply not something I can be passive about!

I think that my biggest problem with "seeing" a very present God, and acting in full accordance with that belief, is not actually a "thinking problem". Like Peter, my spirit is willing—and believing—but it's my flesh that is weak. I need to walk out the faith I already have in tangible, practical, and consistent ways until they become habitual—in other words my heart pursues them even without conscious deliberation.

Of course, this is exactly what Joy has modelled for me for many years. She utilized the power of habit to stockpile treasure in heaven.

Paul writes about this to the Christians in Colossae, when he's encouraging them to grow in the love of Jesus:

> So, chosen by God for this new life of love, *dress in the wardrobe God picked out for you:* compassion, kindness, humility, quiet strength, discipline. Be even-tempered, content with second place, quick to forgive an offense. Forgive as quickly and completely as the Master forgave you. And regardless of what else you put on, *wear love.* It's your basic, all-purpose garment. Never be without it.[202]

Perhaps this is what C.S. Lewis means when he writes about "pretending" as a key element in becoming more

---

[202] Colossians 3:12-14, MSG (Italics mine).

like Jesus.[203] He relates Paul's words to our childhood practice of dressing up like our parents and learning to be like them through imaginative practice. The more I do it; the more I become it.

What do I do when I feel like I've lost some of what I once knew—especially my experience of God being more fully present in my life? The message to the church in Ephesus in Revelation 2:5 that has "lost" their first love, simply advises, "turn around and do the things you did at first." This is what psychologists call "acting as if..."

What author and friend Mike Mason suggests to married couples that have lost the original desire they once had for each other's company, applies to the intimacy of our relationship with God as well:

> There is an old bit of wise and practical marital advice, often quoted, suggesting that couples who begin to feel themselves "out of love" should return to doing the sort of things they did together when they were in love, even if it means sitting whole summer evenings side by side on the porch swing, with no other entertainment but one another.[204]

Practicing the presence of Jesus works just like that.

---

[203] C.S. Lewis, *Mere Christianity (Geoffrey Bles, 1952), Book 4.7: Let's Pretend*

[204] Mike Mason, *The Mystery Of Marriage: Meditations on the Miracle* (Multinomah, 1985). In my opinion, one of the best books ever written on marriage. Christianity Today seemed to agree—made it book of the year back in 85.

14 An Invitation From God

I think the most important practice that I can commit to, in order to build a habit of wanting to look for—and rest in—God's presence, is what Paul refers to as prophecy. Seeing God as present and not absent is, after all, a paradigm shift, and probably nothing helps to reinforce that shift better than prophecy.

Now I must admit, I sense myself tensing as I hear that word—given my background as I have earlier explained surrounding my first encounter with tongues-speakers. By prophecy, I certainly don't mean the "make YouTube video's and get weird" kind of prophecy. I do know that some people seem to have astonishing revelatory gifts. I'm not denying that. I'm just less convinced that many of them understand what it is they see and how it should be helpfully applied.

The kind of prophecy Paul is talking about is the ability to really build people up by "seeing" them the way God does—and that means through God's unfailing invitation toward them. Paul encourages me to "eagerly desire" that gift. I've always felt I need to take that seriously, though it hasn't come naturally to me. I'm not a free-flowing prophetic artist; I'm more of a paint-by-numbers guy.

I could write a book on all the ways that God has led, prodded, tricked me into the practice of this gift, but I'll spare you for now. Eventually, through it all, I think I've learned a few things. At least things that help me.

The first, and most important part, given all I've been talking about, is constantly cultivating a paradigm of God being present in every one of my interactions with people. I try to always entertain this question in my mind, no matter what conversation—or lack of one—is taking place.

"God, what is it that you so love about this one, so beautifully made in your image? What is your invitation to them—your plan to prosper them, give them a hope and a future?"

That's it. That's all I try to do. That changes my paradigm and now I can be a gift to them, whatever I do or say. The last thing I try to do is to be "prophetic."[205] In what comes next, I simply try to, as Paul says to the Ephesians, "make every word a gift."[206]

I just try to "see" them. That alone can be life-changing for both seer and seen.[207]

Often, if I'm able to do just that, something happens inside me. I find that I'm moved emotionally by the love that God has for them. Even as broken as I am emotionally, there's something irrepressible that takes

---

[205] I have, of course, previously tried that—it's usually pathetic.
[206] Ephesians 4:29, MSG.
[207] I won't nominate Avatar for film of the century, but you have to love that phrase, "I see you." Brilliant. They may have got the idea for that phrase from the Zulu word *Sawubona*, meaning, "I see you, you are important to me and I value you." Peter Senge, in his leadership book *The Fifth Discipline*, unpacks how valuable this perspective and resultant custom is.

place through my alignment with God's heart.

And when that happens, I look in their eyes and speak encouragement...as though God is the one speaking. Oh, I don't say, "Thus says God...uh." I just take the risk of speaking straight from what I believe is God's heart into theirs.

I don't care if what I say is something I can naturally perceive or if I'm seeing and saying things that are most likely beyond my cognitive ability to know. It makes absolutely no difference. Sometimes the impact of what I might share has less to do with what I actually say and more to do with the timing of my words—they are just what is needed for that particular point in life.

But, at the end of the day, I'm not putting on a performance, I'm just trying to be the kind of ambassador that Paul says I should be in 2 Cor. 5:20, conveying the message Jesus embodied, "Become friends with God; he's already a friend with you."[208]

Here's the irony: done this way, prophecy perfectly takes my focus off of myself. All I can think of is building up the person I'm with. Any thought of developing a "prophetic ministry" is a million miles away—as it should be. But when I do this, it does more than almost anything to strengthen a sense of God's presence in me and all around me. I begin to see God everywhere.

If the heart of prophecy is forthtelling the incredible invitation of God who is reaching for us, then I know of no greater prophetic figure than my wife Joy. Joy wouldn't see herself that way but if you talk to those who knew her well, who were recipients of the extreme

---

[208] 2 Corinthians 5:20, MSG.

generosity that marked how she lived, there would be no doubt in their minds.

The first lines of a song written by Brian Thiessen, to honour Joy at her memorial, simply state what everyone at the margins would say of Joy:

She'd walk the line for you,

Like no one else wanted to,

All the ordinaries and broken hearts.

Stories keep coming in,

From lost souls that were dead within,

She would look at you like a work of art.[209]

I'd choose that prophecy any day of the week over predictions concerning political saviours or rapture dates.

---

[209] Brian Thiessen, lyrics from song *Where Joy Is Found.* It can be viewed at https://youtube.be/9HXnQWuQlll

15 Stepping Into God's Generosity

When my eyes are open, I see not only a present God, but a generous one as well. There is only one way to respond when I understand that I can trust God for any outcome and that God will ensure that I have everything I need. Of course, that response must be to live in generosity myself.

It's like the lepers in the Old Testament illustration, who stumble upon an abandoned enemy encampment. After gorging on as much food as possible, trying on various bits of armor, and taking selfies, they finally come to their senses. Realizing that their families and former neighbours are literally starving within the city—unaware of the provision that is waiting—they remark, "How stupid can we be? This isn't right...what will come upon us if we don't go and share the good news?"[210]

What happens when I lose sight of God's generosity is that I lose sight of God. I must give or I begin to cease being fully alive—in stopping up the flow of God's generous spirit through me, I prevent it coming to me. What I give or how much are not the most important things. What matters is that I "practice" the habit of

---

[210] You can read this story in 2 Kings 7.

trusting God and God's goodness.

So that I give because I want to and for no other reason. I am, after all, what I want.

I'm truly blessed and have everything that I need. That isn't to say that I have a substantial income: a senior's pension in Canada seems to factor in a senior's reduced appetite—or perhaps the former determines the latter.

While writing today, I have a sense that I should give an extra gift to a wonderful charity that works with street kids in Surrey—where I grew up and later worked as a teacher. Joy was a huge inspiration to one of the founders and we both really are keen supporters of what they are doing...I suppose Joy still keeps tabs on these sorts of things?

At any rate, it's not a huge amount but it is two-thirds of my pension for the month. What better use is there for money other than things like this? Am I going to stuff it in my coffin when I die? So, I give it and think nothing more of it. Later today, I get a message that a movie is being shot where I live—I rent a suite from some dear friends who have a lovely home—and I'll have to move out for a few days.

And, by the way, I will be reimbursed...for the exact amount that I have given earlier in the day.

What I am suggesting here is not some kind of "seed principle" with a multiplier that I can use as leverage against God. In a way, Joy and I have mostly given throughout our lifetime as a form of entertainment. There is almost nothing else that has brought us more pleasure. And God seems to keep making it possible.

One form of sharing God's provision that is possible

regardless of whether I have much or little, is something that is a unique gift of Joy's—hospitality. Being a pretty serious introvert, Joy's invitation list is something I don't usually want to look at. Though to be honest, Joy isn't usually organized enough to make a list.

Her greatest privilege is filling our home with those not generally invited to dinner. She always takes Jesus's story about party invitations seriously. In addition, we almost always have people living with us for extended periods. Only able to deliver two children, her heart always has room for more, and therefore so does our home.

From her reading of scripture, she has half a mind that this may be her best chance of actually seeing an angel.

16 Nothing Left Unsaid

These are the habits that Joy establishes as part of the rhythm of our life together. Now, with her gone, I'm trying to continue on the path of healing for myself. I'm continuing to build habits that keep my eyes open, trusting in a generous God who will give me all I need in this next stage of my journey.

I'm pressing against my tendency to isolate. I'm trying to cultivate an awareness of my longings—to recognize and welcome them. To not hedge my bets against disappointment. I want to believe that this next season of my life can be my best yet.

It's too important to not be intentional about it all. So I'm trying to continue to light a candle at every meal—because Jesus is the light of the world. I have fresh flowers always in the house to remind myself that God's beauty is all around me and freely available.

I read each morning—sometimes out loud as I did to Joy for years—and worship at night...alone. I'm trying to practice hospitality. My guests are polite and accommodating, encouraging my efforts.

I'm trying to keep forming my heart, "practicing the presence of Jesus" as Joy has modelled for me throughout our years together. I'm continuing to trust that the one Joy leads to the other. I'm trying to choose longing over pleasure...or escape.

There is only one practice I haven't been able to continue—one Joy initiates a few weeks before she dies. To be honest, I find it embarrassing at the time, though I'm not sure why.

She wants to re-kindle intimacy by practicing the terms of endearment that come so easily in our first few years together. So she suggests that the first thing we will do when we get up, before anything else, will be to embrace each other, look straight into each other's eyes and say, "Good morning, sweetheart."

I can't say I'm overly excited, or that it produces any magic, but what harm can it do?

On the morning of Joy's last day, when we arise, I give her a hug, say, "Good morning, sweetheart"...and then— and I don't know why I say this—I add, "Thanks for sleeping with me last night."

Little do I know what the day will hold, or that I will never have another opportunity to lay beside her.

But I'm thankful for the routine.

Or I never would have said it.

17 I Think I Caught A Glimpse

It was the Unicorn who summed up what everyone was feeling. He stamped his right fore-hoof on the ground and neighed, and then cried: "I have come home at last! This is my real country! I belong here. This is the land I have been looking for all my life, though I never knew it till now.[211]

For as long as I can remember, like Lewis' Unicorn, I've struggled with a certain unsettledness. Something in me yearns for a home, a place to truly belong. There are times when I feel like I should be happy with how my life has played out for me—and truly I am.

And yet...

I still have a sense—and always have had—that even the best of what I experience here is only a "taste" of what I long for. And if there is a taste, then my heart tells me, there must be a meal.

Through all my years from childhood to my present age, I've felt the tension of this longing. In all the spaces between the other, more surface distractions of life, I

---

[211] C.S. Lewis, *The Last Battle,* (The Bodley Head, 1956), 161.

notice myself listening for its call.

C.S. Lewis, in describing this mysterious "pull," reminds me of what I know is only too true:

> All the things that have ever deeply possessed your soul have been but hints of it—tantalizing glimpses, promises never quite fulfilled, echoes that died away just as they caught your ear. But if it should really become manifest—if there ever came an echo that did not die away but swelled into the sound itself— you would know it. Beyond all possibility of doubt you would say, "Here at last is the thing I was made for."[212]

It's something we rarely talk about with one another, but every one of us knows about this space in our deepest heart that defies being filled—that is, if we're even honest enough with ourselves to admit it.

As Lewis writes, it is "the thing we desired before we met our wives or made our friends or chose our work, and which we shall still desire on our deathbeds, when the mind no longer knows wife or friend or work. While we are, this is. If we lose this, we lose all."[213]

And what is this mysterious "it"? The inconsolable longing of joy.

Yet, as Robert Frost's poem *The Road Not Taken* suggests, taking this pursuit of joy seriously is to choose the path "...less traveled by." I think I understand why this is. First of all, I never heard anyone ever talk about it— certainly not during my growing up years. I certainly have never been strongly encouraged to pursue it. Does it

---

[212] C.S. Lewis, *The Problem of Pain* (New York: Macmillan, 1962), 151.
[213] Lewis, *The Problem of Pain,* 146-147.

make us too vulnerable to dare to mention it?

Second, I think for many of us, we fear this quest will raise our expectations just to see them go unmet. It's just too painful to keep hoping, and to stay engaged with something that continually dashes that hope. It's the "hope deferred" thing. So we hedge our bets.

Besides, it seems that most of all the foot traffic is on the wider, trampled down landscape. At least that one is well lit by the neon billboards. There's no danger of getting lost. And there is always enough noise to keep us distracted...most of it from someone selling something, or trying to return it.

On that path, the echo is drowned out. The yearnings are barely noticeable and they can be easily pushed aside by the endless number of urgent, if less important things.

I choose this route early on. Don't most of us do the same? To survive on this route, I've had to adapt my eyes to seeing things at very close range. There is little time, space, or thought given to an actual destination—no sense looking for that. Instead, my focus is on me, and on using whatever power I've been able to access to make sure that I get what I think I need.

I become a consumer, using what God's world so generously supplies, to provide comforts for my soul. I manufacture facsimiles of joy to stave off my deeper wrestlings—like household idols I can worship to avoid the risk of the real.[214]

Yet no matter how I scrape, scavenge, and even pillage, I can't make these substitutes for joy sustain. University

---

[214] Worship, at its core, is giving recognition to what I truly value and think is important and worthwhile. It's easy to see what I really worship by what I surround myself with and "bow down" to in the way that I live day to day.

professor and celebrated writer, David Foster Wallace, runs through the checklist of the household gods I have tried—even in their church-sanctioned versions—and echoes the truth my heart knows too well.

Let's not fool ourselves, Wallace says. We all worship. The objects of our worship vary widely, from the worthy to the futile. Hardly a religious person himself, Wallace says something extraordinary—he urges us to seriously consider, in his words, "some sort for god or spiritual-type thing...[because] pretty much anything else you worship will eat you alive."

Why? He goes on to explain:

> If you worship money and things—if they are where you tap real meaning in life—then you will never have enough. Never feel you have enough. It's the truth. Worship your own body and beauty and sexual allure and you will always feel ugly, and when time and age start showing, you will die a million deaths before they finally plant you...Worship power—you will feel weak and afraid, and you will need ever more power over others to keep the fear at bay. Worship your intellect, being seen as smart—you will end up feeling stupid, a fraud, always on the verge of being found out.[215]

For me, it conjures up a memory of visiting a Mexican

---

[215] David Foster Wallace, American author and professor of English. This is an excerpt from his 2005 commencement speech, *This Is Water*, to the graduating class at Kenyon College. Maybe one of the greatest commencement speeches of all time? Wallace committed suicide three years later, after having suffered from depression for many years. Wallace is an outstanding example, according to James K. A. Smith, of someone caught within the "cross-pressure" of the immanent and the transcendent. Smith has a fascinating summary of Wallace's thought in *How Not To Be Secular: Reading Charles Taylor* (Eerdman's, 2014), 14-16. And, by the way, should be considered essential reading to understand the secularism of the world we all live in—with all of the challenges it brings to our ability to believe.

prison. Within the walls, there is a tremendous disparity of conditions. Depending on outside contacts—or the lack of them—an inmate can either have constructed a pretty decent house with all the amenities, or be sleeping under the stars.

As I reflect on my "accomplishments", I've managed to gather a fair number of accoutrements. More than most...and they have provided a measure of comfort. But all the while, around me, walls are being built. At the end of the day, rich or poor, I'm still in prison.

Do I dare risk reaching for what could set me free?

I know only too well the challenge of treasures. Whatever you hold too close for too long, eventually holds you. That's what makes idols so dangerous.

As Wallace reminds us, "The insidious thing about these forms of worship is not that they're evil or sinful; it is that they are unconscious. They are default settings. They're the kind of worship you just gradually slip into, day after day, getting more and more selective about what you see and how you measure value without ever being fully aware that that's what you're doing."[216]

For long seasons, I've pushed ahead on this path—head down against the wind. Most of my sideways glances are more directed at discovering new resources to utilize than at taking in the beauty of God's world, even in its unfinished state.

At key times, in one of these glances, something will catch my eye. I glimpse an opening in the woods that lay

---

[216] Wallace, *This Is Water.*

on the side, some distance from the well-established route that I'm on. Is it a path? Sometimes it's hard to be sure...mostly overgrown as it is. It could be nothing—just a hollow in the woods. And yet, even the thought of pursuing it sparks something deep within me that has lain dormant...almost forgotten.

Still, it makes no sense. It most likely will end in disappointment. It's the kind of thing you pursue in your twenties—double or nothing every time. Easy to say when you have no winnings...and no responsibilities.

If I risk it, I'll lose my place in the cue. And besides, much of what I've accumulated so far won't be able to come along with me. The trail is too unused, too narrow. It's as crazy as looking for Zaventem on our honeymoon. It could end in embarrassment. And yet, I'm convinced that this is the path that leads to joy. More art than science, to pursue it demands more trust than calculation.

The skills and accomplishments that have given me leverage on the more travelled route are less helpful here. The searchlight I've used to penetrate uncertainty and maximize my odds, simply doesn't work on this path. The only light that does is a lamp that is powered by love.

But it operates like the Psalmist's "lamp to my feet"— there's always enough light to put my next foot forward but never enough to eliminate the need to trust.

Mysteriously this light is both within me...and yet, lies ahead of me in the distance. The focal length of my eyes has shifted. I see that which is immediately around me and I see a light coming from the future—beyond my reach and yet so real I feel like I can touch it.

This light—love?—hooks into my heart and draws me forward. At any point, I can resist...and I often do. I return to the familiar path, and my familiar routines of self-preservation. And God waits....

Then weeks, months, years later...I see an opening in the woods.[217]

---

[217] Now might be a good time to take a break and read Martin Buber's *I And Thou*, (Charles Scribner's Sons, 1958) for a description of the two paths...and the kinds of relating that they produce.

18 Corrective Lenses

At There is a reason that Jesus's way is often referred to as an *upside-down kingdom*. Because of the patterns I have fallen into throughout the course of my life—patterns which of course have been established for centuries—living life the way Jesus prescribes is very counter-intuitive. You change things by showing weakness instead of strength? You end up with more by giving away, not by gathering? It's simply not how this life works.

Of course, in reality, it is *our* present world—from which we have excluded any acknowledgement of God's presence—that is truly upside down. It is just that we have become so used to it that it now seems "normal" to us.

In 1931, Theodor Erismann, a professor at the University of Innsbruck, devises an experiment. He constructs a set of glasses designed in such a way that they will invert everything seen through them. He then directs his assistant Ivo Kohler to wear these glasses through the next weeks.[218] first, Kohler is understandably and

---

[218] There are distinct reasons to aspire to becoming a professor rather than an assistant. Much safer I would think...

completely disoriented, but then something amazing takes place: within ten days his brain has completely adjusted. He is able to easily navigate through all the expected functions of his day within what is now becoming his new normal—and proves it by riding a bicycle through the crowded streets of Innsbruck.

When I'm re-introduced to God's kingdom—what it looks like when God's desires are fully realized here on earth— at first, it's like being handed a document upside down and encouraged to read.

I'm conditioned to journeying on the wider route; the path less travelled is at first unsettling. The good news is that my mind and heart can adjust. With perseverance and faith, my understandings re-orient.

I see the same dynamic taking place in the many dialogues between Jesus and his disciples. The time of Jesus's crucifixion is drawing nearer, and there are so many key understandings that still need to be completely flipped for the twelve.

A visit by the mother of James and John creates the teachable moment. They're asking Jesus—no doubt before someone else does—for special status to be conferred when Jesus's revolution has succeeded. Of course, the other disciples are incensed...no doubt because they hadn't taken the initiative first.

Mark's gospel records the following interaction as Jesus unpacks the implications of what James and John have done:

You know how it is in the pagan nations, he said. Think how their so-called rulers act. They lord it over their subjects. The high and mighty ones boss the rest around. But that's not how it's going to be with you. Anyone who wants to be great among you must become your servant. Anyone who wants to be first must be everyone's slave. Don't you see? The son of man didn't come to be waited on. He came to be the servant, to give his life as a ransom for many. [219]

The first four sentences, in and of themselves, are not hard for the disciples to grasp. "You know how it is...." He's simply repeating to them what they all know about leadership. In whatever world, the bottom line is that leaders get things done.

Everyone is in agreement.

Then Jesus continues, "But that's not how it's going to be with you." What's he saying? It's tempting to want to hear Jesus then say, "Put a warm, more compassionate tone on your leadership process of moving things and people along. Still get things done, but with less of a Roman scowl."

The use of the word, "slave," though, doesn't let us keep the old glasses firmly on our faces, with a few smudges cleaned up. It flips them entirely. True leadership, Jesus seems to say, is light years away from the power plays that few of us ever question. God's idea of leadership involves the surrender of control—as "everyone's slave" makes clear.

It's not hard to understand what Jesus is saying; it's just hard to believe that it can actually work. I mean, leaders exist to change the world. How will we change anything without bending people's choices to *our* ends?

Of course, we've been "changing the world" under the old paradigm for untold centuries. It's interesting how we

---

[219] Mark 10:42-45, KNT.

keep managing to change it, yet the same patterns and power structures seem to stay pretty much the same. Has not the Western idea of "cultural progress" been sufficiently unmasked by postmodernism as largely chronological snobbery?

Jesus is offering a completely upside-down perspective: how about serving people so wholeheartedly that their hearts are captured with a desire to likewise become servants. If we fast forward to the point where everyone is reaching to become a servant? I guess we've effectively changed the world!

Too slow, the critics will argue. Yet, could it possibly be slower than what we are doing?

Of course, what we realize in listening to Jesus, is that he's completely challenging our understanding of the word "servant." In our world—would it not have been even more true in his?—the word servant is a "bullied" word. Anything strong or noble in the word has almost always been overlooked. To bring "servant" and "leadership" together, there's going to have to be some reclaiming of both.[220]

Having the courage to stay on the narrow path, being led by trust and love, is exactly what is necessary to bring healing and re-orientation to my mind and heart. When the source of my light is shining from the future into the present—rather than from the flashlight of my phone— sometimes the words on my page can be seen differently. This new light gives life to old, once-rigid

---

[220] Philippians 2:5-11 is a great place to start that reclamation by looking at the example of Jesus's service and leadership and God's action with respect to it. For those interested in understanding more of servant leadership, Robert K. Greenleaf's short book, *The Servant As Leader* is a great place to start.

ideas so that they begin to bloom into things that are more nuanced, yet make more sense.

Seen in this new light, ambitions I've spent my life pursuing—often with limited success—can begin to be revealed as rather foolish endeavours. I begin to realize the compelling truth of Jesus's Sermon on the Mount— to seek God's Kingdom and then trust that this fresh light will show me the doorway, behind which is the source of everything I *truly* need.

Viktor Frankl provides insight into how this teaching of Jesus applies to my real life: "Don't aim at success—the more you aim at it and make it a target, the more you are going to miss it."[221]

Whether success or happiness, these kinds of things are only and ever unintended side-effects of giving myself to something greater than myself. Ironically the key to realizing them is to not actually care about acquiring them—at least not to the point of making them my goal.

Instead, Frankl—speaking from a place of great authority on these kinds of things—urges me to commit myself entirely to what my conscience tells me is of the highest value.

"Then you will live to see that in the long run—in the long run, I say!—success will follow you precisely because you had forgotten to think of it."[222]

---

[221] Viktor Frankl—preface to the 1992 edition of *Man's Search for Meaning*. It is *so* worth reading the entire preface!
[222] Frankl, *Meaning*.

19 Where Joy Is Found

"We shall not cease from exploration. And the end of all our exploring will be to arrive where we started and know the place for the first time."[223]

My inward journey hasn't changed the circumstances of my life. It has, however, helped me to see everything differently. I would never say that it's an easy stroll. It's not something I would recommend for the faint of heart.

In fact, it's required every ounce of my courage to stay on this more obscure, "upside-down" path. I often feel disoriented...even frightened. I know that I can't simply take the values from my other journey and have them "fit" here. My paradigm is changing; adjusting takes time and tenacity.

Thankfully I have a companion for much of this journey. It's not perfect: we are often somewhat "out of sync" with one another. Our styles are so completely different—I'm consumed with plotting a course through the forest; Joy is continually distracted from our goal as, for her, the forest inspires wonder.

---

[223] T.S. Eliot, from the *Four Quartets*—which Eliot considered his magnum opus.

Frustrating as she was, I see now what a gift Joy has been to me along this path. Without her, most of my *Roads Not Taken* would have simply been the result of *Roads Not Seen*. So intent on getting somewhere, I've often been too rushed to let somewhere *find me*.

Now she is gone. Belatedly I see the blessing that she has brought to me. One Joy bequeathing another. It's as though God knew[224] I would never be able to discover the path to joy without a tangible illustration of it right before my eyes. Whatever Joy's imperfections, the one thing she always modelled was a wholehearted embrace of the joy set before her. And she would never let me abandon those same hopes despite their place buried deep within my pain and disappointments.

Having tasted this journey, I now have a longing for it. The hook of joy is in me and I don't want to pull it out. I don't always—should I say seldom?—know the way. It still feels somewhat counter-intuitive to me. But if I know anything, I know I'm not alone. When I remember to open my eyes, I do see God's provision everywhere. And while I can't prove it, it seems to me that my Joy is also not far away. Like markers along a path, I see signs of her encouragement—petals sprinkled about, like markers designed to catch my eye and my heart, leading me along.

This is an ancient path. I read of it on the edges of church history accounts. It's spoken about in a quieter voice— it's not heard in the whirlwind or earthquake. It doesn't boast of conquests but rejoices in vulnerability.

For those who dare to seek it out, over time a solemn recognition begins to take root in the heart. As Genesis

---

[224] Having just written this—and seeing how hilarious a statement it is—I just have to leave it in.

tells us—however cryptic its account—this path once was taken in the opposite direction. It was the trail of mistrust and separation, along which the seeds of shame and alienation began to take root in the hearts of those who walked it. A journey away from a garden of joy.

The path we are having the courage to follow is the same one on which we walked away—humanity re-tracing its steps. Much like the Israelites in their journey through the wilderness, trying to re-learn the lesson of simple trust. The issue has always been trust.

I'm seeing now that the point of life has never been to get things done for God. I can't "blast" a route through the wall and back to the garden. The impediment has always been within me. What I'm seeing is that the totality of my life has simply been to bring me to point where I'm ready to embrace trust and love—with all of the vulnerability and risk that it entails. Heaven is ready for me; God is lovingly preparing me for heaven.

And one day, perhaps tomorrow...or perhaps twenty years from now, the mist will clear, and I'll see what now I only sense dimly.

When that day comes, I won't be at all surprised to see a very familiar face. Knowing Joy, I might fully expect that she'll be riding on Lewis' unicorn, welcoming me with open arms.

I can almost hear them saying together, "The reason why we loved the old Narnia is that it sometimes looked a little like this. Bree-hee-hee! Come further up, come further in!"

"Join us in the garden where joy is found."

-Maddie Best/Eden Wiebe

Made in the USA
Monee, IL
25 April 2021

66767780R00213